DATE DUE

UPI 261-2505   PRINTED IN U.S.A.

MAKING THE NEW COMMONWEALTH

By the same author

Sir Charles Wood's Indian Policy, 1853–66
Liberalism and Indian Politics, 1872–1922
The Crisis of Indian Unity, 1917–1940
Churchill, Cripps, and India, 1939–1945
Escape from Empire: The Attlee Government
 and the Indian Problem
Edited, *Tradition and Politics in South Asia*

THE KING AND HIS MINISTERS AT BUCKINGHAM PALACE : (LEFT TO RIGHT) MR. SENANAYAKE (PRIME MINISTER OF CEYLON) ; MR. LESTER B. PEARSON (SECRETARY OF STATE FOR EXTERNAL AFFAIRS, CANADA, DEPUTISING FOR THE PRIME MINISTER, MR. ST. LAURENT) ; MR. LIAQAT ALI KHAN (PRIME MINISTER OF PAKISTAN) ; H.M. THE KING ; MR. CLEMENT ATTLEE (PRIME MINISTER OF GREAT BRITAIN) ; MR. J. B. CHIFLEY (PRIME MINISTER OF AUSTRALIA) ; DR. D. F. MALAN (PRIME MINISTER OF SOUTH AFRICA) ; MR. PETER FRASER (PRIME MINISTER OF NEW ZEALAND) ; MR. NEHRU (PRIME MINISTER OF INDIA).

ON THE EVE OF MOMENTOUS DECISIONS : THE KING ENTERTAINS THE MINISTERS OF HIS DOMINIONS IN LONDON.

By permission of *The Illustrated London News* Picture Library

MAKING
THE NEW
COMMONWEALTH

R.J. Moore

CLARENDON PRESS · OXFORD
1987

Oxford University Press, Walton Street, Oxford OX2 6DP

Oxford New York Toronto
Delhi Bombay Calcutta Madras Karachi
Petaling Jaya Singapore Hong Kong Tokyo
Nairobi Dar es Salaam Cape Town
Melbourne Auckland

and associated companies in
Beirut Berlin Ibadan Nicosia

Oxford is a trade mark of Oxford University Press

Published in the United States
by Oxford University Press, New York

British Library Cataloguing in Publication Data

Moore, R.J. (Robin James)
Making the new Commonwealth.
1. Great Britain——Foreign relations——South Asia
2. South Asia——Foreign relations——
Great Britain 3. Great Britain
——Foreign relations——1945-
I. Title
327.41054   DA47.9.S64
ISBN 0-19-820112-5

Library of Congress Cataloging-in-Publication Data
Moore, R.J. (Robin James), 1934-
Making the new commonwealth.
Bibliography: p.
Includes index.
1. South Asia—Foreign relations—Great Britain.
2. Great Britain—Foreign relations—South Asia.
3. Commonwealth of Nations. I. Title.
DS341.3.G7M66 1987   327.41054   86-31215
ISBN 0-19-820112-5

Set by Colset Private Ltd, Singapore
Printed and bound in
Great Britain by Biddles Ltd
Guildford and Kings Lynn

Preface

THOUGH the transfer of power to India and Pakistan in August 1947 was a turning point in world history, it left in question the future relations of South Asia with Britain and the Commonwealth. The Attlee Government hoped to consolidate the new Dominions' membership of the Commonwealth in the interests of defence and economic development, and as a precedent for the colonial empire. The immediate consequences of the partition—the communal holocaust in the Punjab and hostilities over Kashmir—bedevilled its objectives. Its primary task was to avoid the alienation of either India or Pakistan by its approach to their disputes. Its essential problem was to devise a form of Commonwealth that would accommodate them both, while reconciling the Dominion members of the old 'White Man's club' to their full membership. This book is thus concerned with British diplomacy towards the subcontinent in the aftermath of its partition, and with the tortuous path to the formula of the 'London Declaration' of April 1949, on which the new Commonwealth was founded. The hope of an integrated defence structure was disappointed, but in the context of the Cold War the retention of South Asia to the Commonwealth for 'the pursuit of peace, liberty and progress' has been regarded as the Labour Government's greatest contribution to civilization. This is the first systematic study of that achievement.

My thanks are due to Dr Amit K. Gupta and Robin Radford, whose discoveries have enriched the documentation of my story. The work would have been impossible without the financial support of the Australian Research Grants Committee and Flinders University. This is my fourth book for the Clarendon Press and it is a pleasure to acknowledge the moral support of Peter Sutcliffe, who has the gift of making criticism constructive. I have enjoyed the encouragement of Professor Nicholas Mansergh, doyen of Commonwealth historians.

Flinders University of South Australia,
February 1986

Contents

Abbreviations Used in the Notes

AICC	All-India Congress Committee (papers in NML)
ATLE	Draft Memoirs by Attlee (Churchill College, Cambridge)
BO	British Officer
CA	Constituent Assembly
CAB	Cabinet Papers, PRO
CAB 127/57–154	Cripps Collection, PRO
CIGS	Chief of Imperial General Staff
CM	Cabinet Minutes
CO	Colonial Office
CR	Commonwealth Relations
CRO	Commonwealth Relations Office
CWC	Congress Working Committee
DO	Dominions Office
FO	Foreign Office
FRUS	*Foreign Relations of United States* (Washington)
GNWR	Gordon Walker Papers (Churchill College, Cambridge)
GOI	Government of India
IOL	India Office Library
IOR	India Office Records
L/P & J/10	Political Department Transfer of Power Papers, IOR
L/PO	Private Office Papers, IOR
NAI	National Archives of India
NML	Nehru Memorial Library
NWFP	North West Frontier Province
PBF	Punjab Boundary Force
PREM	Prime Minister's Files, PRO
PRO	Public Record Office
PUS	Permanent Under-Secretary
R/3/1	Papers of the Office of Private Secretary to Viceroy, IOR

Map

1

The New Dominions

'WHATEVER else the transfer of power may or may not have been it was a Commonwealth occasion!', wrote Nicholas Mansergh about the emergence of the Dominions of India and Pakistan on 15 August 1947.[1] Less than a year earlier such an occasion seemed unlikely. Dominion status had been promised repeatedly as the intention of the Raj during its last generation. Yet as the end drew near the India and Burma Offices at Whitehall were beset by doubts, curious at first sight, in terms of India's clubbability. A *ballon d'essai* loosed from the India Office questioned 'whether the Commonwealth is capable of the very considerable effort which would be required to extend its "club spirit" to include peoples of oriental race and modes of thought'.[2] One response within the Office was that the extension would mean 'weakening to a probably serious degree the cohesion of the Anglo-Saxon club as we know it'.[3] From the Burma Office Sir Gilbert Laithwaite echoed the well-known sentiments of his former viceregal chief, Lord Linlithgow, that 'India has not the same natural link with the Empire as have what one might call the "White Dominions" ', for conquest was the source of the association.[4] It was doubtful 'whether we can ever really hope, given the absence of *true* links of association such as those existing with the White Dominions, to have her spontaneous and natural co-operation in the same way as e.g. with Canada and Australia'. What, it must be asked, was involved in the analogy between the club and the Commonwealth, which continued to be assumed until India's permanent membership was negotiated at a special Prime Ministers' Conference in April 1949?

Nothing was quite so symbolic of the British Empire as its clubs. In 1934 the former and unlikely member of the Indian Imperial

---

[1] Mansergh, *The Commonwealth Experience* (1982), ii, 126.
[2] F.F. Turnbull's draft, 4 Oct. 1946, *TP*, viii, 409.
[3] K. Anderson to Turnbull, 14 Oct. 1946, ibid., 446.
[4] Laithwaite to Turnbull, 10 Oct. 1946, ibid., 425. Cf. Linlithgow to L.S. Amery, 21 Jan. 1942, ibid.,i, 23.

Police, George Orwell, wrote that 'in any town in India the European Club is the spiritual citadel, the real seat of British power, the Nirvana for which native officials and millionaires pine in vain'.[5] E. M. Forster was contemptuous of the Chandrapore Club's racial exclusiveness. It was where his young sahib went for a smoke among his 'own sort', the Collector held his fatuous 'Bridge Party', and was the scene of the British community's ludicrous amateur theatricals, and its closing of ranks against the 'native' doctor accused of assaulting a white woman.[6] For Paul Scott's Mr Srinivasan, looking back from 1964 across years when he had been secretary of the exclusive Mayapore Gymkhana, the Club meant much more. It was there, as the guest of the Deputy Commissioner in 1939, that in the precise fit of man and milieu he had 'really understood what it was that men like Robin White stood for':

In the club . . . for the first time I saw the face behind the face of Robin White. It seemed to go awfully well with the shabby leather chairs that looked forbidding but turned out to be amazingly comfortable to sit on. And Robin, you know, *looked* at the servants when he spoke to them. . . . He did not feel superior to them, only more responsible for them. It was his sense of responsibility that enabled him to accept his privileged position with dignity. . . . In one dazzling moment . . . I really felt I understood what it was the English always imagined lay but only rarely succeeded in showing *did* lie behind all the flummery of their power and influence. And that is why I have always loved the club since then.[7]

During India's brief dominionhood, the interregnum of August 1947 to April 1949 that fell between the old Empire and the new Commonwealth, the constitutional lawyer Sir Benegal Rau pondered the Commonwealth-club analogy:

It must . . . be remembered that a club . . . cannot grow or flourish merely by liberal rules of admission; to attract or retain members, it must give them something worth while and satisfying, not necessarily in material privileges, but at least in companionship in the pursuit of high ideals. Above all, there must be a sense of genuine equality among the members; for only then can each country be expected to give of its best and to contribute to the peace of this weary old world.[8]

---

[5] Orwell, *Burmese Days* (1934), ch. ii.

[6] Forster, *A Passage to India* (1924).

[7] Scott, *The Jewel in the Crown* (1966), 185.

[8] Rau, 'Citizenship in the Commonwealth of Nations', Aug. 1948, in his *India's Constitution in the Making* (1960), 340.

In their eleventh-hour reservations about admitting India to the Commonwealth, the mandarins of Whitehall were questioning whether, though entitled to independence, India was fit to join a Commonwealth of equals, accepting joint responsibility for the defence of principles to which they all subscribed. Their memoranda contemplated only two alternatives: Indian independence outside the Commonwealth and equality with Britain and the Dominions within it. Their predilection for the former was, however, a substitute for earlier assumptions that the next stage appropriate to India's constitutional evolution was a sort of subordinate dominionhood.

As early as 1884 Lord Rosebery had asserted that the British Empire was 'a commonwealth of nations', but the term 'British Commonwealth of Nations' was not used officially until 1921, in the Irish Treaty.[9] Jan Christiaan Smuts had called for its use as a new name more accurate than 'Empire' to describe the self-governing Dominions, Australia, Canada, New Zealand, and South Africa. It was reaffirmed in the Balfour Committee's Report of 1926 which, mainly in response to South African and Irish demands, described the Dominions as freely associating members of the British Commonwealth of Nations. Their status was defined in terms of their autonomy within the Empire, their equality with each other and the United Kingdom, and their common allegiance to the Crown. The definition seemed to head off separatist movements in the Dominions. In 1931 it was enacted in the Statute of Westminster, whose preamble referred to the Crown as the symbol of their free association and unity. While the Commonwealth ideal of self-government was applied to all components of the Empire-Commonwealth the realities of status were exemplified by their relationships with the separate Whitehall departments for the Dominions, India and Burma, and the Colonies.

In 1928 Britain aroused the suspicions of Indian leaders across the political spectrum when it sent out an 'all white' Parliamentary commission under Sir John Simon. The boycott of its inquiry into the operation of 'dyarchy', or qualified responsible government in the provinces, yielded a viceregal declaration that Britain's

9 Mehrotra, *The Commonwealth and the Nation* (1978), 4, 16.

ultimate goal for India was Dominion status.[10] Though the statement was made by a Conservative Viceroy, on the authority of
Ramsay MacDonald's Labour Government, it failed to convince
the Indian National Congress of Britain's sincerity. It was attacked
by Conservative and Liberal leaders for whom the achievement of
the goal was remote from practical politics. MacDonald was forced
to re-emphasize Parliament's role as the arbiter of India's political
development. Simon's report was silent on the question of
Dominion status. So too was the India Act of 1935, the mouse from
the Himalayan mountain of the report, three Round Table
Conferences, peripatetic expert committees, and a joint
Parliamentary committee. In 1935 advance in India's central
government was made dependent upon the achievement of an all-
India federation of provinces and princes that the latter were
empowered to veto. If the Union were achieved India would enjoy
Dominion status 'with reserves', HMG retaining power over
defence and foreign affairs. The Grail remained beyond reach
when war was declared in September 1939 and Congress at once
made its co-operation dependent upon a definition of war aims in
terms of India's freedom.

During the first year of war HMG clarified its object as
Dominion status of the Statute of Westminster variety, self-
government within the Empire, without acknowledging the
implicit right to secede from it. After the war Indians would be
consulted on a Dominion constitution but Parliament must remain
the arbiter and would not impose a majority demand upon an
unwilling minority. HMG thus pledged itself to uphold Muslim as
well as princely rights against Congress demands. The no-freedom-
without-unity requirement signalled a constitutional road block. In
1942, with the Empire in Asia imperilled, the block was removed by
the Cripps offer, which fused concessions that Sir Stafford Cripps,
Clement Attlee, and some Labour colleagues had favoured for
years with a Conservative plan to protect Muslim rights. Cripps
offered India a post-war constituent assembly, empowered to make
a Dominion constitution for a Union that might at once secede from
the Empire. The offer required the Union to enter a fixed-term

---

[10] In 1931 it was thought to betoken India's 'inevitable equality' that at the unveiling
of Herbert Baker's four Asokan columns in Government Court, New Delhi, each was
seen to bear the name and floral emblem of a donor Dominion (Irving, *Indian Summer:
Lutyens, Baker and Imperial Delhi* (1981). 294, 342).

treaty, through which Britain would, among other things, protect the princely states while they settled their relations within it. It met the Muslim problem with terms proposed by L.S. Amery, which offered provinces opposed to the Union constitution the right to become separate Dominions.[11] Pakistan was conceded in principle.[12]

The status within the Commonwealth of the plurality of subcontinental Dominions contemplated in the Cripps offer could not have been much superior to that of the 1935 Act's dominionhood with 'reserves'. Its implications were never worked out, for the failure of the Cripps mission brought HMG back to the realities of governing India for the duration in the face of Congress hostility. Amery, Churchill, and R.A. Butler speculated privately that at the next stage of development British forces would hold the ring from an imperial enclave, as dependent Dominions—perhaps Hindustan, Pakistan, Princestan—emerged. The prospect resembled Smuts's later vision of Britain remaining 'the arbiter of India's destiny and the moderating influence in her racial troubles and problems . . . indispensable in her affairs and a vital force in India's internal peace and welfare'.[13]

Labour's India experts had, in contrast, accepted Amery's 'local option' in the belief that it would induce Congress conciliatoriness towards the Muslim League and thus promote unity. Their *bona fides* on the question of India's status were demonstrated in March 1946 when the Attlee Government abandoned the Cripps scheme and despatched a Cabinet Mission to help establish constitution-making machinery through which Indians might by their own choice achieve freedom either within or outside the Commonwealth. As Foreign Secretary Ernest Bevin, who had been in the vanguard of the 1942 initiative, was 'glad that it was a Labour Government that had the courage, the wisdom, to take this step'.[14] It placed Attlee with 'the great men who had helped build this Commonwealth', with 'Durham who had saved us Canada . . . and

[11] Amery cited Dominion precedents: 'This is after all only what has happened in the case of every Dominion, where provinces have stood out for a time, or, as in the case of Newfoundland, New Zealand, and Southern Rhodesia, stood out permanently' (Amery to Hoare, 11 Mar. 1942, Templewood Papers, Cambridge Univ.Lib., XIII: 19).

[12] '. . . the powers-that-be are reconciled to the idea of a Moslem Confederation in the north' (R.A. Butler to Hoare, 6 Mar. 1942, ibid.).

[13] Smuts to Attlee, 26 May 1947, *TP*, x, 538.

[14] Speech of 30 Mar. 1946, in Bullock, *Ernest Bevin: Foreign Secretary, 1945-1951* (1983), 234.

Campbell Bannerman who created the Union of South Africa'. Additionally the Cabinet Mission strove to promote an all-India Union. It ruled that Pakistan was not viable and sought to accommodate the demand for it at a sub-national level of provincial groups. It proposed the free association of the princely states with the Constituent Assembly and, according to their individual choice, their attachment to the Union or their negotiation of subordinate treaties with it.

Late in 1946, when the senior civil servants at Whitehall were ventilating their doubts about the Commonwealth there seemed little chance of India becoming a Dominion. Led by the Congress the Constituent Assembly would surely opt for 'complete independence', the avowed object of Jawaharlal Nehru since 1928. On 26 January 1930, as President of Congress, he pledged himself to that end, and the party had reaffirmed it at Ramgarh in March 1940. On 22 November 1946 he called for the Constituent Assembly to establish an 'independent sovereign republic'. The concept of Dominion status had been soiled by the hands of imperialists.

If, in the ancient world, imperial and international relations were influenced by Cleopatra's nose and the face that launched a thousand ships, Mohammad Ali Jinnah's chest may have played a decisive role in Commonwealth history. Had the tuberculosis from which he died in September 1948 cut short his life two years earlier it is doubtful whether the Muslim League could have marshalled the strength required to secure Pakistan. It was essentially the League's capacity to destabilize Congress governments in Muslim areas that convinced Congress of the necessity of partition and dominionhood.

As early as 1938 Jinnah espoused his theory that Muslim India satisfied the criteria of separate nationhood. In 1940 he demanded the demarcation of contiguous Muslim areas as separate states. Yet it is unlikely that he believed a fully sovereign independent Pakistan should be achieved in a single constitutional step. If Britain were to divide India in the face of Congress hostility and summarily withdraw, Pakistan must face enormous problems of finance and defence. On the other hand, the arrangement of those two subjects in any Union government would be contentious. There are indications that, at least as a step towards a sovereign Pakistan, Jinnah was prepared to accept subordinate dominionhood, while in early 1946 he would accept a limited Union if he were assured of an opportunity to consolidate Muslim India within strong provincial groups. However, by August 1946 he was convinced that Congress was bent on destroying the Cabinet Mission's grouping principle and that HMG lacked the will to impose it. When he called for direct action to secure a sovereign Pakistan atrocities were perpetrated in Calcutta, and communal violence spread like an infection through eastern and northern India. A veritable revolution for Pakistan emerged. Though the League belatedly entered Nehru's Interim Government in October its purpose was to secure Pakistan and it boycotted the Constituent Assembly.

When Jinnah went to London in December 1946 for talks on the impasse he insisted that 'his own aim was simply that of Pakistan, within the British Commonwealth'.[15] He met Churchill, who assured him that 'You have only to stand firm and demand your rights not to be expelled from the British Commonwealth, and you are bound to be accepted. The country would never stand for the expulsion of loyal members of the Empire'.[16] In Parliament Churchill foreshadowed a partition of the subcontinent, with the parts of India remaining in the Commonwealth or not as they might choose.[17] Simon put Jinnah in touch with Opposition peers sympathetic to his cause, and in January 1947 Jinnah had a channel of communication to other Conservatives through the Nawab of Bhopal. Lord Templewood, the main architect of the 1935 Act, answered affirmatively when asked 'if Jinnah came out with a declaration that they want to stay within the Commonwealth . . . they would receive a substantial measure of support from responsible opinion in England'.[18]

Jinnah welcomed Attlee's statement of 20 February 1947, which promised a full transfer of power by June 1948. Failing Indian agreement upon a central government for the purpose there would be a plural succession. The League, which already governed in Sind and Bengal, intensified its efforts to control the Muslim majority provinces that it claimed for Pakistan, and soon brought

[15] Record of meeting, 4 Dec. 1946, *TP*, ix, 153.

[16] Jinnah's interview with Mountbatten, 25 Apr. 1947, ibid, x, 229.

[17] Commons Debates, 12 Dec. 1946, col. 1370.

[18] Sir W. Monckton to Templewood, 15 Jan. 1947, and reply next day, Templewood Papers, IOL.

down the Coalition that governed the Punjab and threatened the Congress ministry in the Frontier Province. At the same time some of the leading princes were, with Conservative encouragement, staking claims for their states to become separate Dominions. Though Attlee's time-limit statement made no mention of the Commonwealth, it produced a struggle for succession by separate dominionhood among Muslims and princes who had received special treatment in the abortive schemes for Union in the 1930s and 1940s. Congress responded by claiming the powers of a Dominion for the Interim Government and the expulsion of the Muslim League members. It could then check the drift to disorder and disintegration. The Dominion status Interim Government should assume full executive power pending the making of a new constitution. Any secession from the Union of dissident Muslim majority areas, which might include Punjab and Bengal truncated by the detachment of their non-Muslim areas, would be delayed until the constitution was framed.

While the niceties of clubmanship were being articulated in Whitehall, the realities of communal politics in India thus ensured that the transfer of power would be 'a Commonwealth occasion'. In the second week of March, when Attlee and his expert colleagues met Viceroy-designate Mountbatten to discuss the Indian problem, they recognized that the time limit for withdrawal could probably be met only by amending the 1935 Act to provide for a transfer of power on the basis of dominionhood.

The hobgoblin of consistency is not to be found in the Attlee Government's policies for India's unity or freedom. Labour's initial policy was the imposition of the Cripps offer, which required a Union and any seceding provinces to become Dominions. It next allowed the dominionhood step to be skipped and approved a Union scheme that repudiated a sovereign Pakistan but nominated a procedure for constitution-making through quasi-Pakistan groups. It soon condoned and then resisted Congress neglect of the latter requirement. It finally reinstated a Commonwealth approach and accepted the necessity of a Pakistan based on the partition of the largest Muslim majority provinces. Moreover, it insisted first upon a constitutional scheme based upon Congress–League agreement, in the absence of which, Cabinet decided in mid-1946, Britain would remain in the whole of India. But within a few months it announced Britain's imminent withdrawal, whether or not the Indian parties agreed upon terms of succession. To a large extent Labour did simply react to local events in India as government became ever more difficult. The various policy statements were attempts to find successors who commanded the support necessary to law and order. Neither that object nor lasting goodwill between India and Britain could be achieved through an imposed constitutional settlement.

Yet the tortuous lines of Attleean policy were drawn within long-established co-ordinates. The Conservatives had always assumed the preservation of imperial interests by India's subordination and military dependence; for example, Linlithgow had looked towards the embodiment of defence arrangements in the constitution, while Churchill had rejected the idea of a treaty, which connoted equality. On the other hand, from the late 1930s Labour's leaders planned to protect imperial interests through a treaty with India as an equal partner in the Commonwealth. In mid-1943 Attlee wrote in a Cabinet paper that 'it will be our aim to maintain the British Commonwealth as an international entity. . . . If we are to carry our full weight in the post-war world with the US and the USSR it can only be as a united British Commonwealth'.[19] The next year Cripps urged Churchill to tackle the Indian problem: 'to keep India within the Commonwealth of Nations . . . is of very great importance to our future position in the world both economically and politically'.[20] In January 1945, when Simon questioned whether Indian dominionhood and the continuing presence of British forces were compatible, Cripps recognized that India's own forces must be adequate for internal security but saw no inconsistency in the retention by treaty of British troops for defence.[21] In March 1946 Attlee's waiving of the Dominion condition of freedom was evidence of his hope that the assurance of equality would encourage partnership within the Commonwealth. The hope was symbolized in the requirement for a treaty between equals for the mutual defence of the Indian Ocean area.

When Labour entered office in the aftermath of the war the essential metropolitan determinants of its imperial policy were

[19] Attlee, 'The Relations of the British Commonwealth to the Post-War International Political Organization', June 1943, cited in Bullock, op. cit., 65.
[20] Cripps to Churchill, 29 Nov. 1944, PREM 4/46/12.
[21] *TP*, v, 298.

clear: massive British indebtedness and a predatory Soviet communism. Britain's global debt of some £2,135m. required the early demobilization of armed servicemen and their return to the mines and the factories. The production of export commodities to pay for imports of materials and food was necessary. Any hopes of economic support from her trans-Atlantic 'ally of a kind' were soon dashed by America's instant termination of lend-lease and refusal of a loan on generous conditions. The terms of the loan eventually granted in August 1946 bespoke America's early post-war priorities: Britain must, from August 1947, agree to convert into US dollars surpluses earned in sterling that year by her trading partners. Upon the signing of the lend-lease agreement in February 1942 US officials had recognized the leverage that it gave for demanding the dismantling of imperial trading preferences. They survived American attacks, while the sterling area emerged from the 'wringer of convertibility' to contribute to the quest for solvency.[22] America was hostile to Britain's colonialism and her co-operation with her European allies in South East Asia, the Dutch, and the French, for the rehabilitation of control over Indonesia and Indo-China. The effect of the economic strait jacket was to reinforce Labour's reliance on her colonies for materials and markets, most notably Malaya for dollar-earning tin and rubber. R.F. Holland has located the rationale of Britain's phased decolonization in Labour's recruitment of the colonial empire in South East Asia and Africa to her post-war economic recovery.[23] Roger Louis has written at length of the *Zeitgeist* of Ernest Bevin's retention of the Empire in the Middle East as 'development', through 'partnership', in the mutual interest—and as a shield to the same in Africa.[24]

The global demobilization of British forces was impaired by apprehension of Soviet expansion and the slowness of the US to develop its policy of containment. In a memorandum of 11 July 1945, 'Stocktaking after VE Day', Sir Orme Sargent, Deputy

[22] Holland's phrase, in 'The Imperial Factor in British Strategies from Attlee to Macmillan, 1945–63', *Journal of Imperial and Commonwealth History*, 12 (1984), 165–86. See also, Newton, 'The Sterling Crisis of 1947 and the British Response to the Marshall Plan', *Economic History Review*, 37 (1984), 391–408.

[23] Loc. cit. Cf. Darwin, 'British Decolonization since 1945: A Pattern or a Puzzle?', *Journal of Imperial and Commonwealth History*, 12 (1984), 187–209.

[24] Louis, *The British Empire in the Middle East, 1945–1951: Arab Nationalism, the United States, and Postwar Imperialism* (1984).

Under-Secretary at the Foreign Office, wrote of the Russian danger in the western Mediterranean.[25] Britain's access to Iraqi and Persian oil, India, Malaya, Australia, and New Zealand was at risk. Italy, Greece, and Turkey must be made bastions of liberalism. Here, in the context of Soviet expansion, was a reaffirmation of the traditional strategic importance of the line of imperial communications. Bevin shared this concern, alluding to 'the lifeline of the Empire' and to Russian aggression 'everywhere'.[26] In breach of the Yalta agreement Russia had denied self-determination to Poland, Austria, Bulgaria, and Romania. In 1945–6 she threatened the 'northern tier' of the Mediterranean—Greece, where British troops remained to prevent a Communist take-over, Turkey, from whom Russia sought a base on the Bosphorus, and Iran, where she wished to make the province of Azerbaijan a separate state. In North Africa she wanted trusteeship over the former Italian colony of Tripolitania. At the end of the war Britain had some 200,000 troops in Egypt. The Canal Zone base was the lynch-pin of her position in the Middle East, reinforced by troops in Palestine (as many as 100,000 in 1947). Bevin not only saw the bases as strategically vital but sought to supplement them by acquiring Cyrenaica.

In early 1946 Attlee favoured Britain's withdrawal from her massive commitments in the Middle East.[27] He did not believe that Britain had the resources to resist Russia in the northern tier and argued that the defence of the line of communications to the East was an anachronism, suitable to an empire based on sea power but not in the age of air and atomic power. The extension of control to the Italian colonies would be financially disastrous. By April 1946 he was overborne by the Chiefs of Staff, the Foreign Office, and the Dominion Prime Ministers. The Chiefs of Staff argued that the age of air and atomic power scarcely altered the fundamentals of strategy. Soviet aggression could only be deterred by the capability to launch an air offensive from the Middle East. When the old Dominions' Prime Ministers met in London in April with Churchill's 'iron curtain' speech ringing in their ears they agreed

[25] FO 371/50912.

[26] Record of meeting, 1 Oct. 1945, cited in Morgan, *Labour in Power, 1945–1951* (1984), 242; Bevin to Attlee, 10 Apr. 1946, cited in Bullock, op. cit., 234; Bevin's memo of 18 April 1946, cited in Louis, op. cit., 276.

[27] Ibid.; Smith and Zametica, 'The Cold Warrior: Clement Attlee Reconsidered, 1945–7', *International Affairs*, 61 (1985), 237–52.

that Russian pressure on the northern tier states must be resisted. They followed Smuts in his insistence that Russia must be kept out of Africa. They agreed to exchange defence liaison staffs with Britain. In May Attlee did announce British willingness to withdraw from the Suez base, given a treaty with Egypt for its defence, but by the end of the year negotiations had failed over Egypt's demand for joint control of the Nile with the Sudan. In October, relief from the military burdens in Greece and Turkey came into sight with an American appraisal that suggested her willingness to take them over. Yet at year's end Britain was still clamped in the vice of economic stringency and military commitment. The manpower shortfall exceeded 600,000, and factories stopped for want of fuel. The major military crisis was in Palestine, racked by Zionist terrorism. As Viceroy Wavell and his immediate predecessor Linlithgow agreed, a Palestine situation must be avoided in India.[28]

At times during 1946 Cold War calculations threatened to blow Labour's Indian policy off course. The intended recruitment of India as a partner in the defence of the Indian Ocean area, from the straits of Malacca to the Persian Gulf, was an extrapolation into the Cold War world of the traditional reliance on Indian manpower, resources, and territory for the *pax Britannica*. Labour's quintessential concern to transfer power to responsible Indians was bound to be phrased in Cold War terminology. A.V. Alexander, the Cabinet Mission's authority on Defence, saw that failure to establish social democracy in South Asia would mean a 'Russian type of Communism with one list of political candidates, a gagged press and acceptance of orders from Moscow'.[29] The form of succession must recognize communal divisions or, as a recent High Commissioner to Britain, Feroz Khan Noon, told Alexander, the Muslims would ask Russia to get Pakistan for them.[30] From time to time the Cabinet considered, always to reject, referring the question of Pakistan to the UN. Both the USA and the USSR wanted to liquidate the British Empire. The referral of the Pakistan question to the UN would be made the precedent for bringing imperial disputes before the international forum. In any event, Britain was disillusioned with the UN, where Russia had used her veto to

[28] Moon (ed.), *Wavell: The Viceroy's Journal* (1973), 396.
[29] Alexander's Diary, 10 May 1946, Churchill College, Cambridge.
[30] Ibid., 9 Apr. 1946.

prevent the Security Council from becoming an effective force for international order. Alexander's diary reveals a determination to resist any Indian settlement that would open the subcontinent to Russian intervention:

The danger to the world at large if [the submersion of the British Empire] came about through Russian measures to me was patent for they would impose a system on the world as they had obviously done today in the Balkans and in Poland. . . . I hoped by now that people generally were beginning to understand the nature of the defence which Mr Bevin had been conducting against such a danger.[31]

In mid-1946, when agreement between the Indian parties was elusive, Cabinet recognized that withdrawal, or partial withdrawal as suggested by Wavell, would damage British prestige and embolden the Russians in Afghanistan, Persia, and the Arab states. Here was not so much Russophobia or a twentieth century 'Mervousness' as a tendency to evaluate Indian policy in terms of its implications for British resistance to Russia in Europe and the Middle East.

Indian policy was effectively emancipated from this Bevinite or Foreign Office perspective at the beginning of 1947. On New Year's Day Bevin attacked the intended time-limit statement:

I must express my strong views with regard to India. . . . I have examined this problem in relation to Egypt, Palestine, the Middle East, and all the Arab States and Persia, and I cannot help feeling that the defeatist attitude adopted both by the Cabinet and by Field-Marshal Wavell is just completely letting us down. . . . you cannot read the telegrams from Egypt and the Middle East nowadays without realizing that not only is India going but . . . the Middle East is going with it, with a tremendous repercussion on the African territories. . . . As Foreign Secretary, I can offer nothing to any foreign country, neither credit, nor coal, nor goods. . . . And on top of that, within the British Empire, we knuckle under at the first blow.[32]

Attlee's response referred not so much to the unavailability of troops as to the fact that to hold India by force would find little support in Britain and, most importantly, be a reversal of long-established policy.[33] Britain had 'always governed India through the Indians'. To rule by force would be 'to go back on the pledges

---

[31] Ibid., 16 Apr. 1946.
[32] Bevin to Attlee, 1 Jan. 1947, *TP*, ix, 236.
[33] Attlee to Bevin, 2 Jan. 1947, ibid., 243.

that have been given by Governments of every political colour'. The whole intention of the time-limit declaration was to make clear to the Indians 'that we are determined to hand over as a going concern . . . and we are placing responsibility on their shoulders'. The declaration was essentially a resort to shock tactics, to make collaborating successors of those who could now establish their capacity to inherit the Raj.

Matured as it was in the grim winter of 1946–7, Attlee's time-limit declaration has understandably been seen in the imagery appropriate to the time—load-shedding. As factories were darkened and silenced because of the coal shortage, so to secure manpower and trim defence budgets the withdrawals from Greece and Turkey were announced, and Palestine referred to the UN. But in defence the object was more to share than to shed the burdens. The northern tier withdrawals were really a victory for Bevin as the Americans succeeded to British obligations there and the Truman doctrine was proclaimed. So was Attlee's reluctant capitulation that January to the Chiefs of Staff's ultimatum, backed by resigna-tion threats, that, in the face of the Russian menace Britain must hold her Middle Eastern bases and make her own atomic weapons. The concomitant Chiefs of Staff's policy for the Indian Ocean area now triumphed, too, against the inclinations of the Civil Service chiefs.

On 11 March Lord Ismay, Chief of the Defence Staff and Mountbatten's Chief of Staff designate, defeated an attempt by the heads of the India, Burma, Colonial, Dominions, and Foreign Offices to put a paper up to Cabinet advocating that relations with independent India should be on a treaty rather than a Common-wealth basis. India was thought unsuitable for Commonwealth membership. She could not be trusted to fulfil the unwritten responsibilities of membership, particularly for Commonwealth defence, while Nehru's resolution for an independent sovereign republic would sever the link with the Crown. Sargent, now PUS for Foreign Affairs, summed up the position:

. . . if India simply remained within the Commonwealth, without our rela-tionships being defined, we should be morally bound to assist in her defence while she would have no obligation to come to our assistance. This was the position in the case of the Dominions. It worked out all right with people of the same outlook as ours, but he could not believe that it would be a satisfactory form of relationship with the Indians who were totally different in outlook and fanatically nationalist.[34]

By contrast Ismay argued:

. . . every effort should be made to keep India in the Commonwealth and . . . the main objective in the next 18 months should be to get friendly relations with India in the subsequent period. When the Indians found themselves independent they might well want to stay in the Commonwealth.[35]

A treaty could not secure satisfactory arrangements for India's contribution to Commonwealth defence unless she were herself a member. There now ensued a coalescence of the Chiefs of Staff's strategic planning for the Indian Ocean area and Attlee's shock tactics. On 13 March, at a meeting of Mountbatten, Ismay, and the India Committee of Cabinet, Attlee picked up the Congress demand for an immediate transfer of power to the Interim Government on the basis of dominionhood.[36] He asked the India Office to examine the 1935 Act as a medium for creating more than one Dominion and instructed Mountbatten to encourage India to remain in the Commonwealth.

The Attlee–Bevin conflict of winter 1946–7 revealed a contrast in strategic perspectives. Bevin's view of India was a corollary of his concern to defend Britain against Russia in the Middle East. Like the Whitehall mandarins he had no real faith in any new Commonwealth, whereas Attlee held firm to the ideals of self-determination and partnership. The outcome of the conflict was a sort of compromise: Bevin secured his Middle Eastern policy and Attlee his South Asian. Policies for the new Commonwealth in South Asia now remained outside the purview of Bevin and the Foreign Office until, early in 1948, the India–Pakistan dispute came before the UN.

The complex saga of Mountbatten's diplomatic coup in negotiating the 1947 transfer of power on the basis of dual dominionhood has been recited in full elsewhere.[37] Here a summary must suffice. Mountbatten was instructed that it was HMG's objective to reach a

---

[34] Record of meeting, 11 Mar. 1947, ibid., 522.
[35] Ibid.   [36] Ibid., 529.
[37] Moore, *Escape from Empire: The Attlee Government and the Indian Problem* (1983).

settlement for 'a unitary Government for British India and the
Indian States, if possible within the British Commonwealth'.[38] He
should 'impress upon the Indian leaders the great importance of
avoiding any breach in the continuity of the Indian Army and of
maintaining the organization of defence on an all Indian basis'. He
must 'point out the need for continued collaboration in the security
of the Indian Ocean area'; at a suitable date HMG would send out
military and other experts to help negotiate an agreement.

Almost at once Mountbatten saw that a unitary transfer of power
was impossible, however 'mad' the Pakistan ideal and however
truncated its territorial realization might be. Within a fortnight he
was exploring the possibilities of a plural succession within the
Commonwealth. The Nawab of Bhopal sought dominionhood for
the states, Jinnah for Pakistan, and Congress for the Interim
Government. Mountbatten's first approach was for an immediate
trilogy of 'autonomous' Dominions (the states, Pakistan, and the
rest of British India) to run experimentally until June 1948, but
with Defence, Foreign Affairs, Finance, Food, and Communications 'reserved to some form of central Government'.[39] Here was a
curious re-emergence of the notion of subordinate Dominions.
Ismay demolished it by explaining that with the award of Dominion
status the Governor-General's powers must become merely
advisory, so that he would lose control of the armed forces. The
transfer of power must, in short, be accomplished in a single
step.

Very soon, too, Mountbatten realized that the step must be taken
earlier than June 1948. The compulsions included the steady dete-
rioration of the administrative machinery, which had prompted the
preparation of Wavell's 'Breakdown Plan' as early as the previous
August and was now exacerbated by the communal struggle for
succession. However, the most potent danger was the threatened
withdrawal of Congress from the fragile and divided Interim
Government, where Congress felt frustrated by the presence of
avowedly anti-national Leaguers and the absence of powers
adequate to deal with the breakdown of law and order.
Mountbatten's acceleration of the transfer of power has sometimes
been read wrongly as a bribe to Congress in return for India's

---

[38] Attlee to Mountbatten, 18 Mar. 1947, *TP*, ix, 543.
[39] Ibid., x, 33.

attachment to the Commonwealth.[40] Recently, it has been associated misleadingly with the spring financial crisis at the metropolis.[41]

Given the need for a quick plural succession Mountbatten's essential problem was to cast it in a Commonwealth form acceptable not only to the Indian party leaders and princes but also to HMG. His greatest difficulty was to retain Congress goodwill, so necessary if post-independence relations with India were to prosper, yet resist its claims of immediate Dominion status for the Interim Government over the whole of India, pending the completion of an all-India constitution and negotiations for the secession of, or treaty relations with, dissident areas. Such a transfer of power would breach British pledges to the Muslims and the princes. Not only some Conservatives but also the Chiefs of Staff favoured striking separate arrangements for dominionhood with non-Congress areas if Congress eschewed the Commonwealth. Mountbatten was adroit in revealing to Congress leaders the lurid consequences of their isolation. At one time he was committed to a scheme, proposed by his own staff and HMG, that might 'Balkanize' India, whilst he was evincing sympathy towards the Congress demand.

Mountbatten's triumph, and the final settlement of the Indian problem, was Congress's acceptance of the partition of British India between India and Pakistan prior to a transfer of power on the basis of dominionhood. The partition was to be made on the votes of the provincial legislatures and was 'notional' in the case of Bengal and Punjab, where precise lines of demarcation would be drawn by Boundary Commissions. The princely states were obliged to join either the Indian or the Pakistan Dominion. Congress was spared the possibility, first raised in the Cripps offer and apparent in Attlee's statement and Mountbatten's staff's Plan Balkan, of losing the substantial non-Muslim areas of Muslim-majority provinces. The chimera of a Bengal Dominion was thus destroyed. So too were schemes for princely Dominions, though HMG faced awkward pressures in Parliament. Mountbatten, as he had doubtless led Congress to expect, deployed all the arts of

---

[40] e.g., Krishan, 'Mountbatten and the Partition of India', *History*, 68 (1983), 22–37; cf. Ziegler, *Mountbatten: The Official Biography* (1985), 380.

[41] Holland, op. cit., 169.

persuasion to commit the princes to one of the two Dominions before the transfer of power.

At 15 August Mountbatten became Governor-General of India only, for Jinnah had chosen to be his counterpart in Pakistan. It was hoped that he could help resolve problems arising from the demarcation of boundaries and the accession, yet to be accomplished, of Hyderabad, Kashmir, and Junagadh. He remained chairman of a Joint Defence Council. The party leaders had been too preoccupied to consider defence treaties. However the new Dominions remained within the orbit of Commonwealth defence and both seemed receptive to plans for a visit, probably in October, by British experts to negotiate agreements.

On the eve of Indian Independence the Chiefs of Staff displayed as little faith in the ideal of a new Commonwealth as their civilian counterparts. They referred to the new Dominions as 'temporary', as questionable allies on the basis of the unwritten rules of Commonwealth co-operation for defence. For them treaties were therefore an urgent necessity and they spelled out their detailed requirements in a brief for immediate negotiation. The new Dominions should, consistently with the old Dominions' agreement in April 1946, exchange liaison staffs with Britain. In return for British defence aid the subcontinent should continue to be 'the main support area in war', offering the co-operation of its armed forces, the use of manpower, strategic air fields, and naval and military bases.[42] India and Pakistan should not only undertake the primary responsibility for their own defence but also accept obligations to send forces to neighbouring territories in case of need. The Chiefs of Staff summed up the subcontinent's place in global strategy:

The Indian Continent has long claimed the moral leadership of the South East Asia countries. Through its dominant geographical position, the Continent also is in a position to affect the security of all nations dependent on the sea communications through the Indian Ocean. The stability and strength of the Indian Continent is thus the direct concern of other nations, since it affects their security. These nations, including those Colonies and Dominions within the Commonwealth association, cannot, therefore, forego a direct interest and anxiety that the authorities in India are not only conscious and alive to this responsibility to other nations, but display the

_____

[42] Chiefs of Staff's paper, 'India—Defence Requirements', 1 Aug. 1947, R/3/1/161.

necessary strength to ensure the peaceful use of the sea communications on which these nations are dependent. The discharge of this responsibility needs strength both to preserve internal order and prevent external domination or aggression.

The Chiefs of Staff wanted an India–Pakistan agreement with Britain for the defence of the subcontinent and the Indian Ocean area. The difficulty was that both India and Pakistan received less territory than they had expected; and they might now lose more through the boundary awards and the princes' decisions on accession. Treaties could only be achieved if disputes between the Dominions were resolved. The Commonwealth could scarcely contemplate defence obligations to defend one of them against the other. The roles of British principals in the immediate post-Independence period would be crucial for the future of the Commonwealth.

For Attlee 'the Commonwealth occasion' of August 1947 was far more than the shedding of an imperial burden or the route to defence treaties. The Labour Government deliberately chose the title 'Indian Independence Act' for the statute that set up the new Dominions. When Churchill objected that a Dominion was not independent as it owed allegiance to the Crown, Attlee stood firm. Under the Statute of Westminster a Dominion was surely as independent as Britain; and Attlee was demonstrating that full independence was achievable within the Commonwealth. Though the nature of the new Commonwealth had scarcely been mooted, for Attlee at least the opening assumption would be that the new Dominions were full and equal members.[43]

The concept of a new Commonwealth required a drastic reconstruction of mental images. At the transfer of power it remained to be seen whether the Commonwealth was capable of extending 'its "club spirit" to include peoples of oriental race'. The doubters included not only the civil and military chiefs at the metropolis but the *koi-hais* who stayed on. Mountbatten threw down the challenge to one of them who presided over 'the Nirvana for which native officials and millionaires pine in vain'. In December Mr H. Rowan Hodge of Calcutta came to consult him about membership of the Bengal Club. Mountbatten said that either 'Indians should be

---

[43] Attlee noted in his memoirs: 'It was my task to show them that independence could be had within the Commonwealth' (ATLE 1/13, Churchill College, Cambridge).

admitted on the same basis as Britons or the name changed to the "United Kingdom Club" '.[44] The reply portended the early renaming of the 'British' Commonwealth of Nations, which he was soon to propose.

[44] Ziegler, op. cit., 461.

2

Dominions in Dispute

THE interlude of dominionhood that began in August 1947 was a holding operation for Britain, India, and Pakistan. In the interests of stability powers had been devolved suddenly but the spoils of empire remained to be divided precisely between the successor nations. To a remarkable degree a British presence persisted to assist with the details of division and smooth the transition to new authorities. At the top the office of governor-general had been intended as an agency for continuity. Jinnah's disappointment of that hope dispelled any illusion that the office would be merely constitutional. Though the divided office remained exactly that in statutory terms the Quaid-i-Azam could scarcely be expected to act only on ministerial advice; nor did such a role suit the dynamic Mountbatten. Jinnah, for example, at once dismissed the Congress Government of the Frontier Province, while Mountbatten soon became chairman of India's Defence Committee. Of Mountbatten's senior viceregal staff Sir Eric Miéville and Sir George Abell left at Independence, though the more junior members, Lieutenant-Colonel V. Erskine Crum (conference secretary), A. Campbell-Johnson (press secretary) and Captain R.V. Brockman (personal secretary) served him until he departed the following June. Ismay stayed on but became increasingly critical of Mountbatten and oppressed by the 'miseries of September and October' when 'close friends were bereaved and destitute, and homeless and helpless'.[1] In September he asked to disembark the once so 'happy ship' and finally left in December. It was not until 1950 that India, and 1956 that Pakistan, brought down constitutions to end their dominionhood.

The details of division were consigned to joint agencies and judicial processes. A Partition Council, in which Congress and League were represented equally, was set up under Mountbatten's chairmanship. It spawned a steering committee and ten expert

---

[1] Ismay to Attlee, 6 May 1949, Attlee Papers, Bodleian Library.

subcommittees to apportion assets and liabilities. Contentious issues were referred to an Arbitral Tribunal over which Chief Justice Sir Patrick Spens presided. Its duties were far from onerous. The division of the army was the work of a Joint Defence Council, which Prime Ministers Nehru and Liaquat Ali Khan attended and Mountbatten chaired. Sir Claude Auchinleck remained as Supreme Commander, with a headquarters to undertake the administrative division of military resources. His authority rankled with the Indians and he resigned in November 1947. The Joint Defence Council lingered until April 1948. The heaviest of all burdens imposed by the partition of India was borne by Sir Cyril Radcliffe, chairman of the Boundary Commissions. As his work was most crucial for relations between the new Dominions it must be examined closely below.

In both Dominions British servants of the Raj stayed on as agents of continuity, while senior Indians and Pakistanis perpetuated British traditions in the civil and military services. In Pakistan the governors of the three largest provinces and the heads of the three armed services were still British in May 1949. In India, too, the Commander-in-Chief was British until K.M. Cariappa took over early in 1949. Two of India's first provincial governors were British. Some 2,800 British officers retained the King's Commission in the Dominions' services, though most had resigned by the end of 1947. Few British civil servants remained in India after Independence but some held important positions in Pakistan and the states.

British diplomatic relations with the Dominions were placed under the aegis of the Commonwealth Relations Office, with the venerable Lord Addison as Secretary of State until Philip Noel-Baker succeeded him in October 1947. At Whitehall the amalgamation of the old Dominions and India Offices as the new CRO failed to remove their historic separateness. Until 1949 there were two permanent under-secretaries, with Sir Eric Machtig holding Section A ('white' Dominions) aloof from Sir Archibald Carter's Section B (new Dominions). The first high commissioners to the new Dominions were not eminent remnants of the Raj. Indeed both came from appointments in the Middle East. The mission at Delhi was set up in the last year of British rule by Alec Symon from the India Office, with Sir Terence Shone, of the Foreign Service and Minister in Beirut, as High Commissioner. Soon after Independence there was a disagreement between Addison and Bevin over the seniority of any successor to Shone. Addison favoured an appointment commensurate with the importance of India to Britain (which he thought second only to that of America) and suggested someone of Ismay's or Malcolm MacDonald's distinction. Bevin, irked by the prospect of policy on the subcontinent remaining beyond his influence, wanted a more routine appointment. Mountbatten exerted himself to secure high-level representation and, at his suggestion, Sir Archibald Nye, then Governor of Madras, was appointed late in 1948. At Karachi, Sir Laurence Grafftey-Smith, formerly of the Levant Service and Minister to Saudi Arabia, was High Commissioner from August 1947 until 1951.

At Westminster the India and Burma Committee of Cabinet was succeeded (with the Colonial Committee) by a Commonwealth Affairs Committee. Attlee chaired it and its members were the Lord Privy Seal, the Lord Chancellor, the ministers for the Colonies, Burma, Commonwealth Relations, and Civil Aviation, together with a Foreign Office representative. It was 'to consider constitutional problems and other questions of policy affecting the Commonwealth and Empire'.[2] The 'India–Pakistan dispute' was soon prominent on its agenda.

Within days of the transfer of power the prospect of Indo-Pakistan partnership within the Commonwealth was cast in doubt by the grim consequences of the Punjab Boundary Award. To expedite the transfer the Independence Act provided for a 'notional' partition of provinces solely on the basis of population distribution among administrative districts. Contiguous Muslim and non-Muslim majority districts were thus assigned provisionally to Pakistan and India respectively. Judicial Commissions were to be appointed by the Governor-General to 'demarcate the boundaries . . . on the basis of ascertaining the contiguous majority areas of Muslims and non-Muslims', and taking 'into account other factors'.[3] The need for Boundary Commissions had been recognized from early May, especially to deal with the problem of the Sikhs in the Punjab. Whereas the League sought partition on

---

[2] Meeting of 9 Oct. 1947, CAB 134/54.
[3] Announcement by Governor-General, 30 June 1947, *TP*, xi, 415.

the basis of contiguous areas to below tehsil (sub-district) level
Nehru urged the need to consider 'many other factors'.[4] Where the
term 'other factors' appeared in draft plans Baldev Singh had
wanted to define them as including property held by non-Muslims
and revenues paid by them. The Governor-General's order left the
term undefined. On 14 July, the Under-Secretary of State, Arthur
Henderson, told Parliament that it was employed 'primarily to
enable the Commission to have regard to the special circumstances
of the Sikh community in the Punjab, where considerations such as
the location of their religious shrines can reasonably be taken into
account up to a point'.[5] It was 'for the Commission itself to decide
what are other factors and how much importance should be
attached to all or any of them'. Radcliffe found that his fellow Commissioners, comprising two Congress and two League nominees in
both the Punjab and Bengal Commissions, were unable to agree, so
that the awards must be his own. The leaders of both parties had
agreed to Radcliffe's appointment and pledged themselves to
accept his awards.

Radcliffe was a highly respected King's Counsel who had served
as Director-General of the Ministry of Information during the war.
He had no background in Indian affairs or politics and suffered
large financial loss for undertaking a task from which he could
anticipate no gain or satisfaction. The 'whole experience' was, as
he later recalled, 'terrible'.[6] It did kindle an abiding interest in the
history of Britain in India, which became a favourite subject of
discourse on public occasions.[7] While he acknowledged the stern
imperial presents of legal and governing institutions he wondered
that India had so little inspired the artistic and literary imagination
of the British. In his admiration of Mountstuart Elphinstone, who
responded to the traditions of the country and twice refused the
governor-generalship, and of Henry Lawrence, who opposed the
annexation of the Punjab and was displaced by the Anglicizing
Dalhousie, murmurs critical of the Raj may be heard. Cast as
Solomon in the Alice-in-Wonderlandish world of the Raj *in extremis*
he was bound subsequently to probe the past for the sources of the
intractable problem that he was called upon to solve. He could

---

[4] Ibid., x, 46.   [5] Ibid., xii, 144.

[6] Radcliffe to A. Michel, 28 Mar. 1965, in Michel, *The Indus Rivers: A Study of the Effects
of Partition* (1967), 194.

[7] Radcliffe, *Not in Feather Beds: Some Collected Papers* (1968).

never relive the experience by rereading the evidence of which he took account, for he preserved no papers. With minor exception, he steadfastly refused to add glosses to his spare awards. The essential conditions of his brief, which he took up on 8 July, were that he must exercise independent judgment to bring down awards by 15 August. The most disputed of his departures from the principle of contiguous majority areas were, in Bengal the award of the Chittagong Hill Tracts to Pakistan, and in the Punjab the award of certain Muslim territories to India. In the former case non-Muslim majority areas were ceded because of their exclusive economic linkage to East Bengal. Although the leaders of the Indian Dominion protested the issue did not impair its relations with Pakistan. In the latter case, however, the award was explosive.

The Punjab was the last province to become subject to British control. When British forces defeated those of the Sikh kingdom of Lahore in 1846 the long arm of the Raj extended beyond the Sutlej to an uncertain belt of tribal territories abutting Afghanistan and encompassed Kashmir and Jammu. For ease of administration the latter portions of the Sikhs' dominions were sold to the Dogra ruler Gulab Singh, whose descendants were on the *gadi* in August 1947. The remainder were ruled indirectly until a revolt in 1849 precipitated their annexation. Half a century later Lord Curzon hived off the frontier districts and placed them, together with the tribal areas, under a centrally controlled North-West Frontier Province. The unitary control over north-western India that Ranjit Singh had effected was thus ephemeral but the episode was etched into the folk histories of its peoples. The Sikhs had memories of separate statehood, a *suba*, to set beside Pathan recollections of a Durrani empire extending beyond Afghanistan to Lahore and Srinagar. Among them was the splendour of Peshawar, ravished by the Sikhs when they sacked it in 1823. Other Muslim empires, too, had dominated the land of the five rivers, most recently the Mogul. In the course of two centuries, then, the north-west had experienced, in turn, Mogul, Afghan, Sikh, and British govern-ance. The Punjab was a palimpsest worn thin by the superscriptions of successive invaders. In 1947 Radcliffe was but its latest partitioner.

With the advance of India towards Independence the problem facing the Sikhs was to find a suitable political form in which to express a deeply-felt cultural identity. The problem was not clearly articulated and vigorously represented in the 1930s and 1940s largely because of Sikh reliance upon British protection. Decreeing them a 'martial race' the British relied heavily upon the Sikhs' recruitment to the army. The Punjab supplied half of Britain's Indian Army and the Sikh proportion of that contribution was twice its proportion of the province's population (12 per cent). Admiring the Sikhs' sturdy independence and loyalty, the Raj favoured them with lands in newly irrigated canal colonies in western Punjab. They became dispersed well beyond their strongholds in central Punjab. Under dyarchy and provincial autonomy they enjoyed separate electorates. As the trans-communal ascendancy of the Unionist Party persisted until 1947, they failed to perceive the grim implications of partition. Some 72 per cent of India's 5.7 million Sikhs lived in Punjab province. A division of the province on a Muslim/non-Muslim district basis would divide them fairly evenly between Pakistan and India. In many districts where they had immovable assets or religious shrines they would be exposed to domination by different creeds speaking other languages.

The starkness of their exposure became apparent in March, when Tara Singh 'sounded the bugle' for the destruction by the Sikhs of the Muslim League. In the remote western districts, where they were outnumbered, the readily identifiable Sikhs suffered massive casualties. There were ten or twelve Muslims to every Sikh in Rawalpindi division, where of over two thousand killings most were Sikhs. Word of atrocities was carried east by emigrant Sikhs to evoke a determination for revenge. Sikh bitterness was in any event inevitable, for no partition based upon contiguous Muslim-majority areas could really satisfy them. They demanded all territories east of the Chenab, which would concentrate 90 per cent of them in East Punjab. This was so impossible a concession to 'other factors' that it would mean jettisoning the principle of contiguous majority areas, the only general principle that justified partition. Tara Singh's proposed partition on the basis of immovable assets, with provision for population exchanges, was rejected out of hand by Mountbatten and HMG, as it understandably would have been by the League. The knowledgeable and astute Governor, Sir Evan Jenkins, was sympathetic to claims for part of the fertile colony land in Montgomery district (with 175,000 Sikhs), for there, and further west in Lyallpur (with 263,000 Sikhs), they had been pioneers. Yet in Montgomery they were outnumbered by the Muslims five to one. He was convinced that Radcliffe could not settle such a claim, though if out of court negotiations with the Muslim League could achieve a compromise then a settlement of the Punjab might be possible. However, communal feeling was so 'unbelievably bad' that he was clutching at straws.[8] Sir Penderel Moon, who was then in neighbouring Bahawalpur, thought successful negotiations between the League and the Sikhs were scarcely conceivable. Jenkins suggested that perhaps the solution to the Sikh problem had been for them to have worked for the severance of the non-Punjabi-speaking Hindu districts of Karnal, Hissar, Rhotak, and Gurgaon from Punjab, and their own consolidation as a separate East Punjab within Pakistan. It was a strategy never considered until too late.

In his award of 13 August Radcliffe is restrained in his reference to the nature and influence of the 'other factors' that he considered.[9] The 'fundamental basis of contiguous majority areas' seemed to him to leave 'the truly debatable ground in the end [lying] in and around the area between the Beas and the Sutlej rivers on the one hand, and the river Ravi on the other'. The problem was further complicated by canal, rail, and road systems, whilst there was the 'stubborn geographical fact' of the contested cities of Lahore and Amritsar. Broadly speaking, the Radcliffe award follows the tehsil boundaries adjacent to the Utj river from Kashmir to the Ravi and along the Ravi to the Amritsar-Lahore district border, which it follows until the Lahore district tehsil of Kasur is bisected by a line to the Sutlej, whence the district boundaries adjacent to the Sutlej are followed to Bahawalpur. The north-east to south-west axis thus produced accorded to Pakistan no non-Muslim-majority tehsil but awarded India the Muslim-majority tehsils of Gurdaspur (52 per cent), Batala (55 per cent), and Ajnala (59 per cent) to the east of the Ravi; the eastern portion of Kasur (57 per cent), the only tehsil divided; Jullundur (51 per cent) and Nakodar (59 per cent) between the Beas and the Sutlej; and Ferozepur (55 per cent) and Zira (65 per cent) to the east of the Sutlej. As Radcliffe destroyed his papers any attribution of 'other factors' to particular decisions must be largely guesswork; but as his decisions bear so heavily upon inter-Dominion disputes an evaluation of the available evidence is necessary.

---

[8] *TP*, xii, 81.   [9] *TP*, xii, 488, encl.

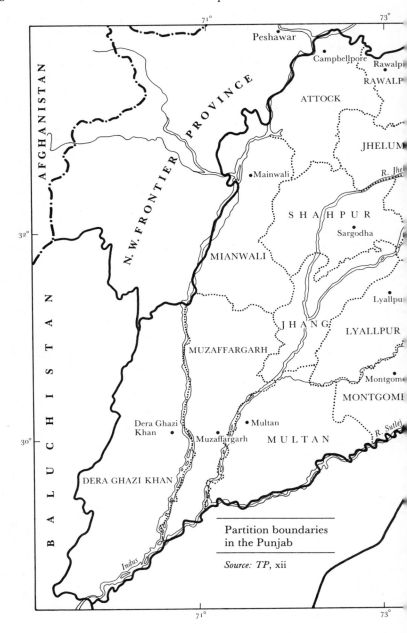

Partition boundaries
in the Punjab

Source: TP, xii

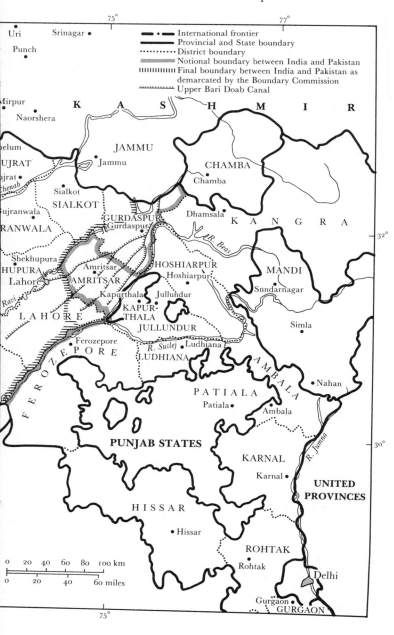

International frontier
Provincial and State boundary
District boundary
Notional boundary between India and Pakistan
Final boundary between India and Pakistan as
demarcated by the Boundary Commission
Upper Bari Doab Canal

Radcliffe's partition of Gurdaspur district gave Pakistan only one of its four tehsils, Shakargarh, west of the Utj–Ravi line. He explains his award to India of the two Muslim tehsils, Gurdaspur and Batala, and the non-Muslim tehsil of Pathankot, all east of the river line, by reference to the Upper Bari Doab Canal system. That system watered Amritsar and Lahore districts. Amritsar district (46 per cent Muslim) could scarcely be denied to India. Lahore district (60 per cent Muslim, and its every tehsil Muslim-majority) must go to Pakistan, both on the contiguous areas principle and as the centre of the north-western railways system. Radcliffe had thus 'not found it possible to preserve undivided the irrigation system of the Upper Bari Doab Canal . . . although I have made small adjustments of the Lahore–Amritsar district boundary [i.e. the partition of Kasur tehsil abutting Sikh-majority Tarn Taran tehsil] to mitigate some of the consequences of this severance'. When he returned to London Radcliffe amplified this point to the Under-Secretary of State, who noted that 'the reason' for allotting the Gurdaspur tehsils to India was 'understood to be that the headwaters of the canals which irrigate the Amritsar District lie in the Gurdaspur District and it is important to keep as much as possible of these canals under one administration'.[10] This 'other factor' is thus made to explain the alienation to India of two Muslim-majority tehsils in Gurdaspur district, one in Amritsar (Ajnala) and the portion of Kasur in Lahore. In fact, as Professor Michel has shown, the UBDC system watered more lands in the Lahore district than in Gurdaspur and Amritsar together, and was necessary to Lahore city's water supply.[11] Had Radcliffe awarded the whole of Gurdaspur district (including non-Muslim Pathankot) to Pakistan then he would have unified the administration of the UBDC system. Pakistan could not have deprived Amritsar of water without denying it to the more remote Lahore. A district-wise partition would have been preserved.

On 8 August Radcliffe's secretary furnished the Punjab Government with a map 'showing roughly' Radcliffe's proposed award.[12]

10 A. Henderson's record of talk, 19 Aug. 1947, cited in Tinker, 'Pressure, Persuasion, Decision: Factors in the Partition of the Punjab, August 1947', *Journal of Asian Studies*, 36 (1977), 695–704, p. 702. For related materials see L/P & J/10/119.

11 Michel, op. cit.

12 Sir G. Abell to Mr Abbott, 8 Aug. 1947, *TP*, xii, 377. The map is reproduced in National Documentation Centre, *The Partition of the Punjab, 1947, Official Documents* (1983), iv, 2.

on three sides by Muslim districts and on the fourth by the Muslim-majority, though Sikh ruled, state of Kapurthala. His treatment of the Gurdaspur problem gave the Sikhs access to Hoshiarpur district. If he were to produce the quasi-political solution to the Sikh problem that his brief's allusion to 'other factors' implied, he could scarcely apply simple principles consistently. His Gurdaspur award is explicable without reference to Kashmir, as he affirmed.

The map that Radcliffe's secretary released on 8 August proposed to partition Ferozepur district, awarding the cis-Sutlej Muslim-majority tehsils of Ferozepur (55 per cent) and Zira (65 per cent) to Pakistan. Radcliffe wrote in his award:

> I have hesitated long over those not inconsiderable areas east of the Sutlej River and in the angle of the Beas and Sutlej Rivers in which Muslim majorities are found. But on the whole I have come to the conclusion that it would be in the true interests of neither State to extend the territories of West Punjab to a strip on the far side of the Sutlej and that there are factors such as the disruption of railway communications and water systems that ought in this instance to displace the primary claims of contiguous majorities.[21]

The reasoning does not confront the exclusion from Pakistan of the Jullundur and Nakodar tehsils in the 8 August map, but their inclusion would have made an untidy frontier, an awkward wedge in Indian territory. In his award Radcliffe is really saying that he believed Pakistan would not benefit from having the cis-Sutlej Ferozepur tehsils, and that the railways and water system justified their cession to India.

It seems possible that the 8 August draft award allotted the Ferozepur tehsils to Pakistan as a *quid pro quo* for Gurdaspur. In both cases control of the headwaters of a canal system was involved, and both departed from the notional award's district-wise demarcation by adopting tehsil boundaries. In the one India crossed the Ravi, in the other Pakistan crossed the Sutlej. Michel speculates on Radcliffe's pursuing a 'tit-for-tat basis' and sees equity in it.[22] Mr A. N. Khosla, chairman of the Central Waterways, Irrigation, and Navigation Commission, wrote to Nehru on 8 August: 'It . . . appears that Sir Cyril Radcliffe's mind may be working in the direction of giving Ferozepore and Zira tahsils having a small

---

[21] Loc. cit.   [22] Michel, op. cit., 181 n. 71.

Muslim majority east of the Sutlej to Pakistan in return for giving
Gurdaspur and part of Lahore district to East Punjab'.[23] There is
no evidence that Radcliffe thought in such terms, though he did
later deny the validity of the concept of 'balancing' the Punjab and
the Bengal awards. He wrote of the Punjab award cryptically to
Michel: 'The many factors that bore upon each problem were not
ponderable in their effect upon each other. The effective weight
given to each was a matter of judgment, which the circumstances
threw it upon me to form; each decision at each point was
debatable.'[24] The meaning is elusive but perhaps Radcliffe was
affirming that each decision was made in isolation by weighing the
factors that bore upon it. If so, then his 8 August plan for the
Ferozepur tehsils had emerged from the 'factors' weighing more
heavily on the Pakistan side and without reference to his decision on
Gurdaspur. They would have included, besides the Muslim
majorities, the immense importance of the Ferozepur headwaters
in controlling the Dipalpur Canal, serving areas in West Punjab
(including the rich Montgomery district). His award drew attention to the point.

Radcliffe's reversal of his 8 August plan must have resulted from
a reweighing of the factors—railways, water systems, and the 'true
interests' of both states affected by Pakistan crossing the Sutlej. The
possibility of viceregal influence having affected the decision must
be considered, for it has been alleged by Pakistanis.[25] There is no
doubt that Mountbatten was himself under pressure to exert
influence.

Khosla's advice to Nehru, which Nehru at once sent to
Mountbatten, was strongly adverse to the award of the Ferozepur
tehsils to Pakistan:

That will be disastrous from the point of view of East Punjab and Bikaner
State from the irrigation point of view and disastrous to India as a whole
from the strategic point of view, because the only line of defence, that is the
Sutlej, will have been pierced by the bridge at Ferozepore and between this
and Delhi there is no natural barrier. . . . Both from the strategic and
irrigation point of view it will be most dangerous to let Ferozepore go to

[23] *TP*, xii, 395.
[24] Radcliffe to Michel, 28 Mar. 1965, Michel, op. cit., 194.
[25] See, e.g., L/P & J/10/119, Raza (ed.), *Mountbatten and Pakistan* (1982), and S.S.
Pirzada, 'Radcliffe Award', National Documentation Centre, op. cit., i, pp. vii–xi.

Pakistan. Whatever may be the decision about area west of Sutlej, no area east of the Sutlej must on any account go to Pakistan.[26]

The point about the supply of water to Bikaner State being controlled at Ferozepur was urged vigorously by the Maharaja himself.[27] He led Mountbatten to believe that if Ferozepur went to Pakistan then he would accede to it. He sent his chief minister and irrigation engineer to lobby Mountbatten and the case was argued before the Boundary Commission. Mountbatten properly declined to intervene. In his award Radcliffe stated that 'an interest of this sort can not weigh directly on the question before us as to the division of the Punjab' for the rights of private property would not be affected and he must assume that whichever state controlled the headwaters would inherit the obligations of the predecessor provincial government. Mountbatten also informed Nehru that he could not send Khosla's representation to Radcliffe, and he repudiated similar demands from all of the Sikh princes to intervene in the Boundary Commission's determination of the Punjab award.[28] Nevertheless, on 9 August Mountbatten's secretary reported to another member of his staff, Mr W. H. J. Christie, that 'H.E. is in a tired flap, and is having to be strenuously dissuaded from asking Radcliffe to alter his award'.[29]

There is evidence that Mountbatten now met Radcliffe at Ismay's house. It appears in a letter that he wrote to Ismay on 2 April 1948, when Sir Zafrulla Khan alleged that he had interfered with Radcliffe's award. Mountbatten wrote:

About this time I met Radcliffe with you at your house for a drink. The main object of this meeting was to discuss the date of the announcement of the Award. . . .

I shall always be grateful to you for having cautioned me not to try and bring any direct influence to bear on Radcliffe concerning the actual Award beyond expressing the following general view.

So far as I remember I said to him that the Sikh attitude had become rather worse than we had anticipated, and that when he was balancing up the boundaries of East and West Pakistan I sincerely hoped that he would bear the Sikh problem in mind. I think I went so far as to say that provided he were really satisfied that the overall decision, both East and West, was absolutely fair to both communities, then I trusted that any generosity to

Pakistan should be given more in Bengal than the Punjab since there was
no Sikh problem in Bengal.

The conversation then turned to the irrigation canals and headworks
and so far as I remember he made some comment about having tried and
failed to obtain agreement for joint inter-dominion working of the headworks and I think he remarked that the boundary was particularly difficult
to adjust round about Ferozepur from this aspect, and I remarked that
provided the overall East and West boundaries were scrupulously fair
between the two Dominions, it seemed to me that he could make any
adjustments necessary for balancing out the boundaries in Bengal and the
Punjab. . . .

If I had had any idea that this particular and relatively small incident
might become a 'Cause Celebre' I should of course have kept a very
accurate record and got it agreed with you and Radcliffe.[30]

Ismay's marginal pencillings on the letter show that his recollection
of the meeting was 'only very hazy', that he could not recall its date
and that he did 'not remember' Mountbatten suggesting 'any
generosity to Pakistan should be given more in Bengal than the
Punjab since there was no Sikh problem in Bengal'. He replied to
Mountbatten that 'my recollection of events is very different from
yours', that Radcliffe was prepared to sign a statement saying the
award represented his own unfettered judgement, and that 'our
consciences are perfectly clear'.[31]

Mountbatten's general injunction to remember the Sikh
problem could scarcely have influenced Radcliffe, whose award
north of Ferozepur had been so largely formulated with that factor
in mind. As Radcliffe totally rejected the principle of balance as
between Bengal and Punjab, the only point added by Mountbatten's remarks was that 'the Sikh attitude had become rather
worse than we had anticipated', that is to say the Sikhs were known
to be preparing for violence and for migration to India. It could
hardly have been thought that the award of the Ferozepur tehsils to
India would moderate their attitude. Nor would that have appealed
to a jurist of Radcliffe's stature as a reason for changing an award.
It seems more likely that the revision that Radcliffe made between
the 10th and the 13th reweighed the factors that the award
acknowledged—railways, waterworks, and the Sutlej as a frontier.

[30] Ismay Papers, III/7/24, Liddell Hart Centre for Military Archives, King's
College, London.
[31] Ismay to Mountbatten, 13 Apr. 1948, ibid., III/7/28.

Ferozepur city was the railway terminus for south-east Punjab, a cantonment town, and a bastion in the defence of India. It had a non-Muslim majority. The Sutlej was a natural frontier. The Ferozepur headworks supplied water to the Eastern Canal, which serviced the non-Muslim-majority Ferozepur tehsils of Muktsar (43 per cent Muslim, 40 per cent Sikh) and Fazilka (43 per cent Muslim, 19 per cent Sikh). The Muslim-majority Ferozepur tehsils lay between the only two Sikh-majority tehsils in Punjab, Tarn Taran (51 per cent) and Mogha (65 per cent), and, indeed, Ludhiana district (46 per cent Sikh). The sorts of factors that contributed to the non-partition of Amritsar district (36 per cent Sikh) also applied to Ferozepur (34 per cent Sikh).

Radcliffe's award, which was finally published on 17 August, is not to be understood in terms of the consistent application of simple principles such as the ascertainment of contiguous Muslim majorities, on either a district or tehsil basis, or predominant national interests in canal headworks. It may be safely said that the modifications to the contiguous-majority principle consistently deprived Pakistan of territories to which that principle entitled her, and that 'other factors' had the effect of enabling the Sikhs to consolidate themselves securely in East Punjab: by according control of the UBDC, which watered Amritsar, to India; by awarding the Ferozepur headworks, which watered Ferozepur, to India; by awarding intact to India the districts of Amritsar and Ferozepur, despite their Muslim-majority tehsils; by awarding the Muslim-majority tehsils of Gurdaspur and Batala in Gurdaspur district, together with part of Muslim-majority Kasur in Lahore district, to India, thereby affording ready communication from Amritsar to Hoshiarpur in the north and to Ferozepur in the south. There is justice in Hugh Tinker's observation that Radcliffe was, in effect, obliged to fashion a 'para-political solution' to the Sikh problem, of which the plan for the transfer of power and partition had taken no account.[32] His award is consistent with that obligation above all others. It gave to India those 'debatable' areas—to tehsil and even part tehsil level—in which Sikhs were a substantial contiguous majority, approaching 25 per cent of the population.

While the partition of India left half of the Sikh community

[32] Tinker, op. cit., 696.

embittered at finding its rich lands and its shrines in an inhospitable
Muslim environment, Radcliffe's Punjab award left populous and
even majority Muslim communities to the mercies of powerful Sikh
minorities in India. Nishtar, Pakistan's Minister of Communications, spoke of the 'parting kick of the British to Pakistan', while
Ghazanfar Ali Khan, Minister of Education, called the award a
'disgraceful injustice which will not encourage us to remain in the
Commonwealth'.[33]

It is difficult to see how Radcliffe could have awarded more
territory than he did to East Punjab, consistently with the
'fundamental basis' of partition. In May Jenkins, whom Pakistanis
have not regarded as a friend, told Tara Singh, 'I did not see how
the non-Muslims could possibly get more than the Ambala and
Jullundur Divisions, the Amritsar district and perhaps parts of the
Gurdaspur and Lahore districts'.[34] In June Moon anticipated 'a
frontier . . . somewhere in the middle of the Lahore Division'.[35]
Lord Listowel, the last Secretary of State, recognized that

Sikh claims are based not on population but on such factors as the
economic position of the Sikhs in certain parts of the Punjab and religious
sentiment applying to certain areas where there are Sikh shrines. Unless
the Boundary Commission were told to give weight to these factors it could
not do more than make marginal adjustments in the boundaries where the
[notional] division of districts has included in the Muslim or Hindu areas
small parts of districts in which Hindus or Sikhs or Muslims were in the
majority.[36]

Radcliffe's award is consistent with the provision of secure Sikh
homelands in central Punjab but there is no evidence that it took
account of the Sikh economic position or religious sentiments
beyond them. In some parts of Lahore district, the Sikhs owned
more property and paid more of the land revenue but these factors
did not outweigh the population principle there any more than did
the Sikh contribution to the trans-Sutlej canal colonies or the
birthplace of Guru Nanak in Sheikhpura. Neither could Radcliffe
have been induced to favour the Sikhs because of any anticipation
of the huge losses they would suffer by abandoning their property in
Pakistan to migrate to India. In another context, his award

---

[33] *Keesing's Contemporary Archives, 1946–7*, 8813.
[34] *TP*, x, 483.   [35] Ibid., xi, 371.   [36] Ibid., x, 371.

observes that 'the territorial division of the province does not affect the rights of private property'.

To a degree the Sikhs were deluded by hopes of 'other factors' enlarging their homelands. Listowel's initial comments on the terms of reference suggest a concern to stave off an intractable problem. He wrote to Mountbatten that 'if you are satisfied that a Boundary Commission, with terms of reference such as will help to keep the Sikhs quiet until the transfer of power, can be set up without provoking the hostility of the two major communities, I shall be very ready to support your view to my colleagues.'[37] Yet the precise nature and timing of the Radcliffe award had relatively little to do with the holocaust that began in August. In May Tara Singh told Jenkins that he did not intend to take revenge on the Muslims for Rawalpindi 'now' but 'after the British went'.[38] He wanted a temporary truce while the Sikhs got 'an area to which non-Muslims could be transferred' and 'remarked darkly that the Boundary Commission might never report at all since he felt that the Punjab might drift into chaos'. Moon recognized that 'civil war' was inevitable.[39]

Though there had been some Sikh migration from Rawalpindi to East Punjab after the March humiliation, neither the British nor the Indian party leaders anticipated large scale movements of population. Late in July the party leaders were appealing to the minorities in East and West to stay where they were. Though the Sikhs were arming themselves from April and the involvement of the Sikh princely states was suspected it was only in the first week of August that evidence appeared of Tara Singh's association with bomb-making, and plans to disrupt canal headworks and railways, and even to assassinate Jinnah during the Independence celebrations. Jenkins and the Governors-designate of West and East Punjab (Sir Francis Mudie and Sir Chandulal Trivedi) advised Mountbatten that the arrest of Sikh leaders would only provoke disturbance. Mountbatten decided against the arrests and postponed the release of Radcliffe's awards until after the transfer of power.

In the last weeks of British rule 'a communal war of succession', in Jenkins's words, broke out. On 1 August Jenkins's secretary

---

[37] Ibid.   [38] Ibid., 483.   [39] Ibid., xi, 371.

reported that 'There is going to be trouble with the Sikhs. When, and how bad, the Governor cannot yet say. Raids on Muslim villages have begun in Amritsar and Lahore district and along the Jullundur–Hoshiarpur border, and there have been four attacks on, or attempts to interfere with, trains in the past two or three days.'[40] A week later Jenkins confirmed that in rural areas of Amritsar, Hoshiarpur, and Jullundur there had been casual attacks and organized raids, in most of which Sikhs were the aggressors and Muslims the victims. Similar outrages were reported in rural Lahore, Ferozepur, and Ludhiana; Gurdaspur could blow up at any time. Amritsar and Lahore cities were disturbed. Daily casualties were 50–100. The Sikh 'homelands' were ablaze.[41]

To maintain civil order in central Punjab a special Boundary Force was announced in late July, in the wake of a spate of arson and stabbing in Lahore and Amritsar.[42] Its 15,000–23,000 officers and men were in mixed units, with operations extending over twelve districts—37,500 square miles, 17,000 villages, 14.5 million people. Its command observed that until 8 August the victims in rural areas were Muslims (though in Lahore city they always held the 'terror initiative'). On 11 August the commander reported that upon his arrival at Amritsar a new Hindu police superintendent had disarmed the Muslim policemen, causing 'panic among the Muslim populace'.[43] The first sabotage of a train occured on 9 August, just outside the Sikh state of Patiala. It was a special, carrying Pakistani employees and their families from Delhi to Karachi. Six carriages were derailed but the passengers were not attacked.

More and more people were on the move, mainly from East Punjab to West Punjab. The Punjab Boundary Force command believed that 'but for the presence of troops an uncontrolled massacre would now be taking place'.[44] Major-General T.W. Rees recorded that 'In the rural areas, the Sikh jathas . . . in the East Punjab were the first to take the field. Later, the Muslims started retaliation. But during the month of August, it was evident to the

[40] Ibid., xii, 306.

[41] On the breakdown of order in the Punjab, see Talbot, 'Mountbatten and the Partition of India: A Rejoinder', *History*, 69 (1984), 29–35.

[42] See Jeffrey, 'The Punjab Boundary Force and the Problem of Order, August 1947', *Modern Asian Studies*, 8 (1974), 491–520.

[43] Ibid., 510.   [44] *TP*, xii, 432.

PBF that, as opposed to their enemies, the Sikhs were thoroughly organized and prepared for such events as took place.'[45] Nehru informed Gandhi that the trouble started about the beginning of August in the rural areas of Amritsar, and 'the Sikhs were the aggressors'.[46] He thought they hoped for 'a Sikh State as a result of this turmoil'.[47] Rees reported that by 21 August 200,000 refugees had arrived in Lahore and another 100,000 were on their way. One refugee centre had 50,000 inmates. Sikhs and Hindus were being driven from Lahore city in the second week of August, as the feeling there became 'unbelievably bad', with the Muslim League National Guard appearing in uniform and the police unreliable.[48] PBF trucks were taking Sikhs and Hindus to Amritsar. What a London *Times* correspondent called 'a vast transfer of populations' had begun.[49]

Jenkins's last letter as Governor to Mountbatten is a sad account of the collapse of law and order in the cities of Lahore and Amritsar, of large bands of Sikhs raiding Muslim villages with extreme brutality, of the railways and roads becoming unsafe.[50] He reported that the Muslims had failed to understand the horror caused by their attacks on Sikhs in March and now thought that reprisals were the answer to Sikh violence. By the transfer of power Auchinleck reported an estimate that about 15 per cent of Lahore city had been destroyed by fire.[51] By 20 August only 10,000 of Lahore's 300,000 Hindus and Sikhs remained. As Jenkins predicted, these reprisals merely provoked further violence. On 23 August a *Times* correspondent in the Punjab reported that Sikh *jathas* were carrying out 'appalling atrocities' including mass murder and mutilation, 'clearing the Eastern Punjab of Moslems, butchering hundreds daily, forcing thousands to flee westward, and burning Moslem villages and homesteads'. Some large towns like Amritsar and Jullundur ('a city of the dead' in the *Daily Telegraph's* words) were becoming 'quieter because there are no Moslems left'.[52] On 26 August the Muslims of Sheikhpura responded, massacring 800 non-Muslims, and razing their houses.

The grim rationality of the holocaust now in progress was, as

---

[45] Jeffrey, op. cit., 505–6.   [46] Ibid., 506 n. 83.   [47] Ibid., 407.
[48] *TP*, xii, 437.   [49] Jeffrey, op. cit., 509 n. 100.
[50] Jenkins to Mountbatten, 13 Aug. 1947, *TP*, xii, 459.
[51] Ibid., 486.
[52] *Keesing's Contemporary Archives, 1946–7*, 9049–51.

Moon has asserted, the forceful extrusion of Muslims from the Sikh homelands to create living space for Sikhs from Pakistan who would have no future under a Muslim regime.[53] The deployment of terror for advantage in the Sikh homelands, where the populations were often evenly balanced, ensured the forced migration of Sikhs from rich holdings in Pakistan, such as Lyallpur, where they lingered long and hopefully. By a forced migration of gigantic proportions the Sikh community evacuated Pakistan. By the end of 1947 well over four million Sikhs and Hindus were to cross the border, with an equal number of Muslims proceeding from East to West. The total migration would run to ten or twelve million. The casualties have been variously estimated at 200,000 (by Moon from Bahawalpur), 600,000 (by Sir Algernon Rumbold at the CRO), and 800,000 (by Grafftey-Smith at Karachi).

As the waves of refugees crossed the frontier in the Punjab eddies were felt in adjacent provinces. By the first week of September some 200,000 non-Muslims from West Punjab had reached Delhi. Sikhs and Hindus in the capital fell upon Muslims in retaliation for their co-religionists' excesses in Pakistan. On 7 September Muslim shops and stalls in Old Delhi were looted and a curfew was declared. By then there had been some five hundred murders. On 9 September Nehru announced that action against rioters would be on a war footing with no mercy for offenders and he condemned the outrages against Delhi Muslims as 'a disgrace to India'. In Pakistan fears were held for the safety of the vast Muslim population of Uttar Pradesh.

While the largest migration in history meant the consolidation in India of the partitioned Sikh community, the consequences of the forced migration of Muslims to Pakistan seemed dire. The countless millions that might ultimately be involved could simply not be accommodated. At the topmost level of government Pakistanis believed that however sincere Nehru and Gandhi might be in their condemnation of offenders, a significant element in India, including Vallabhbhai Patel and the Hindu-extremist Rashtriya Swayamsevak Sangh (RSSS), welcomed the Sikh excesses.

On 10 September Grafftey-Smith received a message from Liaquat

---

[53] Moon, *Divide and Quit* (1961), 280.

for Attlee, with a request that it be reported to the Prime Ministers of Canada, Australia, New Zealand, and South Africa, but not India.[54] Developments in India and relations between the new Dominions were 'now entering a critical phase'. The Muslims of Amritsar, Gurdaspur, Ferozepur, and Hoshiarpur were being liquidated and India was either 'unwilling or powerless to restore order' and protect its Muslims. The message urged Britain and the Commonwealth to consider 'ways and means of saving gravest situation in India'. Here was, in effect, a call for a Commonwealth conference to sort out, presumably by sending observers, the rights and wrongs of the issue. Mountbatten's reading of the situation was that Liaquat wanted to establish the culpability of the Sikhs before the world, for he feared that India would assert that the Muslims were primarily to blame and so provoke a war on the issue.[55] Attlee merely acknowledged Liaquat's message and repeated the request to the Dominions in cables that pointed out the futility of a conference. The British Cabinet, and subsequently its Commonwealth Affairs Committee, agreed that there should be no intervention in the dispute.[56] On 24 September, when Shone conveyed to Nehru a proposal from Jinnah that a team of Commonwealth representatives might be invited to India and Pakistan for joint discussions, Nehru's response was cool. Noel-Baker minuted that India was 'not prepared to accept any Commonwealth intervention of any sort, either by way of an investigation into the facts or by way of formal mediation between themselves and the Government of Pakistan'.[57] He believed it 'impossible to secure any intervention on a Commonwealth basis'. A Commonwealth fact-finding mission might well weaken the links between the new Dominions and the Commonwealth, for like Radcliffe it could not fail to incur the 'odium of arbitration'.

At the end of September Gandhi's novel suggestion was that Attlee should, 'as the author of the scheme of independence of India, free himself from the untenable position of having two hostile dominions in the Commonwealth, if the two cannot live together as

---

[54] Grafftey-Smith to CRO, 12 Sept. 1947, PREM 8/584.

[55] Mountbatten to Gandhi, 29 Sept. 1947, PREM 8/586.

[56] CM (47)76, 20 Sept. 1947, CAB 128/10; Cab. Commonwealth Affairs Cttee meetings, 9 and 31 Oct. 1947, CAB 134/54.

[57] Memo. by Noel-Baker on India–Pakistan Dispute, 26 Oct. 1947, CA(47)8, ibid.

sisters', by ascertaining 'who is overwhelmingly in the wrong'.[58]
He should then withdraw British forces from the offender and, if
that were not effective, then expel it from the Commonwealth.
Only such a remedy could cure 'the drastic disease of the two parts
of India'. Attlee approved a tactful response, drafted by Noel-
Baker, asserting that it was a role 'impossible for me, and indeed for
any man, to fulfil'.[59] Such verdicts 'must be left to the historians'.
Mountbatten reported:

Gandhi appeared to be very disappointed. He said that Mr Attlee, in this
matter, had failed to show himself a really great statesman. He himself was
very perturbed about the future. It had been a great mistake to make two
co-equal Dominions. Mutual hatred had bitten deep into men's hearts and
it was impossible to see how the tragedy would ever end.[60]

The historian of such terrible events feels bound to refer the question of blame to Higher Authority.

From the disruptions of central Punjab in August the infection of
terror and reprisal spread in September until it extended from
Delhi to Peshawar. From his motor car Baldev Singh observed a
'lemming-like' two way procession of refugees; from the air Ismay
observed how superior was the organization of the Sikh exodus.
Where the Muslims straggled the Sikhs moved in military file. The
Indian states, traditional islands of peace in British India's troubled
seas, were not immune. Tales of genocide in Patiala, the largest
Sikh state, have been questioned by Moon, but early in October
Nehru received a report from 'a reliable worker' there:

Story of designs and resistance of Muslims false and fantastic. They died
like goats and sheep. About a lakh [100,000] murdered in whole State;
about 12,000 in Patiala alone. Whole families wiped out. Only innocent
and helpless ones killed. Rape, abduction and processions of naked women
and other atrocities on them. Wholesale looting, with police and military
help.[61]

Sir Terence Creagh Coen, a former Indian Political Servant who
stayed on in Pakistan's Foreign Office until 1953, believed that

    [58] Gandhi to Mountbatten, 26 Sept. and 2 Oct., PREM 8/586.
    [59] Noel-Baker's draft, 21 Oct. 1947, ibid.
    [60] Mountbatten's Report of 7 Nov. 1947, L/PO/433.
    [61] Note from Rajkumari Amrit Kaur, n.d., in Nehru to Patel, 5 Oct. 1947, Das (ed.),
Sardar Patel's Correspondence, 1945–50 (1971–4), i, 50. For the states see also Jeffrey,
op. cit.

'probably the worst of all the 1947 massacres' was that of the Muslims in Jammu.[62] As events in the territories of the Maharaja of Kashmir and Jammu were to become the *casus bellum* between the new Dominions they require sifting in some detail. Our main observation point is Peshawar.

At Government House, Peshawar, Sir George Cunningham observed the steady rise of attacks by Muslims on Hindus and Sikhs in the NWFP. Cunningham knew his India well and he is an invaluable source for events during the eight months of his governorship, from Independence to March 1948. His service on the frontier began in 1914 as personal assistant to the Chief Commissioner and he was subsequently Political Agent in North Waziristan, private secretary to Irwin during his viceroyalty, and Governor of the NWFP from 1937 to 1946. He returned in August 1947 at Jinnah's request. By late August it was obvious to him 'that unless the Punjab slaughters ceased at once it would be impossible to hold back our people; there have been so many revolting stories of the massacre of Muslims in East Punjab'.[63] By mid-month hundreds of non-Muslims had been killed and there were 12–15,000 Hindus and Sikhs in refugee camps. On 23 September Cunningham wrote, 'I have had offers from practically every tribe along the Frontier to be allowed to go and kill Sikhs in Eastern Punjab, and I think I would only have to hold up my little finger to get a *lashkar* of 40,000 or 50,000'.[64] He later gave Mountbatten a synoptic account of the gradual swell of tribal feeling until it boiled over into an invasion of Kashmir.

Towards the end of Sept. stories were rife in Hazara district (I was there myself) that Sikhs were coming in to the neighbouring Kashmir province of Poonch, & were killing & driving out the M[uslim] population. I first heard on Sept. 30th that some of our villagers from Hazara had gone across into Poonch to help the M[ms] and were attacking a Police Thana. On Oct. 13th there was common talk in Hazara of 'Jehad' against Kashmir. I learnt that some of our trans border tribes Afridi Mohmand & Mahsud had been asked to come & help in it. I warned everyone of the danger of starting this. On Oct. 20th I heard that early that morning 900 Mahsuds had started for

---

[62] Coen, *The Indian Political Service: A Study in Indirect Rule* (1971), 139.
[63] Cunningham's Diary, 4 Sept. 1947, IOL.
[64] Ibid.

Tank in lorries. I sent men to stop them but it was too late as they had already crossed one of the bridges in to the Punjab & they then concentrated by various routes on Garhi Habibulla (in NWFP a mile or two from the K. border) whence they started their first big attack on Domel, Baramula, etc. I am not going to say who were the actual people who incited our tribes to stir them up. I know some of them & I suspect others but I honestly don't know (I never felt there was much use in inquiry) where the real initiative came from. Facilities for the tribesmen's actual transit through the province (i.e. lorries & petrol) were no doubt made available to them which would have been impossible if one or two officials had not shut their eyes though orders were issued to all (with the C[hief] M[inister]'s approval) that officials were to take no part in this movement. But I want to make one or two points quite clear (A) From the beginning & to an ever increasing extent as the hostilities developed the tribesmen & the people of our settled districts looked on the K. campaign as a Holy War, they went & fought not because they hoped to get pay (they got practically none) or loot (that idea vanished soon after the Baramula outrages, which were wholeheartedly condemned by all tribes and other Muslims) but because they felt they had an obligation to help their fellow Muslims in K. against in particular the Sikhs. (B) If from October onwards we had advised our Police Constabulary & troops to shoot down the tribesmen as they passed through (which would have been the only way of stopping them) we could probably have enforced the order in some cases under great protest but the result would *without a particle of doubt* have been such an outburst of popular feeling in the Province that not one of our H^s or S^s (I suppose 120,000 of them) would have been left alive.[65]

The Pathan invasion of Kashmir was thus, alleges Cunningham, provoked by the persecution of Muslims in East Punjab and the Maharaja's territories. The linkage requires scrutiny.

The Pathans at large comprise the Western Afghans of Afghanistan, the Eastern Afghans of the Frontier Province, and the highlanders or Karlanri tribesmen of the terrain between them. It is said that

Eastern Afghans, and the Karlanri tribesmen, think of Kashmir as a mistress. Those who love her abide half guiltily in the pleasures of her seduction, but in the very acknowledgement of her beauty their thoughts return to their own and lawful home. The conflict of emotion is enshrined in a proverb: Unto every man his own country is Kashmir.[66]

---

[65] Cunningham to Mountbatten, 8 or 9 May 1948, Cunningham Papers, IOL.
[66] Caroe, *The Pathans, 500 BC–AD 1957* (1976), 257.

The Eastern Afghans include the Yusufzais and others of the Peshawar plain and the valleys to its north. The Karlanris include Mohmands, the ferocious and formidable Mahsuds, the doughty warrior Wazirs, the Afridis and the Orakzai. The Frontier Province as a whole embraced six settled districts under deputy commissioners (Hazara, Mardan, Peshawar, Kohat, Bannu, and Dera Ismail Khan), six tribal agencies (South Waziristan, North Waziristan, Kurram, Mohmand, Khyber, and Malakhand), and three states (Dir, Swat, and Chitral). Whereas the districts were administered, the agencies were secured by influence or indirect rule through *maliks* (chiefs) and the states' rulers were effectively autonomous. In its last years the Raj's main problem with the endemically disordered frontier lay in Waziristan, with the Wazirs and the Mahsuds. Garrisons were stationed at Razmak and Wana, scouts employed elsewhere, and the tribal leaders were paid allowances to keep their malcontents in order. One of Pakistan's first decisions was to withdraw the garrisons and suspend the payments, whereupon a remarkable peace broke out.

The territories of the Maharaja of Kashmir were various and far-flung. They included the central Vale, the Switzerland of the sub-continent, the southern state of Jammu (adjoining Gurdaspur and Sialkot districts), the southern district of Poonch (adjoining Rawalpindi district), the mountainous north-western region of Gilgit and the western areas of Ladakh and Baluchistan (Little Tibet). The territories' total population was about four million, 78 per cent Muslim. Whereas the populations of the Vale and Poonch were each about 90 per cent Muslim, that of Jammu (the ancestral home of the Hindu Dogra dynasty) was about 60 per cent. The Maharaja had not acceded to either of the new Dominions at Independence. As the southern areas of Jammu and Poonch abutted partitioned Punjab, forming a natural route for refugees moving in both directions, the growth of communal feeling was probably inevitable. It began, however, from indigenous causes.

The best authority on the antecedents of the Kashmir disturbances remains Richard Symonds, a Quaker who was on relief work in north Punjab in 1947.

Early in August as the partition of India drew near, there were many meetings and demonstrations in Poonch in favour of Kashmir joining Pakistan. Martial law was introduced and meetings fired on. After one such incident on 27th August in Nila Bat, Abdul Qayyam, a young zemindar, started the revolt with a few friends. Substantial men told me that they would never have joined such a rash enterprise but for the folly of the Dogras who burnt whole villages where only a single family was involved in revolt. Rapidly most of the Moslem ex-servicemen joined Qayyam and in six weeks the whole district except for Poonch city itself was in rebel hands.[67]

Josef Korbel, a Czech who became chairman of a UN Commission on Kashmir, adds significant details.[68] During the Second World War Kashmir had sent over 70,000 men to the Indian Army, some 60,000 of them were Muslim and they mostly returned to farm in Poonch or Mirpur, often retaining their arms. In late July they were called upon to deposit their arms with the police and the Maharaja strengthened his garrisons there with Sikh and Hindu troops. The no-tax revolt that ensued was crushed ruthlessly. Arms were smuggled in from the village 'factories' of the frontier. In the second week of October they rose again and drove the State forces from the Poonch and Mirpur districts, save for Poonch town. Beginning somewhat later than the original revolt in Poonch, communal disturbances flared in Jammu. Sikh and Hindu refugees from West Punjab were arriving in force, apparently encouraged by the Dogra Governor, who, together with the militant RSSS, seems to have entertained ideas of establishing a non-Muslim-majority area. Muslims were driven from their villages and slaughtered *en route* to Pakistan. The nationalist leader Sheikh Abdullah was later to imprison the Governor and to revile Maharaja Hari Singh for their part in the continuing massacre.

In Jammu, the killing of Muslims all over the province continued unabated for weeks under his very nose, the town having been converted into a veritable hell. Innocent children and girls were not spared and the display of sadism to which they were subjected would render insignificant anything that happened on the two sides of the divided Punjab in its hour of madness. All this staggering tragedy on such a vast scale is alleged to have been accomplished by the participation of high-ranking Hindu officials and Dogra military in Jammu as well as His Highness' own trusted relations and his then Prime Minister and Deputy Prime Minister. A widespread belief, certainly not without basis, was that the killing was carried on in pursuance of an organised plan of genocide under which free distribution

---

[67] The *Statesman* (Calcutta), 4 Feb. 1948, cited in Birdwood, *Two Nations and Kashmir* (1956), 50.
[68] Korbel, *Danger in Kashmir* (1966 edn.).

of arms and ammunition was made to communalist organisations like RSS through Hindu officials, high and low.[69]

Ian Stephens, editor of the *Statesman*, wrote that in autumn 1947 the 500,000 Muslims of Jammu 'were practically eliminated'; 200,000 of them 'just disappeared'.[70]

As early as 13 September, armed Pathans had drifted into Lahore and Rawalpindi, and some Swatis had crossed into the Vale. About a week later, according to a deputy commissioner of Dera Ismail Khan, a scheme was launched to send tribesmen from Malakhand to Sialkot, in lorries provided by the Pakistan Government.[71] The report also referred to preparations in early October by Swat, Dir, and Chitral to attack Kashmir from the north-west. The Wali of Swat, a developed state, was an ambitious man. He had sought the governorship of the NWFP. It was now believed that he had been promised Kashmir if he could seize it. Cunningham knew that he 'had put up a lot of money for the expenses of the Kashmir campaign'.[72] He noted, too, that the Pir of Wana had personally recruited thousands of Mahsuds.[73] There is little doubt that at the time when the north-western offensive began, Pathans were active further south in raids all along the Punjab border, from the Indus to the Ravi. The Maharaja and his Prime Minister complained of raiding, looting, and burning from Kathua to Kotli.[74] Beside the clashes between rebels and the State forces, and the incursions of the raiders, Punjabi refugees in Kashmir heightened the communal temperature.

Cunningham's diarized testimony is worth following closely. On 6 October he recorded that there was 'quite a lot of talk now of the danger of actual war between Pakistan and India'. Pakistan was militarily weak, in both men and materials, but winked at 'very dangerous activities on the Kashmir border' that might provoke war. About five hundred villagers from Hazara or Punjab had invaded Kashmir and looted five hundred rifles. By mid-month there was 'a real move in Hazara for *Jehad* against Kashmir'.[75]

---

[69] Abdullah to Patel, 7 Oct. 1948, Das, op. cit., i, 237.

[70] Stephens, *Pakistan* (3rd edn., 1967), 200.

[71] Nehru to Patel, 5 Oct. 1947, and encl., Das, op. cit., i, 50–2.

[72] Cunningham's Diary, 26 Oct. 1947.

[73] Ibid., 26 and 30 Oct. 1947.

[74] Mahajan to Patel, 23 Oct. 1947, and encl., Das, op. cit., i, 64–6.

[75] Cunningham's Diary, 18 Oct. 1947.

Rifles had been collected and a campaign planned for seizing the part of the main Jhelum valley above Domel. A Mohmand *malik* told Cunningham that Rao Bahadur Kuli Khan, OBE, a retired Servant of the Frontier Government, was urging the Mohmands to join in. Cunningham was unsure of the Government's complicity but knew that Muhammad Abbas, one of Pakistan's ministers, was in Hazara and that the trucking of petrol and flour from Peshawar had been sanctioned. A Punjabi member of the Muslim National Guard, Khurshid Anwar, was in fact on the Hazara border organizing an attack.[76] Cunningham discouraged the Afridis and the Mohmands from going to Hazara and on the 17th he challenged his Chief Minister, Abdul Qayum:

He was quite open with me and said that, though he thought it would be a very good thing if Kashmir could be filled up with armed Muslims to the greatest possible extent, our line here must be that all officers and our Police etc give no support or sympathy to the movement, and prevent any kind of mass movement towards Kashmir. It would be difficult of course to stop small parties trickling over. He told me that most of the Pandits in Kashmir favour Kashmir joining Pakistan, because they fear the consequences otherwise. He said the Pakistan Government are nervous about the strategical danger to Pakistan if Kashmir joins India and Indian troops are sent to occupy the Kashmir valley actually overlooking our borders. He thinks that direct action against Kashmir now would tend to make the Maharaja join Pakistan rather than otherwise, and that the Muslims have no desire to kick out Hari Singh from the Gadi if he joins Pakistan.[77]

Next day Pakistan's States' Minister, Agha Saiyid Bad Shah, told him that aggression on Kashmir would provoke Hari Singh's accession to India, which might lead on to war. Shah had just returned from an unsuccessful mission, at Liaquat's behest, to lead the Kashmir Prime Minister, Major-General Janak Singh, towards Pakistan. After three or four promising days, a new Prime Minister, Mehr Chand Mahajan, had arrived and 'told him to clear out'.

Cunningham's diary entries for 20 and 22 October were full of foreboding:

Oct 20th. I am afraid the Kashmir situation is going to be a serious crisis.

---

[76] Ibid., 15 Oct. 1947. On Khurshid Anwar see Collins and Lapierre, *Freedom at Midnight* (1975), 349.

[77] Cunningham's Diary, 18 Oct. 1947.

Heard this morning that 900 Mahsuds had left Tank in lorries for the Kashmir front. We tried to stop them at Kohat, but they had got through to the Punjab via Khushalgarh. About 200 Mohmands are also reported to have gone. I telephoned to Liaquat Ali at Lahore that things were serious and that he ought to broadcast his views so that everyone, officials included, would realise that the Pakistan Government did not approve of any invasion of Kashmir, whether from Punjab or NWFP. He replied that he had already sent instructions to my Chief Minister and others on these lines, and that he thought this would be sufficient. I spoke to the Chief Minister, and he seems to be getting alarmed himself and is broadcasting tonight saying that, although they want Kashmir to join Pakistan, all our officials and people must remain strictly neutral. I hope this may help to convince some of our Police, particularly Khushdil, who appear to have been actively helping the movement, strictly against our orders. The Chief Minister also sent his Secretary to Hazara to try and convince people there that this was his policy. The matter is pretty urgent as tomorrow is the day that is tipped as 'D' Day.

Oct 22nd. Heard this morning that several thousand armed people, tribesmen and otherwise, had gone over from Hazara into Kashmir and had seized Muzaffarabad and Domel. We shall soon see what the reaction of Kashmir and India is going to be to this. I fear it may be very serious. My own position is not too easy: if I give my support to the movement, thousands more will flock to it, and there may be a big invasion; if I resist it, I have to bear the brunt if the movement fails through lack of support.

On 23 October Liaquat made a broadcast condemning Hindu and Sikh excesses in Kashmir and asserting Pakistan's neutrality ('a pleasant little bit of comedy', observed Cunningham). An 'invasion of Kashmir' was in fact in progress, with about 2,000 transborder tribesmen, who had crossed into Kashmir by night in small parties, as many Hazarawals, and many thousand West Punjabis, engaged. On 25 October Cunningham learnt from Iskandar Mirza 'all the underground history of the present campaign against Kashmir':

Liaquat had meant to come here last week and tell me about it personally but was prevented by his illness, which seems to be fairly serious heart trouble. Apparently Jinnah himself first heard of what was going on about 15 days ago, but said 'Don't tell me anything about it. My conscience must be clear'. Iskandar is positive that Hari Singh means to join India as soon as his new road from Pathankot is made, which might be within 3 months. He had got a lot of Sikhs and Dogras into Poonch and Jammu, and has been trying to shove Muslims into Pakistan in accordance with the general Indian strategy. It was decided apparently about a month ago that the

Poonchis should revolt and should be helped. Abdul Qayum was in it from the beginning. BOs were kept out simply not to embarrass them.[78]

Next morning Cunningham noted that the tribesmen were expected to reach Srinagar by the evening.

Cunningham's testimony establishes beyond reasonable doubt that the scheme of invasion originally emerged spontaneously among the tribes as a response to outrages against Muslims in East Punjab and the Maharaja's territories. However, though the central government of Pakistan did not organize the invasion it condoned the active assistance that the provincial government gave to it. In retrospect, and as compared with his own diary entries, Cunningham explained the invasion too exclusively as a Holy War, for there was ample evidence of looting and promises of lands for the tribesmen. He argued strongly that the Pakistan authorities could not have prevented the invasion. The traditional lawlessness of the tribes, their resistance to discipline, their savage butchery as they tarried at Baramula, and Cunningham's own recorded apprehension of them as they passed through Peshawar, all lend support to his argument. Whilst he disapproved of the invasion the alternatives to it seemed dire: a massacre of Hindus and Sikhs in the NWFP; and the forced migration of two million Kashmiri Muslims to Pakistan.

The euphoria of Pakistan at news of the Maharaja's flight from Srinagar on 25 October was dampened two days later by India's airlift of troops to secure the capital. In the interim India had secured the Maharaja's succession. The Pakistan Government now ordered Sir Douglas Gracey, who was acting as Commander-in-Chief in Sir Frank Messervy's absence, to send in its army. Gracey demurred and instead phoned Auchinleck at 1 a.m. on the 28th. It was arranged that a few hours later they would meet at Lahore, where Jinnah was staying with Governor Mudie, an unabashed advocate of military intervention. Cunningham flew down to join in the talks. Auchinleck impressed upon Jinnah that mobilization would instantly trigger the issue of a stand down order to all British officers in both Dominions. Jinnah seemed curiously forgetful of this implication, which Auchinleck had made clear in the Joint Defence Council. On 13 October the Commonwealth Affairs

[78] Ibid., 26 Oct. 1947.

Committee had noted that both governments 'were aware that it was our intention, in the event of conflict appearing imminent or breaking out, to withdraw all British officers employed with the Dominion Forces', and the policy had been avowed in Parliament.[79] Gracey now adverted to the military weakness of Pakistan and Auchinleck emphasized the 'incalculable consequences of military violation of what now is territory of Indian Union in consequence of Kashmir's sudden accession'.[80] Jinnah reluctantly withdrew his orders. Auchinleck's biographer believed that he had 'prevented the outbreak of a war between India and Pakistan'.[81]

Jinnah's retraction was probably prompted more by military realities than constitutional propriety. Messervy was in Britain seeking stores and equipment, while Pakistan was overwhelmingly dependent upon British officers. India had taken over the great bulk of stores, arms, and equipment, the division of which was being delayed. It was still incomplete a month later when Auchinleck resigned and his headquarters were wound up. Auchinleck had minuted:

I have no hesitation whatever in affirming that the present Indian Cabinet are implacably determined to do all in their power to prevent the establishment of the Dominion of Pakistan on a firm basis. In that I am supported by the unanimous opinion of my senior officers, and indeed by all responsible British officers cognizant of the situation.[82]

Neither had Pakistan the administrative infrastructure necessary to wage war effectively. Yet Jinnah felt that he had 'a good moral and constitutional case for intervening by force . . . and that the so-called "accession" of Hari Singh was fraudulent and impossible to accept'.[83]

When Auchinleck phoned Mountbatten to tell of his success with Jinnah he added that he had also persuaded him to attend a round table conference. Jinnah, Liaquat, Mountbatten, Nehru, Hari Singh, and Mahajan should meet at Lahore to discuss the situation.

---

[79] CAB 134/54.

[80] Auchinleck to Chiefs of Staff (London), 28 Oct. 1947, in Connell, *Auchinleck* (1959), 931; Commons Debates, 30 Oct. 1947.

[81] Connell, op. cit., 932:

[82] Auchinleck's Report of 28 Sept. 1947 for Prime Minister, Chief of Naval Staff, CIGS, and Chief of Air Staff, ibid., 920–24. See also Commonwealth Affairs Cttee meeting of 14 Nov. 1947, CAB 134/54.

[83] Cunningham's Diary, 28 Oct. 1947.

Mountbatten agreed to attend. So did Nehru despite some opposition from his Cabinet colleagues, including Patel, who thought that 'to go crawling to Mr Jinnah' would not be tolerated by the people.[84] An Indian agreement to go to Lahore on the 29th reached Jinnah just as he and Liaquat were discussing with Gracey, Mudie, and Cunningham the possibility of helping the Muslims in Jammu with men, arms, and ammunition, short of sending troops.[85] To prevent further butchery Mudie wanted to seek India's acceptance of a Pakistani peacekeeping battalion in Kashmir. Jinnah and Liaquat were alarmed at the probable effect on Muslim opinion everywhere of their failure to act in Jammu. The discussion was aborted by the proposed visit of Mountbatten, Nehru, and the Maharaja, and attention turned to the strategy to be pursued at the conference with them next day. It was agreed that the legality and propriety of the accession should be denied; that a plebiscite should be held to decide whether accession should be to India or Pakistan; and that the plebiscite should be conducted by the two commanders-in-chief, using Indian and Pakistan troops to keep order. However, by the end of the day Mountbatten had sent a message postponing the meeting on grounds of Nehru's ill-health. Jinnah suspected an Indian ruse to delay discussions while more troops were flown in, but Nehru was indeed ill.

On the morning of Wednesday 29 October Jinnah discussed with Cunningham the form that Pakistan's intervention in Kashmir might take.[86] He likened the Dogra ruler's massacre of Muslims to the Turkish atrocities against their Christian subjects in Bulgaria in 1876, and his own position to that of Gladstone. (On another occasion Cunningham was to compare his own problem *vis-à-vis* the tribal invaders with that of a Turkish governor of a French province during the Crusades.) Jinnah felt legally as well as morally free to act in Kashmir in the light of an accession that he deemed 'fraudulent'. He insisted that his British governors and commander-in-chief must 'enter into the full spirit of this struggle for the safeguarding of the lives and rights of the Kashmir people'. Here was a change, for hitherto Cunningham, at least, had instructed his

---

[84] Hodson, *The Great Divide: Britain–India–Pakistan* (1969), 458. Ismay recorded the Cabinet's feeling: 'Why should they, who were so completely in the right, go cringing to Jinnah?' (note of Nov. 1947, Ismay Papers, III/7/66/5a–e).

[85] Cunningham's Diary, 28 Oct. 1947.

[86] Ibid., 29 Oct. 1947.

officers not to assist the tribal movement. He now warned Jinnah of 'the risk that the co-operation of some of my officers with the tribes-men would become known and might be condemned by world opi-nion'. Jinnah accepted this risk and was now regretting that troops had not been despatched. Cunningham advised him of the incom-patibility of a mixed tribal and government intervention: '. . . the only thing to do now, if pressure were required, was to pump in more tribesmen', summoned by 'some recognised authority' in Pakistan and properly supplied with ammunition and rations. At a conference with Mudie and Liaquat in the latter's bedroom (at about the same time that Mountbatten was visiting Nehru in his bedroom) several practical conclusions were reached. About five thousand tribesmen would be maintained, with suitable reliefs, at Baramula. The Punjab would send rations and ammunition, while Cunningham would supply 100,000 rounds from village defence stocks. The tribesmen would be paid in cash upon their return. Poonch would be strengthened with arms and ammunition only, as it had enough men. Tribesmen should proceed discreetly through Hazara rather than blatantly through Punjab. A directing com-mittee composed of senior officials at Rawalpindi and Hazara would control recruiting, operations, and supplies, while if further officers were required they should be given leave.

Towards the end of their discussion Jinnah received a phone call from Mountbatten, who said 'Nehru is in bed; come to Delhi'. When Jinnah replied 'Liaquat is in bed; come to Lahore', Mountbatten agreed to bring Nehru up for a meeting of the Joint Defence Council on Saturday, 1 November. Jinnah and his team therefore turned to the drafting of a telegram denying the validity of Kashmir's accession, and a public announcement. When Cunningham set off for Peshawar that Wednesday afternoon he felt some satisfaction that war between India and Pakistan had been avoided. He thought that Jinnah was conscious of having blundered, for the tribal invasion had thrown Kashmir into the arms of India, and he was now 'desperate to find a way out'.[87] Still, the tribesmen were in the ascendant and the forthcoming Lahore meeting was a promising development. Regrettably, by the Thursday evening Nehru had already withdrawn from it, ostensibly because of continuing illness, but in fact because

[87] Ibid.

Pakistan's announcement condemned the accession as 'based on fraud and violence'. The announcement, which Jinnah broadcast, refused to recognize the accession and referred to the provocation of the Frontier tribes by attacks of Kashmiri troops on Muslims both in the state and across the border in Pakistan. To India it seemed rude and bellicose. It was a diplomatic gaffe. In Ismay's view it became 'really impossible for Nehru to go to Lahore without losing the premiership'.[88]

On 1 November at Lahore Mountbatten and Ismay had lengthy discussions with Jinnah and Liaquat separately. They saw Liaquat in his bedroom. Ill and depressed, he was 'almost disinclined to make any further effort to avoid war'.[89] He contended that the Maharaja had categorically refused to discuss his state's future with Pakistan and had precipitated a crisis by allowing his State forces to massacre Muslims in Poonch, Mirpur, and Jammu. He saw this as the origin of the tribes' raid on Srinagar, which Pakistan could only have prevented at the cost of trouble with the Frontier tribes at large. Jinnah explained his 'fraud and violence' accusation by suggesting that India, or at least Congress, had encouraged the massacres that triggered the crisis and drove Hari Singh into their hands.[90] His main complaint was that India had at once sent in troops, without informing Pakistan until they had arrived. Ismay noted that 'Jinnah produced the somewhat ingenuous admission that if he had known [of the intended despatch of Indian troops] he could have stopped the tribesmen'.[91] This was not, however, to admit Pakistan's ability to control the tribes but to claim that an assurance of joint Indo-Pakistan intervention in Kashmir would have sufficed to placate them. Ismay had been critical from the first of India's failure to signal its intention to Pakistan and seek co-operation.[92] Jinnah could resent with some justification that India's cable had merely told him of the accession and the landing of troops. His difficulty was, however, that the legality of the accession and thus of the Indian military presence and Sheikh Abdullah's Government was impossible to dispute successfully. Mountbatten

[88] Ismay's November note, loc. cit.

[89] Mountbatten's note of a talk with Liaquat on 1 Nov., Das, op. cit., i, 72–3.

[90] Mountbatten's note of discussion with Jinnah on 1 Nov. 1947, ibid., 73–81.

[91] Ismay's November note, loc. cit.

[92] Mountbatten's note of discussion with Jinnah, loc. cit.; Ismay's note on the situation in India, 30 Nov. 1947, Ismay Papers, III/7/66/6a.

offered the prospect of India agreeing to a plebiscite to decide Kashmir's accession, once law and order were restored. Jinnah denied the possibility of a fair plebiscite as long as Indian troops and Abdullah's government were installed. He called for the simultaneous withdrawal of the troops and the tribesmen and the organization of the plebiscite by himself and Mountbatten as Governors-General. Mountbatten was sure that Attlee would never agree to his involvement and entreated Jinnah to come to Delhi for negotiations.

The Lahore meetings of 1 November accomplished nothing. Their failure inaugurated a critical period in relations between the new Dominions. Jinnah was clearly unwilling to seek a negotiated settlement and, like Liaquat, seemed reconciled to the continuation of hostilities. Mountbatten recorded Jinnah's saying

that he had lost interest in what the world thought of him since the British Commonwealth had let him down when he had asked them to come to the rescue of Pakistan. . . . At the end Mr Jinnah became extremely pessimistic and said it was quite clear that the Dominion of India was out to throttle and choke the Dominion of Pakistan at birth, and that if they continued with their oppression there would be nothing for it but to face the consequences. However depressing the prospect might be, he was not afraid; for the situation was already so bad that there was little that could happen to make it worse.

Jinnah's unwillingness to negotiate at this stage seems a mistake, explicable only in terms of a misjudgement of his legal case and political and strategic realities in Kashmir. It is scarcely surprising that he suspected Hari Singh's accession and India's instant supply of troops as the culmination of well-laid Indian plans to grab the state, but whatever their origins the accession and occupation were now established facts. At the moment the tribesmen had been repulsed from Srinagar but they still held Baramula and threatened the Vale. Pakistan could scarcely afford an open war and was obliged to support covertly tribal operations that it could not control. It is difficult to see how Jinnah imagined that the strategic backing for his negotiating position would be improved by playing a waiting game. The suggested basis for discussion at a round table conference that Mountbatten formulated and sent to Nehru on 2 November conceded most of his demands: India would withdraw its troops immediately the raiders returned home; UNO would be asked to supervise a plebiscite; a 'joint India-Pakistan force should hold the ring while the plebiscite is being held'; accession would be decided by an 'impartial reference to the will of the people'.[93] This basis was not presented to Jinnah and it may be that the Indian leaders would have rejected it. But by refusing to probe the possibilities of diplomacy Jinnah overplayed his hand.

In the absence of discussions the Dominion Prime Ministers manœuvred for tactical advantage in broadcasts and public recriminations. Indian troops stabilized the military position. They captured Baramula on 8 November and Uri a fortnight later, but would obviously be unable to pacify Jammu, or recover Poonch or Gilgit (which had thrown off Dogra rule on 31 October) in the immediate future. On 2 November Nehru broadcast an offer of a referendum under UN auspices, 'when peace and order have been established'.[94] Two days later Liaquat's counter-broadcast labelled India's operations as an 'extermination' of the Muslims of Kashmir.[95] On 16 November Liaquat alleged that India's policy was imperialist and that Abdullah was her 'quisling'.[96] He called for the UN to stop the fighting, arrange the withdrawal of outside forces, and set up 'an impartial administration of the State till a plebiscite is held . . . under its direction'. On 21 November Nehru argued that the UN had no troops to replace those of India, who must remain to drive out the raiders.[97] He upheld Abdullah's government and denied its partiality. Four days later Pakistan reiterated that Abdullah was a 'quisling and a paid agent to disrupt the Mussalmans of Kashmir'.[98] It cabled to Attlee that a government under UN or Commonwealth forces was required.

In the first week of December the Prime Ministers met for Joint Defence Council discussions in Delhi and Lahore, with Ismay and Mountbatten struggling to reconcile the opposed terms for withdrawal, administration, and a plebiscite. India's concessions failed to satisfy Pakistan, which would not countenance a tribal withdrawal while Indian troops remained, and demanded more than the presence of the UN as mere observers. India's attitude had begun to harden as the extent of Pakistan's commitment to the

---

[93] Mountbatten to Nehru, 2 Nov. 1947 and encl., Das, op. cit., i, 71–81.
[94] Broadcast cited in S. Gupta, *Kashmir: A Study in India-Pakistan Relations* (1966), 130.
[95] Cited, ibid., 131.
[96] *Dawn*, 17 Nov. 1947, cited, ibid., 133.
[97] Ibid.   [98] Ibid.

tribesmen's operations became apparent.[99] Reports were coming in of large concentrations of 'would-be invaders including tribesmen' in West Punjab near the Jammu border, of Liaquat's encouragement of more raiders to enter Kashmir, and of the raiders' atrocities against non-Muslims.[100] The Pakistani position hardened, too, with news of continuing butchery in Jammu, while the 'Azad Kashmir', or revolutionary government, emphasized that it would fight on unless Indian forces withdrew and an impartial administration was set up. The stalemate was complete.

As winter set in Nehru recognized that the military situation was deteriorating. He wrote to the Maharaja on 21 December: 'It is patent that the present position in which the Pakistan Government and army, though remaining officially in the background, play a dominant role in the invasion of Kashmir, is most disadvantageous to us'.[101] The previous day he had succumbed to pressure from Mountbatten to refer the dispute to UN and carried his Cabinet with him in principle. It was not to be a joint reference to the UN but an appeal for condemnation of Pakistan's 'aggression against India' by its assistance of the raiders.[102] Nehru gave Liaquat written notice of the intended reference immediately. It would be sent forward unless Pakistan agreed to deny the raiders access to its territory for aggression on Kashmir, military and other supplies, and all other kinds of aid. On Christmas eve the news reaching Delhi was dire. The garrison at Jhangar had been attacked by 6,000 raiders and suffered many casualties, and a relief column had been driven away. The Poonch garrison was cut off by land. A formidable gathering of some 6,000 raiders was reported near Uri, loss of which would again expose Baramula and Srinagar. Mountbatten feared that his government might decide to march into West Punjab and appealed to Nehru to call in the UN at the earliest possible moment. Nehru replied, in Alan Campbell-Johnson's words, in 'a cold fever':

The present situation is that the Frontier Province and a considerable part of West Punjab have been turned into military training grounds where vast numbers of tribesmen, ex-service men and others are being armed and

[99] Ibid., 134.

[100] Mountbatten report cited in Hodson, op. cit., 462–3.

[101] Nehru to Maharaja, 21 December 1947, Das, op. cit., i, 124–6.

[102] Hodson, op. cit., 465–9; Indian Complaint to the Security Council, 1 Jan. 1948, in Das, op. cit., i, 345–50.

trained and then sent on to invade Kashmir. The resources of Pakistan are being employed to this end. . . . The only inference to draw from this is that the invasion of Kashmir is not an accidental affair resulting from the fanaticism or exuberance of the tribesmen, but a well-organised business with the backing of the State. . . .

The present objective is Kashmir. The next declared objective is Patiala, East Punjab and Delhi. On to Delhi is the cry all over West Punjab. . . .

From the strictly legal and constitutional point of view it is our right and duty to resist this invasion with all our forces. From the point of view of international law we can in self-defence take any military measures to resist it, including the sending of our armies across Pakistan territory to attack their bases near the Kashmir border. We have refrained from doing this because of our desire to avoid complications leading to open war. In our avoidance of this we have increased our own peril and not brought peace any nearer. . . .

My conclusion is that we should immediately proceed along two parallel lines of action:
1. Reference to UNO. . . .
2. Complete military preparations to meet any possible contingency that might arise. If grave danger threatens us in Kashmir or elsewhere on the West Punjab frontier then we must not hesitate to march through Pakistan territory towards the bases.[103]

Desperate to buy time and avert catastrophe, Mountbatten, with Nehru's knowledge, urged Attlee to fly out immediately and meet the Dominion Prime Ministers but Attlee could see no role that he could play with advantage and wanted the UN to take up the matter. At year's end Jinnah cabled to Cunningham that Indian troops in Jammu were on the verge of committing acts of hostility on Pakistan. Mountbatten felt that war was imminent. On 1 January 1948 India despatched its application to the Security Council. The threat to Uri faded, and with it, for the moment the danger of war.

In the atmosphere of bitterness and recrimination generated by the Indo-Pakistan dispute, Mountbatten made a misguided attempt at the December Joint Defence Council meeting to bring the new Dominions together for external defence. He put up a paper proposing that their Chiefs of Staff should meet for preliminary discussions and that a date should be set for a visit by a British delegation.

---

[103] Campbell-Johnson, *Mission with Mountbatten* (1951), 257; Nehru to Mountbatten, 26 Dec. 1947, Hodson, op. cit., 467–8.

Mountbatten recorded that the Council's reaction was 'disappointing':

> Both Prime Ministers now took the line that it would be valueless to pursue the question of joint defence until their Governments were more in line politically. . . . So far as the British Chiefs of Staff Delegation was concerned, the two Prime Ministers were also of the view that the two Dominion Governments must be in some measure of preliminary agreement on the matters which this intended to raise, before it came out.[104]

The British Chiefs of Staff had always emphasized the need for Indo-Pakistan accord if the subcontinent were to play a role in Commonwealth defence. Now the Dominions were so locked in dispute that their partnership in any new Commonwealth seemed highly problematical.

---

[104] Mountbatten report, ibid., 514. Crum advised Sir Leslie Hollis (Deputy Secretary (Military) to the Cabinet) that at the Joint Defence Council meeting of 22 Dec. both Prime Ministers felt that the strained relations between their Dominions made any such talks inopportune (Crum to Hollis, 30 Jan. 1948, Ismay Papers, III/7/12/2c).

3

Dominions at War

ON New Year's Eve 1947 a British official close to Mountbatten noted in his diary that there was 'in fact a state of undeclared war between India and Pakistan'.[1] Mountbatten was always 'happy . . . that when the possibility of the war spreading really seemed quite imminent' he insisted upon India's reference to the UN.[2] The reference did, as he claimed, constitute 'a detente', albeit short-lived, and the danger of full-scale war receded for a time. Yet there were old India hands who thought he had blundered and that the Commonwealth should have intervened. In November Liaquat had expressed his willingness to have a Commonwealth force in Kashmir. On 20 December Jinnah said:

I fully realize that Britain has no power to intervene in the affairs of any Dominion but at the same time Britain and other Dominions are in a position to use moral persuasion to help settle differences between members of the Commonwealth. It appears to me that His Majesty's Government are so far shirking their responsibility in this respect.[3]

Major J. McL. Short and Sir Penderel Moon, both experts on the Punjab, together with H.V. Hodson, a former Reforms Commissioner of the Government of India, were inclined to the same view. Short produced a paper, 'The Commonwealth is Invaded', which argued that the essential problem was an invasion of both India and Pakistan by the Pathans, who should be expelled by them jointly. Hodson sent the paper to Noel-Baker, and argued that Britain, as leader of the Commonwealth, should approach the combatant Dominions informally and confidentially.[4] Short sent it to Cripps, whose former secretary, George Blaker, replied that both Dominions would resent any offer of armed assistance from the Commonwealth; India was confident of her own ability to deal with

[1] WHJ Christie Diary, 31 Dec. 1947, IOL.
[2] Mountbatten to Cunningham, 29 May 1948, Cunningham Papers, D670/9.
[3] *Pakistan Times*, 20 Dec. 1947, cited in Gupta, *Kashmir*, 225.
[4] Hodson to Noel-Baker, 2 Mar. 1948, Short Collection, F189/20, IOL.

the Pathans but would doubt Pakistan's wish to expel them, while Pakistan would seek ways of using outside troops to disadvantage India.[5] It no doubt seemed to Noel-Baker and Cripps, as to Attlee, that the risks of a British-led Commonwealth intervention were greater than the prospective benefits. Yet the reference to the UN failed to stop hostilities in the short-term. The undeclared war escalated with the commitment of Pakistani regular troops. By the end of 1948 the UN, aided by a military stalemate, had at length achieved a cease-fire. In the course of the year, the UN's extension of India's limited reference into a searching examination of the Kashmir problem came close to alienating Nehru's India from the Commonwealth.

The reference to the UN brought fresh British and international influences to bear upon the affairs of the subcontinent. The overriding object of the Attlee–Cripps–Mountbatten nexus was, of course, the retention of India in a new Commonwealth. Pakistan's membership was simply assumed. In January 1948 it became the responsibility of Philip Noel-Baker, leader of the British delegation to the UN, to formulate policy there. He has been well described by Lord Garner:

A Quaker by origin, he had served with distinction in the Friends Ambulance Unit during the First World war . . . [His] over-riding interest was in the maintenance of peace. He had worked in the League of Nations Secretariat, had been PPS to Arthur Henderson as Foreign Secretary and had written much on disarmament. He had limitless compassion, unquenchable faith and courage and inexhaustible energy. Above all he had a great heart. He was an idealist with all the virtues of the pure in heart—but also some of the drawbacks. He reached for the stars, but was not one to calculate nicely and under-rated the art of the possible. . . . The very sweetness of his nature prevented him from showing the ruthlessness that politics sometimes demanded. He was unfortunate too that his passion was for international pacification but that in this field he was overshadowed by the burly figure of Bevin, of whom he was a great admirer.[6]

Noel-Baker was accompanied to Lake Success by Ismay as his 'Principal Adviser'. Bevin, too, now had a role to play. In May 1947 he had secured Foreign Office representation on the India and Burma Committee, and in September Attlee had arranged for him

---

5 Blaker to Short, 4 Mar. 1948, ibid.
6 Garner, *The Commonwealth Office, 1925–1968* (1978), 282.

to see all important telegrams on India and Pakistan. Now a new channel of influence was opened, for Britain's Head of Mission at the UN, Sir Alexander Cadogan, was instructed by the Foreign Office, of which he had been PUS. Policy was thus subject to the idealism of a pacifist and the Cold Warriors' preoccupations with Russia and the Middle East.

In the circumstances of 1948 Bevin was bound to be concerned with the Kashmir crisis in any case. Palestine had been before the UN since February 1947. In November a scheme of partition had been endorsed there, but a civil war between Arab 'Liberationists' and Zionists was in train throughout 1948. British troops, finally withdrawn in May 1948, were unable to control a situation for which they were nominally responsible and they suffered the odium of both sides. On 6 January Sargent advised Attlee that Bevin was 'worried lest the British should appear to be siding with India. With the difficult situation in Palestine, they must be on their guard against aligning Islam against them'.[7] On 19 January the Foreign Minister and the head of the Pakistan delegation at the UN, Sir Muhammad Zafrulla Khan, told Noel-Baker that the Pakistan Government did 'not contemplate any flirtation with the Soviet Government', but 'if the United Kingdom pursued a policy which seemed to Pakistan opinion unduly favourable to India then the present Ministers might be swept away and new Ministers might go over to Russia'.[8] In 1948 the diplomatic universe was, as Raymond Aron has written of the Cold War world, 'like an echo chamber: the noises of men and events are amplified and reverberated to infinity'.[9] On 25 February the Communists staged a coup in Czechoslovakia and in June the blockade of Berlin began. In March Bevin achieved Western European Union with the Brussels Treaty. He wrote to Attlee that he was 'seriously concerned' that any British proposals at the UN might alienate India or Pakistan and thus offer Russia an opportunity for penetration.[10] It was virtually

[7] Sargent to PM, 6 Jan. 1948, FO 800/470. See also Kirkpatrick to PM, 13 Jan. 1948, ibid. For Pakistan's concern for Palestine, see S.A. Dar, 'Foreign Policy of Pakistan, 1947–8', in Dani, *World Scholars on Quaid-i-Azam Mohammad Ali Jinnah* (Islamabad 1979), 341–7.

[8] Cadogan to Sargent, 10 Feb. 1948, FO 371/2690; Noel-Baker to Attlee, 20 Jan. 1948, PREM 8/821.

[9] Aron, *Peace and War: A Theory of International Relations* (1966), 373.

[10] Bevin to PM, 11 March 1948, FO 800/470. The Chiefs of Staff had recently cautioned the Cabinet against adopting a policy at UN that might prejudice the

inevitable that a British policy that did not simply endorse India's appeal should be suspected as a contribution to Cold War diplomacy. Even in June 1947 Krishna Menon had questioned Mountbatten about Bevin's intentions towards Pakistan:

Mr Bevin said . . . [at the Labour Party Annual Conference] that the withdrawal from India meant consolidation of Britain in the middle east. Is our frontier still the hinterland of this imperial strategy? Does Britain still think in terms of being able to use this territory and all that follows from it? There is a considerable amount of talking in this way and if Kashmir for one reason or another chooses to be in Pakistan, there is a further development in that direction.[11]

In a brilliant exposition of Pakistan's large log of grievances Zafrulla Khan dissuaded the Security Council from making the quick and decisive condemnation that Nehru had sought. Zafrulla painted a canvas of horrors, of genocide in East Punjab and the Sikh states, and of the occupation of the small state of Junagadh by Indian troops when its ruler had acceded to Pakistan. In a private discussion with Noel-Baker he alleged that Mountbatten had behaved perfidiously over the Punjab award: the Radcliffe award, completed by 7 August, had been tampered with to Pakistan's disadvantage; aware of the violence that it would stimulate Mountbatten had delayed its publication until after Independence; and he had thus reneged upon his undertaking to Jinnah that the Sikh leaders, whose plan for a rising was known to the police, would be arrested upon its publication.[12] Cunningham heard similar allegations from Jinnah, who was 'very bitter about the whole thing'.[13] Anti-Mountbatten feeling rose to fever pitch in the influential Muslim League daily newspaper, *Dawn*. Pakistan was bound to read any signs of British sympathy for the Indian case at the UN as a consequence of Mountbatten's influence and a part of his Commonwealth diplomacy.

India's case rested upon the legality of the Maharaja's accession. India claimed that it justified her airlift of troops, legitimized

possibility of defence collaboration with India. See A.I. Singh, 'Post-Imperial Attitudes to India: The Military Aspect, 1947–51', *Round Table* (1985), 360–75.
[11] TP, xi, 201.
[12] Noel-Baker to Attlee, 20 Jan. 1948, loc. cit.; Mountbatten to Jenkins, 19 Mar. 1948, Ismay Papers, III/7/19/2a; L/P & J/10/119.
[13] Cunningham's Diary, 9 Feb. 1948.

Abdullah's administration, and established the guilt of Pakistan in abetting the tribal invasion. Pakistan condemned the accession as fraudulent. The dispute thus raised profound questions: What principles were appropriate to post-Independence accessions? And how did they relate to that of the Maharaja? The rules of this game were elusive of definition. For British India Radcliffe inherited a statutory demarcation by district according to the distribution of Muslims and non-Muslims. His modifications to the principle of population contiguity were highly important but the territories at issue were small by comparison with those of the three princes whose states were the cause of contention after Independence: Junagadh, Hyderabad, and Kashmir. They were enjoined to consult the will of their people and the facts of geography. For a full year the large state of Hyderabad, with a Muslim ruler and court, pursued the illusion of independence, although it had an over-whelmingly Hindu population and was surrounded by Hindu neighbours. Soon after the emergence of the dual Dominions the Muslim ruler of the petty Kathiawad state of Junagadh eccentrically acceded to Pakistan. His subjects were mostly Hindu, as were those of adjacent princes, and his port was open only seasonally. Pakistan accepted the accession, seemingly admitting thereby the principle of the ruler's absolute right of decision. A revolt occurred, the Nawab fled and early in November India sent in troops and set the accession aside. India was apparently asserting the rights of the state's people and the principle of contiguity.

In Kashmir the principle of contiguity could be applied to the advantage of either India or Pakistan. India was, in effect, upholding the ruler's right of choice and Pakistan was demanding that his people be consulted. Was Pakistan, as India believed, seeking to force his hand by a tribal invasion? Or, as Pakistan argued, did India force it by offering to rescue him from the consequences of his inability to pacify his subjects? The Azad Kashmir Government was, in fact, proclaimed four days before the accession. There are indications that the Maharaja and some of his court favoured full independence, as at a later stage did Abdullah. Such a course would have provoked both Dominions. Kashmir was the source of three rivers, abutted powerful neighbours, Russia and China, and contained the trade routes to Central Asia. Mountbatten was wont to assert that in July he had urged the Maharaja to accede to one or other Dominion by 15 August.[14] In fact his visit was in June, when he advised him against haste, suggesting that he await the deliberations of the Pakistan Constituent Assembly (which first met on 11 August). The Indian Dominion was less patient. In early July Patel, as States Minister in the Interim Government, pressed him to join India 'without any delay'.[15]

For Nehru, the Kashmiri Brahmin, the Vale was heaven on earth. He later wrote to Lady Mountbatten:

Kashmir affects me in a peculiar way; it is a kind of mild intoxication—like music sometimes or the company of a beloved person. For years and years I could not visit Kashmir because of prison, etc, and the desire to come here again became a passion and an obsession. It is not just the beauty of the scene, though I love beauty and beautiful things, but even more is the very air of Kashmir which has something mysterious and compelling about it.[16]

In advance of Congress involvement in states matters he had been President of the Indian States Peoples' Movement. Sheikh Abdullah also became prominent in it. The Sheikh's political career had secured a sound basis during a successful movement for political rights that assailed Hari Singh in the early 1930s.[17] Though at first a sympathizer with specifically Muslim grievances, expressed through the missionary Ahmadiyya sect, his National Conference achieved a transcommunal and largely secular appeal. From the late 1930s it was closely associated with the National Congress and Abdullah with Nehru's policies. By contrast the Kashmir Muslim Conference led by the more conservative Ghulam Abbas was linked with the League. In the backward polity of Kashmir Abdullah enjoyed periods of significance interspersed with incarceration. In 1946, when he led a Quit Kashmir movement, Hari Singh effectively abrogated the constitution. At Independence Kashmir's political leaders were still in gaol. It was a pointer to Nehru's concern for Kashmir that he dashed there in 1946 at the stage when the Congress Working Committee was finalizing its response to Britain's proposals for an Interim Government. At a critical moment on the eve of the transfer of power, Mountbatten felt

[14] e.g., Mountbatten's note of discussion with Jinnah, 1 Nov. 1947, loc. cit.
[15] Patel to Maharaja, 3 July 1947, Das, *Patel's Correspondence*, i, 32–4.
[16] Nehru to Lady Mountbatten, 27 June 1948, cited in Ziegler, *Mountbatten*, 445.
[17] Copland, 'Islam and Political Mobilization in Kashmir, 1931–34', *Pacific Affairs*, 54 (1981), 228–59.

obliged to fix Nehru's attention on the problems of India's 400
million people rather than Kashmir's four million and to dissuade
him from visiting the state against the Maharaja's wishes.

As Independence drew near the Congress leaders sought the
removal of the Maharaja's Prime Minister, Ramchandra Kak, and
the release of Abdullah. Kak was known to oppose accession to
India. He was suspected of hostility to Abdullah, and of influencing
the Maharaja in favour of Pakistan. Kak's English wife later argued
that in August 1947 he believed that accession to either Dominion
would provoke a revolt. He yielded to pressures to resign on 11
August and was detained and accused of corruption. He was
replaced on a temporary basis by the Dogra General Janak Singh.
By mid-August the Darbar had requested the loan from India of
Lieutenant-Colonel Kashmir Singh Katoch, the General's son, to
serve as Commander-in-Chief of the State forces. Patel urged
Baldev Singh, the Minister of Defence: 'You know the difficulties
of the State, and I feel that at this juncture it would be most useful to
have an officer of our own Army as Commander-in-Chief of the
Kashmir Forces'.[18] The new commander was installed early in
October. By mid-month a new Prime Minister, Justice Mehr
Chand Mahajan, had been installed. Mahajan, a former judge of
the High Court at Lahore and a member of the Punjab Boundary
Commission, was an Arya Samajist, with, in the words of India's
Agent to Kashmir, 'all the mentality and fanaticism of that body'.[19]
Mahajan claims that he was first invited to the appointment in May
and finally accepted it in September when Patel 'practically ordered
me to accept the offer'.[20] On 10 October Patel phoned him at midnight and arranged his departure for Srinagar within hours. As
States' Minister Patel was also active in September and October to
establish regular scheduled air services with Kashmir and in
'expediting as much as possible the linking up of the State with the
Indian Dominion by means of telegraph, telephones, wireless and
roads'.[21] Wireless equipment was loaned to facilitate an all-weather
air service to Srinagar and Jammu.

In an appraisal of 27 September Nehru expressed the conviction

[18] Patel to Baldev Singh, 13 Sept. 1947, Das, op. cit., i, 37.

[19] Dalip Singh to Patel, 7 Nov. 1947, ibid., 85.

[20] Mahajan, *Looking Back* (1963), 126.

[21] Patel to K.C. Neogy, 17 Sept. 1947, and to Maharaja, 2 Oct. 1947, Das, op. cit., i,
39 and 43.

that India must secure the Maharaja's accession within a month:

It is obvious to me from the many reports I have received that the situation there is a dangerous and deteriorating one. The Muslim League in the Punjab and the NWFP are making preparations to enter Kashmir in considerable numbers. The approach of winter is going to cut off Kashmir from the rest of India. The only normal route then is via the Jhelum valley. The Jammu route can hardly be used during winter and air traffic is also suspended. Therefore it is important that something should be done before these winter conditions set in. This means practically by the end of October or, at the latest, the beginning of November. Indeed, air traffic will be difficult even before that.

I understand that the Pakistan strategy is to infiltrate into Kashmir now and to take some big action as soon as Kashmir is more or less isolated because of the coming winter.[22]

The logistical problem was, of course, apparent to the Darbar and to Indian ministers, and from early October there were strenuous attempts to ensure that arms, ammunition, petrol, and aviation spirit were available to the state. Patel urged the use of air freight upon Baldev Singh. As early as 7 October he argued that 'the question of military assistance in terms of emergency must claim the attention of our Defence Council as soon as possible'.[23] However, Nehru's astute appraisal emphasized a more fundamental problem:

I rather doubt if the Maharaja and his State forces can meet the situation by themselves and without some popular help. They will be isolated from the rest of India and if their own people go against them, it will be very difficult to meet the situation. Obviously the only major group that can side with them is the National Conference under Sheikh Abdullah's leadership. If by any chance that is hostile or even passive, then the Maharaja and his Government become isolated and the Pakistan people will have a relatively free field. . . .

Indeed, it seems to me that there is no other course open to the Maharaja but this: to release Sheikh Abdullah and the National Conference leaders, to make a friendly approach to them, seek their co-operation and make them feel that this is really meant, and then to declare adhesion to the Indian Union. Once the State [accedes] to India, it will become very difficult for Pakistan to invade it officially or unofficially without coming into conflict with the Indian Union. . . .

---

[22] Nehru to Patel, 27 Sept. 1947, ibid., 45.
[23] Patel to Baldev Singh, 7 Oct. 1947, ibid., 57.

It seems to me urgently necessary therefore, that the accession to the Indian Union should take place early.[24]

Nehru had explained this strategy to Mahajan on 19 September 'but he only partly appreciated' it. Mahajan later recalled that Nehru had insisted upon Abdullah's release and immediate administrative reforms but that he himself could not see the need for reforms prior to accession.[25] Abdullah was in fact released even as Nehru was writing his appraisal. Mahajan's outlook was close to that of the Maharaja's authoritarianism.

The National Conference detainees were released in a general amnesty, though Ghulam Abbas and his Muslim Conference associates remained in gaol. In the first week of October Nehru learned that Abdullah and his followers had 'decided for the Indian Union'.[26] At his request (conveyed by Mahajan through the Maharaja) the Sheikh visited Delhi. He was eager to co-operate but insisted upon immediate constitutional reforms. Patel urged Mahajan on 21 October:

It is obvious that in your dealings with the external dangers and internal commotion with which you are faced, mere brute force is not enough. We, on our part, have pledged to give you the maximum support and we will do so. But I am afraid, without some measure of popular backing, particularly from amongst the community which represents such an overwhelming majority in Kashmir, it would be difficult to make such support go to the farthest limit that is necessary if we are to crush the disruptive forces which are being raised and organised.[27]

The Hindu monopoly of security service appointments must end and an approach must be made to responsible government. Patel asked Mahajan to come to Delhi, bringing the Maharaja if possible, in order to 'hammer out something which would rally popular support in defence of the State both from without and from within'. There seems little doubt that Patel was seeking an opportunity to confront Hari Singh with the dire consequences of his indecision, to secure both his accession and constitutional government in return for India's total support against insurgents from Pakistan and within. However, on 23 October Mahajan replied that it was

24 Nehru to Patel, 27 Sept. 1947, loc. cit.
25 Mahajan, op. cit., 126.
26 Dwarkanath Kachru to Nehru, 4 Oct. 1947, Das, op. cit., i, 54.
27 Patel to Mahajan, 21 Oct. 1947, ibid., 61–2.

'hardly the time to think of any constitutional issues'.[28] Kashmir was now 'practically working on a war basis', the border situation was worsening every day, almost the whole of the Muslim military and police had deserted or behaved improperly, and 'we are surrounded on all sides'.

Against this background of Indian involvement in Kashmir during September and October the denouement of the 25–27th is not surprising. At a Defence Committee meeting on 25 October, over which Mountbatten presided, it was decided to secure Srinagar by an airlift of Indian troops. V.P. Menon was despatched to Srinagar to discuss with the Maharaja his request for troops, the need for the Sheikh's co-operation, and the question of accession. The Maharaja, preparing to flee to Jammu, was highly co-operative. Menon returned to Delhi to report and then took an Instrument of Accession to Jammu for the Maharaja to sign. The conditions for sending troops were the Maharaja's accession for defence, foreign affairs, and communications, the democratization of the internal administration, and the appointment of the Sheikh to the administration together with Mahajan.[29]

On the evening of the 26th the Defence Committee decided to accept the accession subject to its ratification by a plebiscite when the law and order situation permitted. At dawn on the 27th a squadron of a hundred planes carried troops and supplies to Srinagar. The provision for a plebiscite seemed to forearm India against accusations of upholding a tyrant's will against that of his subjects. It would also ensure his dependence upon the Sheikh. At a stroke Pakistan's play for Kashmir was defeated by the Maharaja's accession to India, while the Maharaja's power was undermined by the installation of Abdullah and the proposed plebiscite.

From the first the British delegation to the UN adopted a policy that India considered pro-Pakistan. Noel-Baker and Ismay left for Lake Success in January unencumbered by any policy formulated by the Cabinet or its Commonwealth Affairs Committee. Ismay's views must have carried great weight. He had been absent from India when the decisions of 25–27 October were taken. Upon his return he was 'furious' at the role Mountbatten had played.[30] After reflection

[28] Mahajan to Patel, 23 Oct. 1947, ibid., 63.

[29] Mahajan, op. cit., 155.

[30] John Lascelles to Sir Alan Lascelles, 30 Oct. 1947, in possession of Lady Chandos.

he had accepted the need for the airlift in the interests of the security of Srinagar (especially in the light of the tribal massacre at Baramula).[31] But he remained critical of the failure to acquaint Jinnah of the operation in advance and thus invite a bilateral intervention. The proposals that Mountbatten put to Nehru after the abortive Lahore meeting on 1 November may well have been his work (as were most of Mountbatten's important drafts). They had provided for the withdrawal of India's troops as well as the tribal raiders, the installation of forces from both Dominions, and a plebiscite under UN auspices. During a visit to Peshawar on 21 November Ismay was exposed to the views of the Frontier leaders, their wish for a settlement, and their conviction that if the tribes had not acted then Kashmir would have slid into the Indian Union.[32] He must have felt that without a fair settlement of the question of accession the Pathans would refuse to withdraw and Pakistan would not press them to do so.

Anxious not to seem to seek the return of the Raj the British delegation tried to avoid taking the lead in the Security Council. It hoped that the President of the Council or the US delegation would initiate proposals there. On 8 January Noel-Baker and Ismay visited Warren Austin, the US representative at the UN, to emphasize the danger of war and the importance of a cease-fire. They urged the need for a plebiscite under military supervision:

. . . Pakistan troops would be the most suitable [for] . . . the one indispensable condition of peace in Kashmir is to guarantee the security of the Moslems. The whole affair . . . started with the massacre of Moslems instigated by the Prince. When threatened with reprisals . . . he took political refuge by requesting the accession of Kashmir to India.[33]

They elaborated their views at a meeting with officials of the State Department on 10 January.[34] They envisaged the early establishment of a committee of the Security Council to work out a plan for peaceful settlement and the dispatch of a commission to implement it. The plan should include the UN's appointment to Srinagar of a neutral commander and a commission of experts, working with a

---

[31] Ismay's note of 30 Nov. 1947, Ismay Papers, III/7/66/6a.
[32] Cunningham's Diary, 21 Nov. 1947.
[33] US Representative at UN to Secretary of State, 8 Jan. 1948, *FRUS*, 1948, v, 274–5.
[34] Ibid., 276–8.

governing council of Indians and Pakistanis. Kashmir would be divided into zones of military occupation, with Pakistan troops in the south, Indian in the north, and a mixture in the Vale and Srinagar. There should be a thousand international troops in Srinagar and scores of UN observers in the occupied zones. Thus would be satisfied the primary condition of giving 'Pakistan sufficient assurances of a fair plebiscite in order that the tribesmen might be induced to go home'.

During the next month, the British delegation pursued this approach, with US support, in the face of Indian objections. On Noel-Baker's initiative, the Security Council agreed that its President should conduct negotiations with representatives of the Indian and Pakistan delegations. At the same time, in formal presentations to the Council, Zafrulla Khan and Gopalaswami Ayyangar, together with Sheikh Abdullah, put diametrically opposed arguments and proposals. In essence, Ayyangar and Abdullah sought as a priority a UN pronouncement on the wrongs of Pakistan's abetment of the tribesmen, while Zafrulla wanted the simultaneous settlement of the military and the political issues. By the end of January the President's attempts at mediation had foundered on Pakistan's insistence on, and India's objection to, the provision of an interim administration with inter-Dominion forces to maintain law and order. Neither Abdullah nor the Indians would accept that in the eyes of the world the conduct of a plebiscite under his administration might seem less than fair. Noel-Baker held Indian stubbornness and a hardening of Nehru's attitude to be responsible for the impasse. By 9 February the Indian delegation felt that the Security Council's handling of the Indian reference was so unsatisfactory as to require an adjournment. Nehru wanted it to return to Delhi for consultations. Noel-Baker felt that India must be pressed harder on conditions for a plebiscite. At the same time the State Department, advised by the US Ambassador in Delhi, was doubtful whether India would ever accept aspects of the British approach. It began to demur at the proposed UN interim administration—a virtual trusteeship for an indefinite period—and to look for a compromise with India on the form of the existing regime and the introduction of Pakistan troops. Again, in order to stop the fighting it saw the need to give prominence to a requirement that Pakistan withhold assistance from the raiders.

During a recess in the UN's consideration of Kashmir, from 12

February to 9 March, there was a change in the British approach. This was influenced in part by the American reappraisal in the middle of February, in part by the intervention of Mountbatten, but most significantly by an analysis of the problem by Attlee, Cripps, and the Commonwealth Affairs Committee.

In the first half of February Nehru complained to Mountbatten that the British and American line at Lake Success seemed to be governed by power politics; that is, by concern to rehabilitate their position with the Muslims of the Middle East in the wake of the Palestine catastrophe, and to cultivate Pakistan as a counterpoise to Russian penetration from Central to Southern Asia. He was nonplussed at the UN's apparent reluctance to accept India's basic complaint against Pakistan's aggression. He wrote to his sister that he 'could not imagine that the Security Council could possibly behave in the trivial and partisan manner in which it functioned. . . . The United States and Britain have played a dirty role, Britain probably being the chief actor behind the scenes.'[35] He would defy the UN rather than 'surrender either to the gangster tactics of Pakistan and the raiders or to the attempts at bullying by Britain and the United States'.[36] He deeply resented a patronizing letter from Attlee about Kashmir.

Mountbatten became worried that the attempts of Attlee and Noel-Baker to dispense even-handed justice was alienating India from Britain and the Commonwealth. The British delegation should recognize the need for the raiders to be condemned and consider more sympathetically the possibility of a plebiscite being conducted without setting aside Abdullah's legally constituted government. On a visit to India at this time Kingsley Martin, editor of the *New Statesman*, realized Mountbatten's embarrassment: it was he who had pressed Nehru to refer Kashmir to the UN but Britain had given India no backing there, and in consequence India might leave the Commonwealth.[37] In the same vein, on 17 February Krishna Menon, India's High Commissioner, wrote to Attlee that

---

[35] Nehru to Mrs Pandit, 16 Feb. 1948, cited in Gopal, *Jawaharlal Nehru: A Biography* (1979), ii, 27–8. See also records of Mountbatten's interviews with Nehru and Patel, 10–14 Feb. 1948, Collins and Lapierre (eds), *Mountbatten and Independent India, 16 August 1947–18 June 1948* (1984), 166–71.

[36] Nehru to Menon, 20 Feb. 1948, Gopal, *Nehru*, ii, 27.

[37] Cunningham's Diary, 22 Feb. 1948.

he was 'very concerned that there is an increasing drifting apart in the relations of India and UK'.[38] On 19 February Attlee answered Mountbatten's representations in part by cabling that India's demands on Pakistan might easily be placed in the foreground as part of an agreement that also provided conditions for a plebiscite. At the same time Noel-Baker sent to the British High Commissioner an appreciation of the Kashmir problem that gave his answer to the Indian complaints, and asked that it be shown to Mountbatten.[39]

Noel-Baker affirmed that 'the suggestion in the Indian Press that "power politics" influenced the Security Council is nonsense'. China, Argentina, France, Columbia, Belgium, Spain, the USA, Canada, and the UK were at one in essentials and sought only peace: 'But it was felt that Pakistan could hope to succeed [in stopping the fighting] only if it could point to agreed arrangements under which armed action against Muslims would cease and people of Kashmir would be genuinely free to choose between India and Pakistan'. No doubt Pakistani officials had given facilities to the tribes but in view of the sympathy for them in Pakistan they could not have done otherwise.

To that extent Pakistan is blameworthy as Maharaja was at least in part to blame for original rising of his subjects. . . . But for the Security Council formally to condemn either side or to call on Pakistan to take action in advance of agreement on a general settlement would merely make it more difficult for Pakistan Government to take effective action to stop the fighting. . . . Indian delegation expected Security Council to order Pakistan to hold the ring while the Indian army crushed by military force population of Mirpur, Poonch, Muzaffarabad, and presumably Gilgit. That this was the intention was made quite clear to Council by Sheikh Abdullah although Ayyangar presented his case less bluntly and more skilfully.

Noel-Baker alleged that since October the Government of India had changed its position from accepting a provisional accession, establishing order, and holding a plebiscite under UN auspices. Now it would crush the opposition to the regime, uphold a plebiscite under Abdullah, and regard international assistance as an infringement of sovereignty.

[38] Menon to Attlee, 17 Feb. 1948, Attlee Papers, 67/210, Bodleian Library.
[39] Noel-Baker's appreciation of the Security Council's Approach to the Kashmir Problem, 22 Feb. 1948, Ismay Papers, III/7/15/3a-b.

Mountbatten referred the appreciation to his staff for appraisal, in preparation for an interview with Noel-Baker's deputy, Patrick Gordon Walker, who was visiting India.[40] The staff paper reported Nehru and Ayyangar's conviction that the British delegation had gone to Lake Success with their minds made up and were still dissuading other delegations from expressing views sympathetic to India's. Indian opinion suspected British policy of being directed by a view of 'the gloomy two-world split' and of seeking a western bloc against Russia from fears of her advance into Afghanistan and the Middle East. Noel-Baker, like Jinnah, viewed the Kashmir situation communally and showed a 'predilection for Pakistan's case'. India could not be expected 'to take the view that her urgent request (made in the face of armed invasion) can not be dealt with as a preliminary to examining the wider issues involved'. Noel-Baker's policy 'can only effect a worsening of Indo-British relations and postpone or destroy the prospect of a plebiscite being held in Kashmir'. If it produced a UN decision adverse to India then Nehru would be swept from office and replaced by an extremist government.

> There can be little doubt that, if His Majesty's Government continue to pursue their present policy in this matter peace will not come to the sub-continent. . . . If . . . good Indo-British relations are to be preserved, with all the effect that that would have on Commonwealth solidarity, it would be desirable for the United Kingdom Delegation, when it returns to London, to follow a policy different from that expressed in Mr Noel-Baker's appreciation.

As evidence of India's reasonableness over the wider issues, Mountbatten should say to Gordon Walker that the Government was willing to broaden Abdullah's interim administration and to accept UN representatives to supervise the plebiscite. They might also agree to withdraw Indian troops, except for small strategic forces, but they would not accept a total withdrawal or the entry of Pakistan troops.

Mountbatten actually gave a copy of the staff paper to Gordon Walker. He also arranged for them both to meet Nehru, Patel, and Ayyangar on 25–26 February, which gave Gordon Walker a direct appreciation of the limits to the Indian leaders'

---

[40] Mountbatten's Staff Memo. No. 8/48, 25 Feb. 1948, ibid., III/7/15/2. Records of meetings of Mountbatten, Gordon Walker, Nehru, Patel and Ayyangar, 25–6 February 1948, Collins and Lapierre, *Mountbatten and Independent India*, 172–7.

flexibility. The Indian advance towards a compromise had been assisted by the diplomacy of the sympathetic American Ambassador, who had represented to Nehru (much as Noel-Baker had intimated in his appreciation) the impression of the Security Council that a fair plebiscite could scarcely be expected from Abdullah's government. While Mountbatten's intervention may have helped to get across Indian views that were not well put at Lake Success, it was bound to offend Noel-Baker. Though at first disposed to send a direct rejoinder to the staff paper, Noel-Baker accepted advice in Whitehall that such correspondence would be unconstitutional, and that Ismay should write privately. Ismay's letter to Mountbatten issued a stern rebuke:

It seems to me very wrong, in principle, for a Governor-General or a Commander of any kind to let *anyone* know the nature of the advice that has been offered him by his Staff. But it is surely doubly wrong when—
(a) the Staff in question consists of very junior officers;
(b) their advice is extremely critical of one of His Majesty's principal Ministers; and
(c) the disclosure of their advice is made to the direct subordinate of the Minister concerned.[41]

As for the staff paper's substance, Ismay contrasted the views held in Delhi with those of the outside world: 'The whole question of anyone in the Council playing power politics on this issue is so ridiculous that I can only describe it by Winston's latest gem: "A quintessence of assininity". . . . The free peoples want the subcontinent of India to be peaceful, prosperous and progressive; Soviet Russia wants chaos and anarchy.' He did, however, agree that when the Security Council next met it should 'make it clear that Pakistan have failed in the first duty of a sovereign independent State, in that they have not been able to prevent an incursion across that State into territory which temporarily, at any rate, belongs to one of their neighbours'.

The Commonwealth Affairs Committee took up the Kashmir question on Friday 27 February. Noel-Baker reported India's complaint that the Security Council had failed to condemn Pakistan. The Council saw its task as wider than 'the narrow issue put to them by the Government of India' and feared that mere condemnation of Pakistan might aggravate the situation.[42] In fact the

---

[41] Ismay to Mountbatten, 10 Mar. 1948, Ismay Papers, III/7/18/2a.
[42] CAB 134/55.

Indian delegation had not pressed for a condemnation in advance of
discussing terms of a settlement but had alienated the Council 'by
presenting proposals which gave the impression that they were not
concerned to ensure that a fair plebiscite would be held in
Kashmir'. However, there were now signs of Indian concern for a
settlement and a 'more accommodating temper'. In discussion the
strength of India's resentment and the merits of her case were
emphasized (probably by Cripps). Attlee's independent discussions with Krishna Menon and the senior official H.M. Patel (who
was visiting Britain with a mission to purchase military and other
supplies) had suggested that India would not contemplate any UN
settlement plan that smacked of a rebuff to her. It was agreed that
unless both parties invited Britain to intervene she should not do so.

On Monday, 1 March Gordon Walker reported India's 'bitterness' towards the Security Council and suspicion that Britain had
supported Pakistan in order to impress opinion in the Middle East.
HMG must remain strictly neutral as 'Any deviation from this line
might ultimately drive one or other disputant out of the British
Commonwealth. . . . There were signs that India was now moving
towards willingness to accept permanent membership of the Commonwealth. . . .'[43] Discussion produced the heads of a scheme,
which, while avoiding 'formal intervention', might be presented to
H.M. Patel and to Zafrulla, who had come to London to see Attlee.
The scheme should take advantage of the recent 'marked change' in
India's attitude, building upon her willingness to include Azad
Kashmir representatives in the administration, accept a UN Commission to supervise a plebiscite, and reduce her military presence.
Still, the crux of the dispute would remain: Pakistan's insistence
that a full Indian withdrawal was necessary in order to stop the
tribesmen from fighting. The draft scheme that resulted called on
Pakistan to seek the raiders' withdrawal and refrain from helping
them, on India to withdraw from Poonch and reduce her forces elsewhere, and on both governments to stop fighting. A UN Commission should observe these arrangements and hold a plebiscite under
powers delegated by a coalition government. The Committee
realized that the weakness in the scheme was the reliance on local
forces that Pakistan would regard as partial, yet India would
certainly resist the entry of Pakistan's troops.[44]

[43] Ibid.   [44] Meeting of 2 Mar., ibid.

On 5 March Attlee reported that the responses of Patel and Zafrulla had not been encouraging.[45] While the latter wanted Abdullah replaced by a neutral administration and India's withdrawal, Nehru had committed himself publicly to the Sheikh's administration. Nevertheless, the Committee agreed that the proposals should form the basis of HMG's policy at Lake Success. They met India's demand by implying some condemnation of Pakistan for having failed to prevent the entry of armed raiders into Kashmir, while the provisions for a UN Commissioner to hold a plebiscite went far to meet Pakistan's case. If the plebiscite terms assuaged Pakistan's fears then she might be persuaded that the continuation of the present administration was a necessary face-saver for India.

Rather than risk alienating a Dominion by mediating, the British worked behind the scenes in New York, with the help of the Americans and the Chinese, whose representative Dr Tingfu Tsiang, the President of the Security Council for March, adopted their proposals in substance. On 18 March he called on Pakistan to secure the withdrawal of the tribesmen and its own nationals and proposed a plebiscite administration directed by a UN representative under the authority of a State government so constituted as to represent all major political groups. Zafrulla, whose interview with Attlee on 3 March had alerted him to a change in British policy that he never ceased to lament, instantly objected to the scheme: the presence of Indian troops and the perpetuation of Abdullah's authority were sufficient to vitiate the possibility of a fair plebiscite. Grafftey-Smith cabled to the CRO in terms that courted a rebuke, implying HMG's disregard for justice and recourse to expediency:

. . . it appears that India's refusal to accept any change in administration of Kashmir or any participation by Pakistan troops in the maintenance of law and order or any 'neutral' control of civil or military affairs have been accepted as final, with the result that the efforts of HMG in the UK are now directed towards a solution which recognises these resistances as valid.[46]

Attlee had observed previously that Grafftey-Smith was 'becoming a partisan of Pakistan'.[47] He now sent a sharp minute to Carter:

[45] Ibid.
[46] Grafftey-Smith to Noel-Baker, 18 Mar. 1948, PREM 8/813.
[47] Attlee minute of 27 Jan. 1948, ibid.

I am disturbed by the increasing lack of objectivity in the telegrams sent by our High Commissioner in Pakistan. . . . He seems to adopt completely the Pakistan attitude. It is not true that India has refused to accept any change in the administration of Kashmir or any neutral control over civil affairs notably as regards the taking of the plebiscite. He proceeds to charge His Majesty's Government with basing their policy on acceptance of the Indian position. . . . I object also to his suggestion that we are moved by expediency only, especially in relation to a question where the rights and wrongs are by no means as clear as one would gather from his attitude.[48]

Carter sent on the substance of the rebuke and explained to Attlee that it was 'extraordinarily difficult to keep both the High Commissioner in Delhi and the High Commissioner in Karachi from adopting an over-partisan attitude'.[49] They were banned from setting foot in Kashmir. Grafftey-Smith recalled later that he was also 'officially unwelcome in the considerable parish of my colleague in Delhi'.[50]

On 22 March Noel-Baker wrote to Attlee hopeful of an agreement between the Indian and Pakistan delegations being negotiated on the basis of Tsiang's proposals within three days.[51] This was far too hopeful. Cunningham noted that Tsiang's resolution would 'never be accepted by Pakistan; too obviously drafted in Indian ink'.[52] Zafrulla complained bitterly about the substance of the resolution and the manner of its preparation:

. . . he was convinced that the Indians had had a great deal to do with preparing the draft. Tsiang had told him that he understood the Indians would accept it except for certain minor details. In spite of British protestations, he knew they had been in consultation with Tsiang on the draft. Tsiang had, in front of Zafrullah Khan, told Noel-Baker that one of the provisions was put in at the suggestion of Noel-Baker. . . . Zafrullah was worried about the English position. He said they had changed their tone. He had had a talk with Attlee in London who had tried out on him some of the ideas contained in the Chinese draft. He was personally convinced that Mountbatten also had a hand in it and indicated that Mountbatten was concerned that Britain by her previous stand had come close to forcing India to renounce her dominion status.[53]

[48] Attlee minute of 22 Mar. 1948, ibid.
[49] Carter to Attlee, 24 Mar. 1948, ibid.
[50] Grafftey-Smith, *Hands to Play* (1975), 136.
[51] Noel-Baker to Attlee, 22 Mar. 1948, Attlee Papers, 68/170.
[52] Cunningham's Diary, 24 Mar. 1948.
[53] US Mission memo. of conversation, 22 Mar. 1948, *FRUS*, 1948, v, 316–18.

His main objection was to Abdullah's administration. The President of the Azad Kashmir Government cabled the unacceptability of a plebiscite under Abdullah's administration and with the Indian Army on Kashmir soil.[54]

Attlee believed that Pakistan must be persuaded to accept Tsiang's proposals, which he told Krishna Menon were 'in general harmony with our views'.[55] He thought India had shown 'a very reasonable spirit'. On 26 March he instructed Noel-Baker that 'We should not allow the Pakistanis to think that they can veto any proposal that does not give them all they demand. Time is running on. If agreement can not be reached we should state quite clearly that we believe the proposed basis of settlement to be one which should be accepted.'[56] Mountbatten wrote privately to Cripps that the shift in policy had helped counter anti-British sentiment:

On the whole the atmosphere in India is greatly improved thanks to the attitude which the Prime Minister and you took up over Kashmir. Unfortunately they still feel that the British Delegation at UNO is pro-Pakistan. In any case the appalling tension under which we were living when the whole of HMG were regarded as being anti-Indian has been lifted, and I can never tell you how grateful I am for this change. I hope you will keep these remarks to yourself for I feel they are rather unconstitutional, but I wanted you to know how grateful I was for the line you have taken up.[57]

Despite his apparent firmness Attlee did acquiesce in amendments to Tsiang's proposals with a view to conciliating Pakistan. They included the appointment of opposition party representatives as ministers in Abdullah's government, the enlargement of the powers of the UN plebiscite administrator, the reduction of Indian troops, and safeguards against intimidation. While Pakistan was not placated India became exasperated by the revisions.

Pakistan's leaders were appalled by Britain's change of policy during the UN recess. Jinnah saw Tsiang's resolutions as contrived by the British, who in a crisis always abandoned Pakistan in favour of India because the latter seemed more important. He explained to the US Ambassador that 'all Pakistan wanted was a fair plebiscite',

[54] Telegram of 20 Mar., ibid., 318–19.
[55] Attlee to Noel-Baker, 26 Mar. 1948, Attlee Papers, 68/249.
[56] Ibid.
[57] Mountbatten to Cripps, 2 Apr. 1948, CAB 127/139.

which was impossible with Abdullah in office and Indian troops in occupation.[58] He attributed the Security Council's 'somersault' to 'British wire-pulling instigated by Cripps whose operations . . . had many "wheels within wheels" '. It was impossible to get the tribes out of Kashmir on the terms proposed. Liaquat told the Ambassasdor that the resolutions 'showed complete lack [of] understanding [of] Oriental psychology' for with Abdullah in power the populace would fear his vengeance if they voted against him.[59] A few weeks later he confided to Sir Oliver Goonetilleke of Ceylon the lessons of the Kashmir dispute in terms of Commonwealth membership:

This change . . . was due to fact that India had threatened to leave the British Commonwealth and the United Nations and he was convinced that Pakistan was being sacrificed to keep India within the British Commonwealth and the United Nations. What benefit was it to Pakistan to be a member of the British Commonwealth? She would almost certainly receive better treatment from the United Kingdom Government if she left the Commonwealth and became completely independent. He warned Goonetilleke never to let Ceylon get into a dispute with a larger member of the Commonwealth because Britain would always side with the larger member.[60]

Dawn saw Britain's motive as the retention of India to the Commonwealth as a counterpoise to Russia and asked: 'Why have not steps been taken to develop friendly relations between Pakistan and Moscow?'[61]

Neither of the Dominions accepted Tsiang's resolutions in the form that the Security Council adopted them on 21 April. Nevertheless it was decided that the Commission for which it provided should proceed to India and Pakistan, placing its good offices at their disposal in the hope of securing peace and holding a plebiscite. It was not to arrive until 7 July. With the passing of Tsiang's resolution and the creation of the United Nations Commission for India and Pakistan (UNCIP) Britain's attempt to settle the dispute at UN had run its course. However, developments in the fighting in Kashmir, and the overlapping of the dispute with the question of

[58] US Ambassador in Pakistan to Secretary of State, 10 Apr. 1948, *FRUS*, 1948, v, 328–30.
[59] US Ambassador to Secretary of State, 17 Apr. 1948, ibid., 335–6.
[60] UK High Commission in Ceylon to CRO, 6 May 1948, PREM 8/819.
[61] *Dawn*, 27 Apr. 1948.

Hyderabad's accession to India, placed Britain's relations with the two Dominions under continuing strain. Their remaining in the Commonwealth was indeed at issue.

In February–March there had been some feeling at the senior levels of military command in both Dominions in favour of an early cease-fire. Pakistan's frustrations at managing covert operations to support tribesmen who were often ill-disciplined and unpredictable were matched by India's logistical difficulties and recognition that in certain areas, such as Poonch and Gilgit, they were fighting an entrenched local population. However, India's inclination for a truce evaporated as Pakistan's objection to Tsiang's original resolutions produced modifications that seemed to undermine Abdullah. The Indians had survived the winter without serious setback, holding Uri, the city of Poonch (where they were besieged), and resisting attacks on their position in Naoshera. Communications were improved for a springtime offensive and Baldev Singh looked forward to expelling the raiders by mid-year.

On 20 April Gracey (who had succeeded Messervy) reported:

It is obvious that a general offensive is about to start very soon now. . . . If Pakistan is not to face another serious refugee problem with about 2,750,000 people uprooted from their homes, if India is not to be allowed to sit on the doorsteps of Pakistan to the rear and on the flank at liberty to enter at its will and pleasure; if the civilian and military morale is not to be affected to a dangerous extent; and if subversive political forces are not to be encouraged and let loose within Pakistan itself, it is imperative that the Indian Army is not allowed to advance beyond the general line Uri-Poonch-Naoshera.[62]

On 4 May Grafftey-Smith cabled home that units of the Pakistan Army were now fighting in Kashmir, mainly to prevent a mass immigration that would destroy the Pakistan economy.[63] It was estimated that if the Indian Army overran Poonch and Mirpur some three million Muslims would flee west. Again, if it broke through to the Mangla headworks on the Jhelum it could cut off the supply of water. Already, on 1 April, India had stopped supplies at Madhopur and Ferozepur. HMG responded with suitable gravity to news of the deployment of three regular battalions. Noel-Baker,

---

[62] Cited in Ali, *Emergence of Pakistan*, 305. Cf. Mountbatten's record of interview with Gracey, 2 May 1948, Collins and Lapierre, op. cit., 184–5.
[63] Grafftey-Smith to CRO, 4 May 1948, PREM 8/819.

with Attlee's concurrence, proposed to seek official confirmation of it from the Government of Pakistan.

At this stage, on 13 May, Ernest Bevin intervened, urging that the matter should not be pursued and hoping that it would not be raised publicly until the UN Commission arrived to mediate.[64] He had become disturbed by Pakistan's belief that Britain's fears for her relations with India were inhibiting a fair settlement. There was a danger of a Pakistani 'overture to Russia—and the consequences of that would be most serious not only locally but in the whole of the Middle East'. Next day the United States recognized the state of Israel, which represented a rift in Anglo-American policies towards the Middle East. In a 'Strategic Appreciation' the Foreign Office weighed the consequences in terms of possible Muslim solidarity against the West: 'It has been the object of British and United States policy to keep Pakistan and India in the Commonwealth, or at least to arrange defence and trade agreements which will keep them within our orbits. But the attitude now adopted by the United States on Palestine must sooner or later have the opposite effect.'[65] Bevin envisaged the possibility of a 'tremendous anti-European and anti-Western movement embracing the whole Arab and Moslem world'.[66]

Bevin's intervention delayed for almost two months public knowledge of the Pakistan Army's involvement, of which Zafrulla acquainted UNCIP when it arrived on 7 July. However, early in July the Indian leaders were aware that Pakistani regulars were engaged in the crucial defence of Domel and Muzaffarabad, which Nehru expected to have fallen. By July there was growing Indian resentment of British policies and of the roles of British individuals in relation not only to Kashmir but also to Hyderabad. Nehru wrote to Cripps:

The Kashmir episode and Hyderabad and the large number of British officers, both civil and military, who seem to be working against India in Pakistan have had a bad effect on the people. Personally I have felt that the British Government itself has been fair and impartial but I have rather doubted how far this has been reflected in the activities of their representatives abroad. Most of these representatives belong to the old school who

[64] Bevin minute of 13 May 1948, ibid.

[65] FO Strategic Appreciation, 24 May 1948, cited in Louis, *British Empire in the Middle East*, 114.

[66] Ibid., and n. 23.

have not got over their ancient animus against nationalist India. Pakistan is full of them, indeed they run Pakistan to a large extent. Many of those who have been peculiarly anti-India in the past have now found shelter in Pakistan.[67]

There is perhaps a large unwritten history of British intrigues for a separate Dominion of Hyderabad but in early July 1948 the immediate issue was relatively small. There were reports that English privateers were running guns into Hyderabad by night flights from Pakistan. Krishna Menon complained officially that such flights had been made over Indian territory by UK registered aircraft. Noel-Baker reported to Attlee that there was circumstantial evidence that a Mr F.S. Cotton, managing director of a UK registered company, was responsible for flying five Lancastrian aircraft in a shuttle service.[68] Grafftey-Smith has recorded that Cotton was Australian-born.[69] It is clear that the case was not provable in court but that HMG would act with vigour to prevent British involvement in such operations. Krishna Menon next complained to Cripps that there were UK officers in the Hyderabad Army.[70] There were in fact seventeen of them and they were advised to resign in the event of hostilities with India, for their service would then become prima-facie treasonable.[71]

Of greater moment than these individual involvements with Hyderabad was authoritative British criticism of Indian treatment of the state. On 27 July Churchill acquainted Attlee of his intention to raise, during the summer adjournment debate in Parliament, the question of Britain's historic pledges to the princes that with the lapse of the Crown's paramountcy at Independence they would become free to decide the political future of their states.[72] He would argue that both Kashmir and Hyderabad must, in honour, be supported by HMG in their wish to 'have their fate decided by a plebiscite under the auspices of UNO'. He acquainted Cripps of his intended criticism of his personal breach of trust, adding, perhaps with tongue in cheek: 'It is my hope that you will find yourself able to support the broad democratic solution which I propose, and

[67] Nehru to Cripps, 3 July 1948, CAB 127/143.
[68] Noel-Baker to Attlee, 5 July 1948, PREM 8/1007.
[69] Grafftey-Smith, op. cit., 117.
[70] Menon to Cripps, n.d. [Aug. 1948], CAB 127/139.
[71] Noel-Baker to Attlee, 4 Oct. 1948, PREM 8/799.
[72] Churchill to Attlee, 27 July 1948, CAB 127/115.

which I understand would be accepted by all those in Hyderabad and Kashmir whom Nehru's Government is now attacking or about to attack'.[73] Noel-Baker's brief for Attlee emphasized that since the transfer of power the negotiations between the Nizam and India had 'been conducted entirely without the assistance or intervention of the United Kingdom Government'.[74] Attlee, aware that Nehru and Patel would deeply resent Parliamentary debate on a matter that they deemed internal to India, asked the Speaker to rule on 'the scope of any Debate which may ensue with regard to India and Pakistan, in view of the fact that they are now self-governing Dominions'.[75] The Speaker alluded to the Rule on Questions that prevented the putting down of questions referring to the national affairs of Dominions but he allowed an unlimited debate. Churchill proceeded to an all-out attack on India's treatment of Kashmir and Hyderabad, asserting a contradiction in her upholding the prince's right to accede in the former case and denying his right not to accede in the latter. Nehru's offer to the Nizam—Hyderabad's accession to India or its extinction—was Hitlerian, he argued. Attlee's handling of a situation potentially explosive for the Commonwealth was masterly. He could assert with truth that when Kashmir was before the UN, 'We did our utmost to obtain the fullest and fairest methods for holding a plebiscite for the people to decide, and that is now going forward'.[76] As for Hyderabad, he could point out that Churchill had overlooked the fact that in November 1947 the Nizam had signed a standstill agreement with India, yielding for a year the regulation of the state's relations with the outside world. Since then India had urged the Nizam to settle the question of accession by a plebiscite based on adult suffrage but the Nizam had refused to do so. Attlee turned the argument effectively against Churchill, who never did anything 'to draw closer the bonds between India and Pakistan and the rest of the Commonwealth' and whose 'intervention . . . in the Indian problem' even knowledgeable Conservatives deplored.

On 13 September India settled the Hyderabad problem at a stroke by a swift and decisive police action. An appeal by the Nizam had been before the Security Council for three weeks but it had not

---

[73] Churchill to Cripps, 28 July 1948, ibid.
[74] 'Points for use in the debate on the adjournment', 29 July 1948, ibid.
[75] Commons Debates, 30 July 1948, col. 1719.
[76] Ibid., col. 1740.

been discussed. Attlee rode out the almost universal press condemnation of India and effectively contained critics who thought
the recourse to force unworthy of a Dominion. Ismay, who had
been unhappy about India's treatment of difficult·states' issues
since Independence, felt that this was 'the last straw'.[77] Lord
Halifax, the Conservative elder statesman on India in whom he
confided, agreed with him. India's action was 'almost unbeliev-
able, but I am not sure that I like your remedy of casting them out of
the "family party" '.[78] Ismay warned Attlee that he felt he must
speak out. Attlee replied in his own hand that there was 'a good deal
to be said on the side of the Indian Government'.[79] The Nizam was
'thoroughly unsatisfactory' and had become captive to the militant
Muslim Razakars. The spread of disorder was revealed in docu-
mentary evidence that he would open to Ismay. If India had been
wrong to send in troops then surely Pakistan stood condemned in
Kashmir. The action was now a *fait accompli* and Nehru was 'taking
a wise line': 'In these circumstances I should not think that a con-
demnatory statement from you would be useful especially as I think
that there is a reasonable chance of getting a settlement of the
Kashmir trouble'. Ismay kept his silence, as publicly did R.A.
Butler, another authority on India who was unhappy. Attlee told
Butler that he felt Nehru was 'trying to carry out his principles' and
assured him, enigmatically, that 'in this matter we have exercised
all the influence that was possible'.[80]

Attlee, Cripps, and Mountbatten worked strenuously to retain
Indian goodwill during the difficult months that followed
Pakistan's admission of her military presence in Kashmir. In mid-
July HMG acted on rumours of the involvement of British technical
officers in Kashmir by seeking assurances that such personnel
would be withdrawn immediately: HMG 'cannot be a party to the
use of their armed personnel in Kashmir'.[81] Nevertheless, India
complained both officially and in private top-level correspondence
about British officers in the Pakistan Army, who if they were
not combatants in Kashmir were, by planning, organizing, and

[77] Ismay to Attlee, 21 Sept. 1948, PREM 8/807.
[78] Halifax to Ismay, 16 Sept. 1948, Ismay Papers, II/3/99.
[79] Attlee to Ismay, 22 Sept. 1948, ibid., III/7/43.
[80] Attlee to Butler, 29 Sept. 1948, Attlee Papers, 73/176.
[81] GRO to UK High Commissioner in Pakistan, 16 July 1948, PREM 8/801.

commanding the aggressors on Indian soil, accomplices in illegal actions. Krishna Menon appealed to Cripps for HMG to bring pressure upon Pakistan to withdraw by threatening to stand down all British officers as 'We have now an undeclared war being waged by Pakistan against us in Kashmir. The presence of British officers in the Pakistan Army now assumes a grave position.'[82] Mountbatten, who had left India on 21 June, asked Cripps to meet him after the first anniversary celebration of India's Independence at the Albert Hall on Sunday 15 August. They were the main speakers at the gathering of four thousand well-wishers of India. Cripps paid tribute to Nehru and Patel as 'great statesmen' and observed 'an almost universal feeling of good will' between Britain and India.[83] The few regrettable exceptions included 'a few dyed-in-the-wool Blimp-like reactionaries' who had 'no regard for the damage they did in setting one people against the other'. Mountbatten's speech dwelt on India's schemes for material development. His private comments to Cripps referred to the existence of 'full scale war between the two Dominions, as yet undeclared' and the need for HMG to advise 'Jawaharlal in his great difficulty'.[84] That night he wrote a long letter to Nehru, imploring him not to declare war on Pakistan and 'show some patience with UNO'.[85] He appreciated that the only wholly satisfactory conclusion for India was for UN to 'condemn Pakistan publicly', but that would prejudice Pakistan's agreement to a cease-fire. He urged Nehru to respond favourably if UNCIP called for a cease-fire. He reassured him, too, of HMG's sincere friendship towards India: 'The decisive voices in the British Cabinet are extremely sympathetic and well-disposed towards India'. Attlee's remarks in Parliament and Cripps's Albert Hall speech were evidence of the fact.

Next day UNCIP's appeal for a cease-fire was announced. It called for a truce, the withdrawal of Pakistan's troops and the tribesmen, the subsequent reduction of India's troops, and their observance of the cease-fire line pending a final settlement. The conditions for a plebiscite under UN auspices, which had been defined by the Security Council on 21 April, were not repeated. Nehru accepted UNCIP's resolution within days but Pakistan

82 Menon to Cripps, n.d. [Aug. 1948], CAB 127/139.
83 *The Times*, 16 Aug. 1948.
84 Mountbatten to Cripps, 11 Aug. 1948, CAB 127/139.
85 Mountbatten to Nehru, 15 Aug. 1948, Das, op. cit., i, 220–2.

failed to follow suit. India's leaders found increasing difficulty in reconciling British professions of friendship with HMG's refusal to stand down its officers in Pakistan. HMG adhered to the code that it had formulated in September 1947: officers in both armies would be stood down simultaneously upon the declaration of war. HMG did secure the assurance of both Dominions that they would not use British officers in Kashmir. Their involvement in planning would not be grounds for a stand-down order. If the order were applied to Pakistan several regrettable consequences would follow: some officers would defy it; anti-British feeling would develop; Pakistan might leave the Commonwealth; and the Muslim world would be alienated. Most importantly, there would be a collapse in Pakistan 'from the chaos of which the Communists would profit'.[86] The Pakistani reliance on British officers was, in fact, immense. There were still 800 British officers in Pakistan's forces, including 179 from the British Army and 226 from the old Indian Army. On the other hand India had nationalized its forces rapidly, so that only 350 British officers remained, 82 of them from the British Army, and 195 from the ex-Indian. In India they all held advisory or technical posts. Whereas at Independence there were two Indian major-generals and twelve brigadiers, by the end of 1948 there were thirteen Indian generals and thirty brigadiers. In unofficial approaches to Cripps Sudhir Ghosh expressed the view that all civil and military officers should be withdrawn from both Dominions.[87] On the other hand Krishna Menon appealed to Attlee against the injustice in the existing context of 'treating Pakistan and us alike'.[88]

Rajagopalachari, now Governor-General, complained to both Mountbatten and Cripps that 'British officers in Pakistan have become violent Pakistanis'.[89] He emphasized the implications for the future of the Commonwealth:

How can we press on Indian public opinion any change of the Constituent Assembly's decision that India should be a republic independent of the Commonwealth? The only justification for remaining in the Commonwealth has crumbled. If peace cannot be maintained between units of the Commonwealth, there is nothing left to say on its behalf.

---

[86] Noel-Baker's memo. for Attlee, 20 Aug. 1948, PREM 8/800.
[87] Ghosh to Cripps, 30 Aug. 1948, CAB 127/129.
[88] Menon to Attlee, 1 Sept. 1948, Attlee Papers, 73/73.
[89] Rajaji to Cripps, n.d., copy sent by Cripps to Attlee, 18 Sept. 1948, ibid., 73/130.

Cripps appealed for India 'to show great statesmanship and tolerance' with the less powerful Pakistan: 'The more *we* try to interfere the less satisfactory and lasting any settlement of the situation will be'.[90] Rajaji was not convinced:

There is so much talk and discussion about the Commonwealth. The occasion is psychologically most opportune to end the Kashmir tangle. Officially and admittedly the Pakistan Army is operating against a sister Dominion, India. What meaning or justification can the Commonwealth have for India if after the disclosures before the UNCIP the Commonwealth is not able to say to Pakistan 'Cease Fire'?

It may be ungracious and difficult to withdraw British officers and the like. Sometimes a big thing is easier than a smaller thing. It would be effective now if Britain and the Commonwealth could ask Pakistan to cease fire for otherwise Commonwealth would have no meaning. Pakistan cannot afford to disobey. Peace and terms will automatically follow.[91]

Attlee's response was characteristically curt: 'I cannot think that his suggestion is very realistic'.[92] It was, however, in line with Moon's impatience with Pakistan's 'unreasonable intransigence'.

Now that Hyderabad has so ignominiously collapsed (confounding all our Edens and Butlers who so rashly indulged in elocutions on the subject) the way should be prepared for a settlement in Kashmir. . . . I think Pakistan could have been persuaded to accept UNO's cease-fire proposal, if the Hyderabad issue had not still been open. They did not want to disembarrass India just when India was going to attack Hyderabad. The proposals should be put to them again and if they don't accept they should be turned out of the Commonwealth Club.[93]

Attlee and his colleagues proceeded more cautiously.

With the approach of a Commonwealth Prime Ministers' Conference to be held in London from 11–22 October, the first to be attended by the South Asian Dominions, hopes were concentrated upon a settlement by direct negotiation between Nehru and Liaquat. On 7 October V.P. Menon cabled Mountbatten that a series of high level discussions, with Nehru and Abdullah present, had canvassed all possibilities, including Kashmir's independence,

---

[90] Cripps to Rajaji, 18 Sept. 1948, ibid.
[91] Rajaji to Cripps, 18 Oct. 1948, CAB 127/146.
[92] Attlee to Cripps, 23 Oct. 1948, ibid.
[93] Moon to Short, 20 Sept. 1948, Short Collection, F189/22.

a plebiscite, arbitration, and partition.[94] The last alternative, 'on the basis of the territories at present occupied or controlled by Pakistan or India', was favoured. If Attlee and Mountbatten 'made a supreme effort to bring both parties together . . . a settlement can be achieved'. At the same time Mudie advised Liaquat to pursue a settlement in London on the basis of an impartial plebiscite under British troops or, better, by partition on the line of the Chenab.[95] The demands in terms of partition thus offered little hope of settlement for each side claimed the Vale. Yet both clearly wanted a settlement because of the economic drain of the war.

After India's action in Hyderabad there was also apprehension in Pakistan of her launching an all-out war. Pakistan's leaders sought a defence pact with Britain. Liaquat approached Attlee through his British Deputy Commander-in-Chief, while Zafrulla asked Noel-Baker for a bilateral alliance if India resisted an engagement.[96] The British response was cool, from fear of alienating India. Mudie, who urged Liaquat to seek a declaration from the Commonwealth Prime Ministers to defend a Dominion if it were attacked by another, feared that the Indian leaders may become obliged to back their anti-Pakistan propaganda with action. He sketched the consequences of all-out war in world terms:

A war between India and Pakistan would not only be a great human tragedy, but it would have consequences of the greatest importance to the peace of the world. Whatever the relative merits of the two armies, the size of India's army and even more their possession of ordinance factories and economic resources, which Pakistan does not have, and their ability to blockade Kashmir, would make India's eventual victory almost certain. The Sikhs and the RSS Sangh would be let loose in the West Punjab as they were in the East. Muslims in the fertile districts would be massacred or driven off to starve in the deserts and hills, west of the Chenab. There would inevitably be a violent reaction in the Muslim countries of the Middle East, which might easily be taken advantage of by Russia. India would have acted in defiance of world and particularly of Commonwealth opinion, and Pakistan would have practically ceased to exist. Even if, for some reason, India remained and was retained within the Commonwealth, she would be isolated and without a friend. Being in fact out of the Commonwealth she would inevitably fall within the Russian sphere.

---

[94] Menon to Mountbatten, in Symon to Carter, 7 Oct. 1948, PREM 8/1008.
[95] Mudie to Liaquat, 6 Oct. 1948, Mudie Papers, IOL F164/49.
[96] F.K. Roberts minute, 30 Sept. 1948, FO 800/470; A.I. Singh, op. cit., 365.

Already communism is a serious threat in the South, and on and within her border she would have a Muslim population thirsting for revenge and willing to take help from Russia or any one else who could help them against the Hindus. If Russia made a serious attempt to absorb India, I do not see that there is anything that India could really do about it. As long as Pakistan exists and remains within the Commonwealth, the position is totally different. There is little or no communism in West Punjab, though there is some in East Bengal, and an attack by Russia on Pakistan would mean war with both Britain and the USA. Pakistan within the Commonwealth is the barrier preventing Russia from controlling India and, with India, the Indian Ocean and the Persian Gulf. If Pakistan were destroyed, the whole of Asia would go communist.[97]

Liaquat commended this 'penetrating analysis'.[98]

Bevin played a prominent role in the attempt at an 'out of court settlement'. He was aided by the efforts of the US Secretary of State, General George Marshall, and the US representative to UN. Bevin's meetings with Nehru and Liaquat in London were matched by Marshall's discussions with them in Paris. Bevin advised Marshall that it was

of vital importance to India, Pakistan, Kashmir and the whole world that a settlement should be quickly reached, preferably by direct agreement between the two parties, and we do not think that this is impossible. . . . This would give them a great moral ascendancy and if you could emphasise on Nehru the tremendous affect it would have on the course of events in Asia and the whole world, and if he would accept that, this would be a great achievement. Both India and Pakistan must appreciate that they are faced with the risk of the Russian menace and if they would make a supreme effort to settle their differences it would make a great contribution to peace.[99]

Marshall reported that Nehru 'seemed primarily interested in having my views on the world situation and, most particularly, on Russian objectives'.[100] He felt that the talk added to Nehru's appreciation of 'the Russian menace'. But Nehru felt 'most sensitive' about Kashmir, that 'he had a real grievance there', and that legally and morally India was in the right.

The British. attempt at an out-of-court settlement came to

---

[97] Mudie to Liaquat, 6 Oct. 1948, loc. cit. See also Mudie to Sir M. Hallett about Russia and Indo-Pakistan relations, e.g. 11 Nov. 1948, ibid., F164/48.

[98] Liaquat to Mudie, 11 Nov. 1948, ibid., F164/49.

[99] Marshall to Acting Secretary of State, 15 Oct. 1948, *FRUS*, 1948, v, 429–30.

[100] Marshall to US Embassy in UK, 20 Oct. 1948, ibid., 431–2.

nothing. When Bevin, Cripps, and Noel-Baker discussed Kashmir with Nehru he insisted on the ethical rights of India's case and the established fact of Pakistan's aggression.[101] India had accepted but Pakistan rejected UNCIP's cease-fire resolution. The British ministers were unable to elicit from Nehru plebiscite conditions that he would accept.[102] He seemed emotional, intransigent, and insistent that India must control the main artery to Central Asia. He did agree to meet Liaquat over dinner with Attlee and Bevin but nothing was achieved. He also responded to a final plea from Cripps to meet Liaquat face-to-face, but their long post-prandial talk in Paris at the end of the month was fruitless.[103] Nehru stood firm in offering Liaquat two alternatives: either Pakistan's acceptance of UNCIP's August resolution or a partition, with western Poonch and some northern areas including Gilgit going to Pakistan. Liaquat firmly rejected the latter. He sought Nehru's acceptance of the UN plebiscite conditions defined in the Security Council's April resolution, which Nehru regarded as derogatory of Kashmir's accession and Abdullah's administration. Bevin was gloomy: 'He very much feared that next Spring the Indians, encouraged by the success of their operation against Hyderabad, would start fighting in Kashmir . . . and that this might open up considerable possibilities to the Russians to exploit the situation in order to obtain a foothold in northern India'.[104] Bevin thought Liaquat more reasonable than Nehru and appealed to him to take the lead in organizing an Arab bloc.[105]

During the stalemate that followed Britain favoured the appointment of an American mediator but the Americans favoured a Commonwealth one: 'Since problem is one in which Commonwealth has long established interest and since recent Conference created cordial atmosphere, [State] Dept inclined view selection prominent Commonwealth statesman would be constructive'.[106] The approach

[101] Nehru to Ayyangar, 19 Oct. 1948, Das, op. cit., i, 247–8.

[102] Memo. of conversation with Bevin etc., by US Counsellor of Dept. of State in Paris, 27 Oct. 1948, *FRUS*, 1948, v, 434.

[103] Cripps to Nehru, 26 Oct.; Nehru to Cripps, 27 Oct. and 2 Nov. 1948; CAB 127/143; Memo by US Representative on UNCIP, 1 Nov. 1948, *FRUS*, 1948, v, 440–2; Nehru to Patel, 27 Oct. 1948, Das, op. cit., i, 249–50.

[104] Memo. of conversation by US Counsellor with Bevin, 27 Oct. 1948, loc. cit.

[105] Hugh Dalton's Diary, 15 Oct. 1948, cited in P. S. Gupta, *Imperialism and the British Labour Movement, 1914–1964* (1975), 299.

[106] Acting Secretary of State to US Delegation at UN, 11 Nov. 1948, *FRUS*, 1948, v, 448–9.

was suspended in mid-November when it was learned that UNCIP had sought informal discussions with Zafrulla and Sir Girja Bajpai (Secretary-General of India's Ministry of External Affairs) on terms for a plebiscite. Liaquat and Nehru authorized unofficial talks on the understanding that UNCIP would report that the August resolution should stand but be supplemented by recommendations for plebiscite conditions.[107] The prospects of UNCIP's success were enhanced by the military situation in Kashmir.

In mid-November Indian troops at last relieved the beleaguered town of Poonch and secured all territory to the east of the Poonch–Naoshera line (including Mendhar tehsil, the granary of Kashmir). Pakistan feared an all-out Indian offensive. Attlee appealed to Nehru for restraint.[108] If the Indian troops advanced they could cut Azad Kashmir in half. Grafftey-Smith reported fears that the aggravation of the Kashmir refugee problem 'may mean collapse [of] Pakistan'.[109] If India were not restrained Pakistan would in genuine despair experience 'nationwide revulsion of feeling favourable to Russia'. There was an 'imminent risk General Gracey will feel obliged to throw in all Pakistan land and air forces'. General Nye, who had recently arrived in Delhi as High Commissioner, was instructed to discuss Pakistan's alarm with Nehru. As a senior military officer, and fresh from his appointment as Governor of Madras, he was the man for the job. The US Ambassador reported:

Nehru argued heatedly that although no offensive under way India had every moral legal right therefor and if one were launched Pakistan could have no reason complaining because Pakistan troops occupying Indian territory. Nye then said even if India had right to attack, as military man he could assure Nehru such offensive would end disastrously despite Indian superiority in numbers equipment training, etc. Further, he would stake his military reputation that India could not even in summer defeat Pakistani and tribesmen in Kashmir because of degree to which terrain and communications factors favored Pakistan. Even if his estimate were wrong, and India won military victory, it would be temporary unless India maintained indefinitely large garrisons in all Kashmir. GOI could be certain that at favorable moment tribesmen and Pakistani would again

---

[107] Cripps's 'Note for Record', 11 Nov. 1948, CAB 127/115.
[108] Attlee to Nehru, 18 Nov. 1948, in US Secretary of State to Acting Secretary of State, 20 Nov. 1948, *FRUS*, 1948, v, 455.
[109] Cited, ibid.

ravage Kashmir unless political settlement reached by Pakistan and India.

Nye assured me he endeavored drive home point that only final solution was political and military solution impossible for either side unless India should decide on war against all Pakistan. He told Nehru he did not believe any Indian Government would consider this because would be difficult for India survive as nation if it had face indefinitely millions hostile Moslems within and without.

In reply my inquiry Nehru's reaction Nye said latter seemed unhappy and apparently did not feel in position to refute his arguments. He added he sincerely believed everything he told Nehru and with other British here would seize every opportunity impress on GOI leaders fact they must work out with Pakistan political solution of Kashmir as no other possible.[110]

Attlee reported to Cabinet that Nye believed no general Indian offensive was intended that winter, but that Pakistan proposed an offensive if India's existing operations persisted.[111] Fears were expressed that if the situation deteriorated Russia might encourage Afghanistan to raid across the frontier.

Until that time Pakistan had not attacked India's supply lines from East Punjab through Jammu, but now she concentrated her forces so as to sever them, thus isolating India's forces in Kashmir. On 14 December the Pakistanis began a thirty-six-hour bombardment of strategic communications and supplies. India's obvious response would be to push armoured units into West Pakistan and attack Lahore, which would have precipitated a general war. However, General Bucher instead suggested to Nehru that he should signal Gracey to co-operate in a cease-fire.[112] Nye believed that now his own earlier advice to Nehru and Bucher's 'steadiness and wisdom . . . bore fruit'.[113] Cripps proposed to Nehru that the Governors-General should meet to consider the crisis and Attlee again appealed to him for restraint.[114] Nehru wrote to Cripps resentfully:

I think we would have been much nearer solution of the Kashmir problem if the representatives of the United Kingdom in the Security Council had not been consistently hostile to India. There is strong feeling on this here.

[110] US Ambassador to India to Secretary of State, 28 Nov. 1948, ibid., 458.
[111] Cabinet meeting, 9 Dec. 1948, CM (48) 79, CAB 128/13.
[112] Birdwood, *A Continent Decides* (1953), 234–5.
[113] Sir William Strang's note on discussions with Nehru, 16–20 Jan. 1949, in his report on tour of South East Asia and the Far East, 27 Feb. 1949, CP(49)67.
[114] Nehru to Cripps, 17–18 Dec. 1948, CAB 127/143.

Also the whole show on the military side in Pakistan is run by British officers who are more intractable and hostile to us than the Pakistanis. You will appreciate how this affects us.[115]

Krishna followed up.

The request to us not to advance when the major strength of Pakistan's entire army is in Kashmir or just across the border came very inappropriately. . . . Our direction not to launch an offensive is still in force. But we are faced with a major offensive, the cutting of our communications and heavy shelling. Are we expected to sacrifice our troops and allow the offensive to creep nearer and nearer while we sit with folded hands?[116]

War, he insisted, might become inevitable and the British officers in Pakistan would be responsible for it. But on 23 December, even as Krishna wrote, India formally accepted UNCIP's plebiscite conditions, followed on Christmas Day by Pakistan. A cease-fire began on New Year's Day.

While the Kashmir dispute remained—and still remains—to be settled, the truce enabled India and Pakistan to contemplate at peace their future in the Commonwealth. It was a major achievement of the Attlee Government to have avoided the alienation of either of the warring Dominions from the Commonwealth. But at the end of 1948 the future, the nature and structure, of the Commonwealth was an open book.

[115] Nehru to Cripps, 17 Dec. 1948, ibid.
[116] Menon to Cripps, 23 Dec. 1948, ibid.

4

All the King's Men?

IT was Mountbatten's delicate diplomacy for a quick transfer of power on the basis of dual dominionhood that first triggered consideration in London of the new Commonwealth. As an old friend of Mountbatten's and an eminent constitutional lawyer Sir Walter Monckton suggested in May 1947 that Nehru's aversion to Dominion status might be overcome by finding some means of accommodating a republic within the Commonwealth. He sought guidance from Cripps and the Crown Law Officers on the key question:

The King is King of the UK and separately of the individual Dominions etc. Is it possible to superimpose on this the conception of him as the recognised King or head of the family of the British Commonwealth? and for the Indian sovereign state to be associated with the family and Commonwealth and in some way to owe allegiance to HM as King of the whole but not of India as a unit?[1]

Cripps sent out a reply from Sir Hartley Shawcross, the Attorney-General, which indicated their joint opinion 'that we could improvise some arrangement which would enable India to owe some sort of allegiance to the Crown as the head of the Commonwealth'.[2] Shawcross emphasized that 'the statute of Westminster itself refers to the Crown as the symbol of the association'.

Sir Norman Brook, Secretary to the Cabinet and as such Secretary of Commonwealth Prime Ministers' Conferences, wrote to Attlee on 12 May that it seemed 'anomalous that Sir Walter Monckton should be directing himself to this problem in India on behalf of Nehru while no sustained effort is being made at home . . . to find a solution on behalf of His Majesty's Government'.[3] It was not merely a question for India alone, for Eire was in an anomalous position as an independent republic within the

[1] Monckton to Ismay, 2 May 1947, encl. in *TP*, x, 367.
[2] Shawcross to Cripps, 9 May 1947, ibid.
[3] Brook to Attlee, 12 May 1947, ibid., 418.

Commonwealth, South Africa periodically chafed at Dominion status, while Burma had been promised 'independence within the Commonwealth', and Ceylon was asking for it too:

... surely we should at least consider whether the true balance of advantage may not lie on the side of a larger yet looser association rather than a smaller but more compact Commonwealth of 'Dominions' and 'Colonies'.... We may well fail in the attempt to find a new basis which would hold the whole of our existing group together; but it seems to be wrong to allow the opportunity to go by default.

He suggested referring to Professor R.G. Coupland or H.V. Hodson for advice and setting up a small ministerial group to decide major policy questions and guide a team of experts. On 14 May, Attlee took up the matter with vigour and urgency in a minute to his senior colleagues, Cripps, Bevin, Morrison, Alexander, Jowitt, Addison, and Creech Jones.[4] The urgency is no doubt to be explained by what Mountbatten called 'Nehru's bombshell', that is his recoil from the plan for the transfer of power that Cabinet had approved. That day, trying to explain the setback, Attlee told the India and Burma Committee that 'the raising at this stage of the possibility of early attainment of Dominion status by India ... seemed to have produced a radical change in the situation'.[5] His minute rehearsed the general unattractiveness of 'the phrase if not the content of "Dominion status" '. He emphasized one of the 'curious anomalies' of Dominion status, that the Dominions were represented in Britain by high commissioners, who ranked after the representatives of Liberia or Guatemala:

3. There is, therefore, need for reconsideration of the present position. The critical position in India, Burma and Ceylon makes this an urgent need. There is no time for a lengthy examination by constitutional lawyers. What is required is a political decision. This needs to be taken here by the Cabinet with a view to seeking the opinion of the Dominions and if possible getting a decision without the lengthy formalities of an Imperial Conference.
4. What I think is required is the finding of a formula which will enable the greatest number of independent units to adhere to the Commonwealth without excessive uniformity in their internal constitutions or in their relationship to Great Britain, the Commonwealth and one another. Some such phrase for instance as 'The Associated States of the Commonwealth' might

[4] Ibid., 436.   [5] Ibid., 437.

provide an umbrella under which a number of independent States might be brought together—Britain, Eire, the existing Dominions, Rhodesia, India (whether single or multiple), Burma and Ceylon.

Attlee envisaged an early meeting of a small group of ministers, assisted by a few experts. A meeting of senior ministers was held on 2 June on the arrangements for handling British relations with India after Independence, and it was agreed to establish the Commonwealth Relations Office to subsume both the India and Dominions Offices. The larger question was not considered until a week later.

The four-week delay in the discussion of a matter that seemed to Attlee 'urgent' is to be explained mainly in terms of the dual Dominions solution. The eventual status of India and Pakistan could be handled at leisure. Ceylon's leaders had been pressing for Dominion status, which would enable them to meet challenges from their left, and by early June they too had been promised 'fully responsible status within the British Commonwealth of Nations'.[6] In these circumstances the remaining urgent case, Burma, did not seem sufficient cause for rocking the Commonwealth boat.

The Secretary of State for Burma advised its Governor on 24 May:

Burma is a small and weak country and its inclusion within Commonwealth on terms of equivocal acceptance of forms and obligations of membership is not likely in eyes of UK and Dominions to appear to bring sufficient advantages to them to outweigh disadvantages to them . . . of undertaking obligations towards Burma which automatically flow from membership while prejudicing essential features of Commonwealth as hitherto understood.[7]

With India, Pakistan, and Ceylon in the Commonwealth bag as Dominions the Burmese must be told that if Burma chose republicanism her membership of the Commonwealth would be 'doubtful . . . however closely she may be prepared to ally herself'. On 3 June the Governor was asked to postpone any decision of Burma's status until Aung San, President of the Anti-Fascist People's Freedom

---

[6] HMG's announcement of 10 June 1947, cited in De Silva, ' "The Model Colony": Reflections on the Transfer of Power in Sri Lanka', in Wilson and Dalton (eds), *The States of South Asia* (1982), 77–88, 82. See also De Silva, 'Sri Lanka: D.S. Senanayake and the Passage to Dominion Status', *Sri Lanka Journal of Social Sciences*, 3, n.d., 1–14.

[7] CAB 134/117.

League (AFPFL), had heard the broadcasts by Mountbatten and the Indian leaders. Nehru's acceptance of dominionhood 'may carry great weight with Aung San and . . . it would be wise to give him the right to think things over in light of the broadcasts'.[8] The Prime Minister also sent a personal message to Aung San on 3 June emphasizing the disadvantage to Burma, in the financial, economic, foreign affairs, and defence fields, of leaving the Commonwealth.[9] Attlee had already offered loans, help with reconstruction, and support in international relations to a Burma Dominion and he clearly hoped for success by standing firm on 'acceptance of the Crown and of the position of HM'. Now the Governor was asked to hammer home the advantages of Commonwealth trade and modern armaments: 'We can be of great assistance to her . . . over equipment, training facilities, supply of skilled technicians, development of modern weapons, technical developments in military and air, etc'. Commonwealth membership would give strength to the international voice of a small country squeezed 'between two great countries like China and India'.

When the meeting of senior ministers on Commonwealth relations eventually occurred on 9 June it adopted a leisurely approach.[10] Attlee rehearsed the argument of his minute, emphasizing the need for a 'formula' alternative to dominionhood as the basis of Commonwealth membership. His suggested Committee of Ministers, to include the Foreign Secretary, the Lord Chancellor, and the Dominion Affairs Secretary, with himself as chairman and other ministers attending as invited, was approved. Brook was its secretary. It was to be assisted by a Committee of Officials, initially chaired by Sir Edward Bridges (Secretary of the Treasury) but from 1948 by Brook. Attlee suggested as a new title for the British Commonwealth 'the Associated States of the Commonwealth', but Cripps's proposed 'Commonwealth of British and Associated Nations' seemed preferable. The position of high commissioners would be considered. However, the essential problem was seen as the recognition of the Crown, that is, whether an independent sovereign republic could be accepted within the Commonwealth. India might well raise the question, as Eire had already done, 'in a very special form'. There was agreement that 'it would

[8] Secretary of State for Burma to Governor of Burma, 3 June 1947, ibid.
[9] Ibid.
[10] *TP*, xi, 118.

be necessary to insist that membership of the Commonwealth should imply recognition of the Crown, at least to the extent at present accorded by the Eire Government, i.e. in the sphere of external relations'. The Offical Committee was to tackle the thorny problem of 'the future structure of the British Commonwealth' at meetings in July and August and, more especially, in the preparation of reports for the Ministerial Committee. However, the latter was not brought together until April 1948, when the preparation of the Indian constitution approached its final stage.

Later in the day of Attlee's meeting with his senior colleagues the India and Burma Committee learnt that Aung San had intimated his intention to move a resolution in the Constituent Assembly for Burma to become a sovereign independent republic.[11] He had found 'that the forces of public opinion were too strong for him, and that his Party were determined to accept nothing less than complete independence. Acceptance of Dominion status would split his Party, and drive its left-wing elements into the hands of the Communists.' At the same time, the Executive Council had called for immediate Dominion status as granted to India, without prejudice to the ultimate decision of the Constituent Assembly. The case was similar to India's, but whereas Nehru had sensibly left open the question of future status, Aung San's party seemed to view dominionhood only as a device of very temporary utility. The Committee rejected such an exploitation of dominionhood, whose whole conception would be brought into contempt if Burma left the Commonwealth within weeks. As a final diplomatic effort Burma would be told that she might have immediate dominionhood 'only on the understanding that the Dominion status so achieved would have to remain unaltered for a period of time'. Clearly, it was important in dealing with constitutionalist Ceylon not to soil the prize of dominionhood. Though a Burmese Goodwill Mission visited Britain and further explored the matter they made it clear that the leaders of AFPFL felt 'bound by the ignorances and prejudices of their rank and file to persist in their determination to take Burma out of the Commonwealth'.[12] Listowel assured Mountbatten, who urged the adoption of the solution he had applied in India, that it had been 'fully weighed' and abandoned with the 'utmost reluctance' only when the Burmese leaders 'made it

[11] Ibid., 121.
[12] Listowel to Mountbatten, 27 June 1947, ibid., 376.

perfectly clear that there was no possibility of their changing their minds about leaving the Commonwealth'.[13] The 'prostitution of dominion status' was at issue.

For a time Governor Rance, Mountbatten, and others, including it seems Attlee himself, continued to hope for Burma's membership of the Commonwealth on the new formula yet to be devised. Rance had cabled home of the wider bearing of the Burma case:

> I feel that the example of Burma in leaving the Commonwealth may well be followed by other subject countries treading the path of political development. There is a natural psychological urge in such countries to demonstrate their independence and political adulthood. . . . But if it is declared to the world by the case of Burma that there are only two choices—within the Commonwealth on Commonwealth terms particularly where one of these is allegiance to the King or outside on their own it may well be that opinion will harden. The Leftist trend in Burma is I believe common to all Eastern countries now rising to nationhood and with humble respect to His Majesty allegiance to the King may prove not immediately but ultimately a difficulty.
>
> The conclusion I reach therefore is that the time seems ripe for a new conception of association within the Commonwealth not necessarily owing allegiance to the Crown especially for those countries which have no ties of blood culture or religion. I believe that in Burma we are faced with a time of decision not only affecting Burma and Great Britain but with much wider repercussions. In my opinion it is a question not only whether HMG has a *dynamic* policy for SEA but whether HMG can produce a new conception of Commonwealth to meet new conditions.[14]

At his request, these views were reported to Mountbatten and the Governor-General of Malaya, Malcolm MacDonald. Mountbatten agreed that 'the time was now ripe for investigation of a form of association within the British Commonwealth', and 'the British Empire must move with the times'.[15] He was 'worried whether at some future date we shall not find the Union of India also wishing to leave the Commonwealth'.[16] A 'looser form of association' must be considered. MacDonald carried the authority of a former Secretary of State for Dominion Affairs (1935–8 and 1938–9), for the

---

[13] Listowel to Mountbatten, 18 July 1947, ibid., xii, 166.
[14] Rance to Listowel, 9 June 1947, CAB 134/117.
[15] Mountbatten to Listowel, 27 June 1947, *TP*, xi, 368.
[16] Mountbatten to Listowel, 25 July 1947, ibid., xii, 227.

Colonies (1938–40), and High Commissioner to Canada (1941–6).
He supported Rance's views in a long and important cable:

. . . Burma's departure would have much repercussion. It would be
regarded throughout Asia—not only in countries for which we are
responsible, but also elsewhere—as unchallengeable evidence of the
weakening of British influence. Peoples in this part of the world, believing
that Britain is losing her authority and power, would think less of her, give
less weight to her policies and there would be less importance [attached] to
her friendship. That certainly would be the tendency in Malaya, with
unfortunate results on our capacity to get our ideas accepted. Amongst all
Asian peoples, nationalist movements are growing, and our influence in
Asia now depends largely on how successfully we can work with these
movements and retain their confidence. The departure of Burma from the
Commonwealth, especially if it were followed by the departure of India,
would probably be the beginning of an immense decline in our prestige and
position in South East Asia.

If British influence slips, some other external influence will inevitably
take its place. A possible alternative might have been American influence,
if that is counted for much in this part of the world. But, at present at any
rate, it seems that the power which rises in our place will undoubtedly be
that of Communism, with the Chinese Communist Movement (which has
promiscuous cells over much of South East Asia) acting directly or
indirectly as the agent of Russian Communism. This movement is already
making considerable headway and its victory is assured if British influence
is gravely weakened.

. . . effect in a country like Malaya, for example, will be great. Whereas,
if Burma and other more advanced countries in Asia drop out of the Commonwealth one by one, there is little chance of Malaya choosing to stay in
when the time comes for complete self government here: if means can now
be devised by which Burma and others willingly stay in the Commonwealth, the Malays will probably be happy to regard this as a pattern for
their own future status.

Such a development would not only preserve our interest and influence
in SE Asia. It would also make possible the creation of a British Commonwealth of Nations including nations and peoples of many races, colours
and civilizations. It would build a badly needed bridge of understanding
and partnership between the peoples of the West and East. If we can realize
this splendid conception, the moral influence of Britain, as well as its
material security, would be vastly increased.

I think that this is one of the great testing moments of British statesmanship. Our genius for political government enabled our predecessors in the
last generation to transform a large insecure part of the Colonial Empire
into a Commonwealth '*of free and equal nations*'. The ruling people in these

nations, however, are white men, most of them of British stock. The test now is whether we can transform the 'coloured' part of the Colonial Empire also into a commonwealth of free and equal nations. This is obviously a more difficult task.

We must accept what the Governor says in his telegram about the attitude of the Burmese to the Crown, and face this problem realistically. What he says about the Burmese probably applies in a greater or lesser degree to other Asiatic peoples in the Empire. . . . I wonder whether we can find a solution to this problem which, in part at any rate, abolished the institution of the Crown whilst fully preserving the personality of the King throughout the Asiatic nations of the Commonwealth.

I suggest that the starting point of our examination of this problem might be the Constitution of Eire. Perhaps I may be permitted to recall that I was Secretary of State for Dominion Affairs when Mr De Valera introduced his Constitution, and was responsible for advising the Cabinet of the day that we should not regard the Constitution as putting Eire outside the Commonwealth. One reason why I advised the Cabinet to adopt that line was that it seemed likely that when the time came for India, Burma and other non-white countries in the Empire to attain dominion status, some, at least, of them would adopt a similar attitude to the Southern Irish towards the British Crown. It seemed wise to accept a compromise in Eire which might, in due course, open the way to a similar compromise enabling India and other Empire countries to stay as full partners in the Commonwealth. . . .

If this argument is sound, can we devise an arrangement on the general principle of the Eire precedent, by which a Burmese republic remains member of the Commonwealth, recognising the King as head of the Commonwealth and accepting His Majesty as the Supreme Constitutional authority through which it should act in many matters touching external affairs?[17]

Such hopes for Burma were dashed by the assassination of Aung San and all of his ministers on 19 July. Attlee later ruminated that 'if U Aung San had lived they might have stayed in, but the murder removed the one man who might have done it and ridden the storm'.[18] The foremost expert on the subject, Professor H.R. Tinker, consigns such might-have-beens to the realms of mythology. The documents, he shows, disprove the 'legend' that Aung San's death marked a turning point or that Burma would have stayed in the Commonwealth if India's intention to do so had been known earlier.[19] Burma achieved full independence in

[17] MacDonald to Creech Jones, 27 June 1947, CAB 134/117.

[18] Quoted in Harris, *Attlee* (1982), 361–2.

[19] Tinker (ed.), *Burma: The Struggle for Independence, 1944–1948* (1984), ii, p. xxx, n. l.

October and withdrew from the Commonwealth in January 1948. Thereafter its relations with Britain were governed by treaty.

The Official Committee comprised representatives of the Foreign, Home, Commonwealth Relations, Colonial, Burma, and Cabinet Offices. They were drawn from the deputy under-secretaries rather than the permanent heads who, in the previous winter, had questioned the wisdom of India's membership of the Commonwealth club. At their first meeting, on 4 July, they considered the status of high commissioners in London. The problem was that whereas all ambassadors ranked in precedence above His Majesty's ministers (save the four most senior), high commissioners ranked below them. The Committee resolved it, to the dissatisfaction of the Foreign Office, by ranking them in separate groups but at the same level. Thus was removed an existing resentment that would become acute with newly independent states of the Commonwealth. As a basis for future discussion of the existing Commonwealth relationships and possible alternatives to the Dominion model, it was agreed that the various departments should prepare brief reports on nationality, defence, trade, foreign affairs, diplomatic representation, consultation, and the position of the Crown.

At its second and last meeting for 1947 the Committee tackled the nature of the Commonwealth relationship in the light of the departmental memoranda. Bridges' conclusions, suitably supplemented by specific comments on Defence by Sir Leslie Hollis, Deputy Secretary (Military) to the Cabinet, and on Burma by Laithwaite, were embodied in a report to the Ministerial Committee.[20] The Commonwealth system had developed gradually from a basis of common sentiment and common interest. It rested on mutual trust and confidence, and had no constitution save the Statute of Westminster. Britain should attempt to build up trust and confidence in relations with the new Asian members. India, for example, should be treated on a footing of complete equality with the older Dominions. Differences of race and colour would present difficulties but they should not prove insuperable. The British origin of much of the Commonwealth was but one of the ties, which also included a common educational background and the experience of working together. The appointment of British governors by India

[20] Second meeting of Official Cttee on CR, 8 Aug. 1947; Memo. on 'Commonweatlh Relations', 15 Aug. 1947; CAB 134/117.

and Pakistan was, after all the political differences of recent years, evidence of a common sentiment from which trust and confidence might grow. Rather than 'looking to see in what way the Dominion relationship should be modified', or seeking to create an inferior kind of Commonwealth, the existing system should be assumed and the necessary risks run in order to make it work. Only such modifications as proved unavoidable should be made.

However, the Committee agreed, there was one matter that might not admit of development or adaptation and would therefore require a decision of principle. This was the position of the Crown, as expressed in the Statute of Westminster, '. . . inasmuch as the Crown is the symbol of the free association of the members of the British Commonwealth of Nations, and as they are united by a common allegiance to the Crown . . .'. The Eire case, in which the Crown was recognized only for external purposes, was a compromise possible only because of the unique historic relations of her people to the British, her strategic position, and the economic link. Even if Burma wished to remain in the Commonwealth on a basis other than dominionhood 'the dilution in the position of the Crown to meet her particular case' would not be warranted. Yet 'There would be a much stronger case for some further consideration of the position of the Crown in relation to the Asiatic Dominions if a situation arose in which this was the only obstacle to India remaining within the Commonwealth. Our present view would be very strongly against raising this issue at the present time.' That the Committee's conclusions in favour of a wait-and-see policy prevailed is evidenced by the fact that from the presentation of its report in mid-September there was no further ministerial call for advice for six months.

On 17 March 1948 Brook wrote to acquaint the King's secretary that the Official Committee had met again the previous day.[21] Ministerial interest in the possibilities of adjusting the existing structure had revived 'mainly because of the possibility that the Constituent Assembly in India may devise a form of constitution which is not easily reconcilable with the Commonwealth relationship'. Difficulties of diplomacy during the Kashmir war might also provoke the severance of Commonwealth links at any time. In addition, it had become clear that Eire would soon repeal the External

---

[21] Brook to Sir Alan Lascelles, 17 Mar. 1948, CAB 21/1804.

Relations Act, thereby cutting its last links with the Crown and thus the Commonwealth. Two non-official papers on the concept of linking independent nations with the Commonwealth by 'association' rather than membership were attached to the agenda papers for 16 March.[22]

As chairman of the Official Committee and secretary of the Ministerial Committee Brook played a leading role in the making of the new Commonwealth. His talents were understated by his Oxford tutor, Maurice Bowra, who wrote that he 'had beautiful hand-writing, a very clear mind, and a gift for sorting a difficult subject into its main elements under the right headings'.[23] He led his Committee with skill and the balance and clarity of his reports for Ministers carried great weight. It is often difficult to decide the sources of the ideas that appear in the reports, for besides his discussions with his official colleagues, his exchanges of views with the constructive Patrick Gordon Walker, and Indian suggestions were brought to bear in them.

On 16 March Brook sketched from the chair three alternatives to be pursued if India or Pakistan declined to remain a Dominion.[24] First, the Commonwealth relationship might be diluted to achieve the maximum accommodation of potential members, including republics. The Committee rejected this alternative as the Crown was the only formal link uniting the Commonwealth. Secondly, membership might be confined to those nations prepared to accept the existing relationship as it stood, leaving others to secede and enter treaties with Britain as Burma had done. While the Committee saw advantage in preserving the common outlook, heritage, race, and experience of the existing association, their endurance could not be assumed. The influence of the Commonwealth and the very survival of its Dominions core would be greatly prejudiced by the secession of India and Pakistan. 'To regard the Commonwealth as essentially European in race and British in culture and outlook would, indeed, be wholly inconsistent with our Colonial policy, which contemplated, as an aim of political development, the ultimate attainment by the dependent territories of responsible self-government within the British Commonwealth.'

---

[22] Both papers (discussed below) appear in the CR Cttee file for 1948 (CAB 134/118).
[23] Bowra, *Memories 1898–1939* (1966), 148.
[24] Minutes of first meeting of Offical Cttee on CR for 1948, CAB 134/118.

As Brook put it in a report based on the discussion, 'It would be inconsistent with our Colonial policy to regard the Commonwealth as a "white man's club", to which non-European nations may only be admitted if they accept unquestioningly the rules and conventions created by an ealier generation for a different type of member'.[25] Further, in a polarizing world the policy of Western Union implied the association of Europe with its overseas territories outside the orbits of the United States and the Soviet Union. The elimination of Brook's first two alternatives indicated the need for a close evaluation of his third: 'to devise a special form of association with the British Commonwealth for those countries for whom the normal form of Dominion status was unacceptable'. The existing relations between states that preserved their allegiance to the Crown would be unchanged, but a new concept of 'association' would maintain the linkage of other states to the Commonwealth.

One of the two non-official papers before the Committee was a lecture on 'The Implications of Eire's Relationship with the British Commonwealth of Nations' that Dr Nicholas Mansergh, Abe Bailey Research Professor at the Royal Institute of International Affairs, had delivered on 25 November 1947. Mansergh sought guidance for the future from an historical analysis of Eire's relations with the Commonwealth. He drew a parallel between Eire's position in 1921, when she had sought a relationship based on independence from the Crown but compromised on a form of Dominion status, and that of newly emergent nations in 1947: 'In Asia today, and in many parts of Africa tomorrow, the British Commonwealth will be confronted with nationally self-conscious peoples balancing in their minds the relative advantages of equal partnership within the Commonwealth and independent existence outside it'.

As with Eire in 1921 they might feel allegiance to a foreign Crown to be unacceptable, preferring to be republics outside the Commonwealth but associated with it. In the Irish case British insistence on the Crown as the basis of association produced a steady divergence between the form and the substance of the relationship. In 1937 the principle of external association was in fact established, though there was provision for the Crown to accredit Irish Ambassadors to foreign countries. Britain continued to regard Eire as a Dominion

---

[25] Draft of report on 'The Commonwealth Relationship', 24 Mar. 1948, ibid.

though she regarded herself as a foreign state. The breakdown of understanding produced contrary expectations and impaired the relationship. As de Valera affirmed in September 1947, 'We are associates of the States of the Commonwealth; but if they regard the existence of the King as a necessary link, if they consider that it is a bond they have, then we have not got that bond. . . . We are externally associated with the States of the British Commonwealth.' Mansergh defined the concept thus:

External association is in a sense a *via media* between Dominion status and Treaty Relationship, but it is a mistake to think of it as a colourless compromise. Rightly regarded, it is the positive answer to a certain set of circumstances. Its foundation should be the desire of two or more independent countries to form a close and lasting association. In that, it is similar to Dominion status, but distinct from a treaty relationship which is normally founded on a short-term coincidence of interest in a limited and particular field. On the other hand, as distinct from Dominion status, it rests, not upon a sense of underlying unity in history, development and tradition, symbolised by allegiance to a common Crown, but upon a sense of partnership between two peoples with different histories and different loyalties, but sharing common interests, common aims in world politics and, above all, a common sense of values.

He contrasted its potentialities with the rigidity of the treaty relationship, as with Burma.

Burma, it is stated in the Burma Independence Bill, shall become on 6th January, 1948, 'an independent country neither forming part of His Majesty's Dominions nor entitled to His Majesty's protection'. By that decision, Burma is likely in the long run to lose considerably, for while the material foundation remains the same the sense of intimate and growing partnership may well be lost. No one would wish to question the very real measure of goodwill that exists towards Britain in Burma to-day, but goodwill tends to be transient. Under the Treaty of Relationship which has now been established, it will find little scope for expression in day to day relations over a period of years. Whatever may be the intentions and hopes of the signatories, treaties are usually interpreted in a literal and restrictive sense. They are not a stepping-stone to a closer and more intimate relationship, just because they provide no machinery for making relations more intimate. It is here that the concept of association could have made a valuable and distinctive contribution. Even had it been based upon a treaty whose essentials corresponded in almost every particular to the details of the treaty just signed, association with the Commonwealth would have allowed for a continuing and expanding consultation and co-operation in all matters of common concern. As a direct consequence the area of common interest might have widened as the years went by and the friendship deepened. Therein lies the supreme merit of association as against treaty relationship. It allows, it is designed to allow, for growth.

Mansergh envisaged that from a stated and defined basis of association there would grow, by continued contact, conventions that would 'enrich and deepen the association'. The secession of Burma should be taken as a lesson, not complacently, revealing the need for a 'new approach', to meet a problem 'perhaps as much psychological as political'. Though Mansergh's starting point was 'external association' he clearly envisaged that members and associates of the Commonwealth would grow closer to each other, towards 'a Commonwealth of the future, in which there are both member States and associate States, and the distinction between them being one, not of status, but of history, tradition and cultural background'.

Perhaps because it emphasized the failures of British policies for Ireland and Burma Mansergh's lecture did not receive the attention that was given to the other non-official paper before the Committee. It was by a former Indian Civil Servant who claimed agreement with Mansergh's views. Mr J.P. Stent, now employed in economic planning at the Foreign Office, sent his paper on 'The British Commonwealth and Asia' to Cripps and Noel-Baker. Cripps commended him to Attlee as 'a very intelligent man who has corresponded with me in this respect in the past'.[26] The paper was 'well worth reading and might indeed form a good point of departure for a discussion'. Stent was concerned that, regarding Dominion status as 'involving some degree of subjection, some derogation from complete independence', India and Pakistan would eventually follow Burma out of the Commonwealth. Ceylon would be difficult to retain as a member and Malaya might not remain. British influence in Asia would diminish and Communism would step into the void: 'These are not mere visionary possibilities and almost any sacrifice would seem to be worth while to prevent their realization. The key to the whole problem lies in the future status of India and Pakistan.' In order to hold them to the Commonwealth they should be offered a 'free and independent partnership on a purely voluntary basis in a new entity, a new conception of the

[26] Cripps to Attlee, 28 Jan. 1948, PREM 8/735.

Commonwealth, a new "Union" or "Association" of the British Commonwealth and countries of Asia'. Stent considered several alternative titles for the new entity. His choice of 'The Commonwealth of British and Asian Peoples' suggests the inclusion of republics rather than their external association on the Mansergh model, but it is clear this was not his intention. For 'the British Commonwealth proper would continue in being', and would not be 'dissolved in the larger whole'. His concept would be more accurately described as an 'Association of the British Commonwealth and Asian Peoples'. He proposed making the purposes of the association the subject of a pledge, which would include the preservation of peace, mutual co-operation for defence, trade, and economic progress, the pursuit of liberty and democracy, the abolition of racial discrimination, etc.

On 12 April, when the Ministerial Committee met for the first time, it agreed that the Official Committee should proceed at once with detailed consideration of a new 'Commonwealth of British and Associated Nations'.[27] However, difficulties with the concept were anticipated. 'It was not, for instance, clear what difference there would be between associate membership of such a Commonwealth and the position of a foreign country in formal alliance with the Commonwealth countries.' The Official Report (dated 21 July) on the concept of association found its 'main advantage' to be that it preserved unchanged the Dominions core of the Commonwealth.[28] The report examined the concept in its two alternative applications: as a means of providing for 'associate members' in addition to Dominion members of a new Commonwealth; and as providing for the external association of independent states with the old Commonwealth. The disadvantages of the first case included the real danger that some Dominions, notably South Africa and Canada, might, like India, Pakistan, and Eire, prefer the status of an associated state, thereby throwing 'the inner and outer groups of the new Commonwealth . . . out of balance with each other'. If the new Commonwealth found that 'its main weight came to lie with the "associated" States' then it would not endure for long. Furthermore, the practical difficulty of defining the relations between the associated states and the Dominions would be extreme, as the latter

[27] Minutes of first meeting of Cabinet Cttee on CR, 12 Apr. 1948, CAB 134/118.
[28] 'Commonwealth Relationship: Fourth Report by Official Committee', 21 July 1948, ibid.

would differ among themselves over the rights to be extended and the obligations expected in respect of the former. It would thus be 'difficult to cause the evolution of the Commonwealth relation to move in the direction of "a Commonwealth of British and Associated Nations" '. Neither could external association be regarded by the Dominions core 'as a stage in the evolutionary development of the British Commonwealth'. Such association would rest wholly on considerations of self interest and would not inherit the emotional and sentimental ties of the old Commonwealth. It was 'hard to see how it would be possible to define in generally acceptable terms the commitments which the members of the Commonwealth would have to be prepared to undertake, individually and jointly, on behalf of the "Other Nations" '. In sum, neither form of association seemed to offer any benefits that could not as easily be secured by treaties.

The negative conclusion on 'association' that Brook reported on 21 July and the Ministerial Committee approved on 27 July[29] was essentially the same as that of the Commonwealth Relations Office in early March and Attlee himself in January. The CRO had been pessimistic about the degree of co-operation, notably in the 'most important aspect' of defence, that would result from association, while formal commitments on defence would be anathema to some Dominions.[30] Attlee had referred the matter to Harold Laski for advice and received a nineteen-page 'Note on the Possible Association of an Independent State with Great Britain'.[31] It failed to find any *via media* between a treaty relationship and Commonwealth membership resting on common allegiance to the Crown. The advice confirmed Attlee in his own views, which he expressed in a note that was unusually long for him:

I have read the paper entitled 'The British Commonwealth and Asia' with interest, but I am not clear how the proposals therein differ from an ordinary alliance. . . . The real difficulty which arose in the case of Burma and may arise in the case of India is that of theoretical republicanism. It is also latent in our relations with Eire and South Africa. I say theoretical because there is really no practical issue. Eire has travelled furthest on this road and is in practice a republic only retaining the connection with the Crown for the formal purpose of accrediting ambassadors to Foreign

29 Minutes of third meeting of Cabinet Cttee on CR, 27 July 1948, ibid.
30 Memo. by the CRO, 9 Mar. 1948, ibid.
31 Dated 1 February 1948, PREM 8/735.

Powers. But in actual fact all the Dominions are as far from control by Great Britain as a republic entirely separate would be. . . .

Actually common allegiance to the Crown is, as Laski points out, the only real link connecting parts of the Commonwealth. It is a very strong link in the cases of Canada, Australia and New Zealand. In these countries there would be strong resentment at any attempt to remove it. . . . There is probably a great deal of latent loyalty to the Crown in India. . . . There is no doubt that Mountbatten's connection with the Royal House helped him very much in India.

I am inclined to think that in India and Burma if some face-saving device could be adopted there would not only be willingness but eagerness to remain within the Commonwealth. . . .

To try to substitute some other link would, I think, be apt to raise all kinds of difficulties. . . . There is . . . nothing inherently impossible in a republic forming part of a monarchy.[32]

There is no evidence that Attlee circulated his note. It is testimony to his patience and thoroughness that holding such views he acquiesced in the protracted evaluation of the concept of association until it was finally laid to rest in July. For the note reveals his firm attachment to the link with the Crown as the basis of the Commonwealth.

At its first meeting, on 12 April, the Ministerial Committee added a fourth alternative to those courses of action proposed by the officials—dilution, the status quo, or association. It was 'redefinition' of the existing constitutional relationship so as 'to meet the doubts which Indian political leaders felt about the acceptability of Dominion status in its present form', for 'Republicanism was alien to the Indian tradition and it should not be assumed that the relationship between India and the Crown could not be defined in such a way as to command general acceptance in India'. It might be possible to redefine the Commonwealth relationship so as to meet the special needs of individual Dominions. The Official Committee was instructed to take up the task. It identified the five essential features of the Commonwealth relationship as the position of the Crown, common citizenship, economic co-operation, consultation on foreign policy, and collaboration in defence.[33] The last three

[32] N.d. or signature but from context clearly written by Attlee between 1 and 9 Feb. 1948, ibid.

[33] 'Commonwealth Relationship: Third Report by Official Committee', 21 May 1948, CAB 134/118.

aspects had never been precisely formulated and it was doubtful whether the rights and obligations involved in them were susceptible of definition. Common citizenship was the subject of legislation already prepared in a British Nationality Bill (to be discussed below) and offered no scope for further redefinition. The Crown, 'with its historical associations and emotional significance', really reflected 'both the undefinable quality' of the Commonwealth relationship 'and its variable character'. Thus the redefinition of the relationship, in the sense of expressing the principles basic to it, was an unpromising approach.

Brook's reports to the Ministerial Comittee (21 May and 21 July) proposed approaching the task of 'redefinition' from a different angle. Changes of 'usage' and 'convention' were suggested to 'ease the existing relationship' and make it more acceptable to new members. As some Asian peoples might regard membership of a *British* Commonwealth of Nations as connoting subjection, the adjective might be dropped. The unpopular term 'Dominion' might lapse and be replaced by 'Member of the Commonwealth'. Equality of members should be emphasized, so that the British Prime Minister would be referred to as a 'Commonwealth Prime Minister'. Brook also considered 'the minimum formal ties which a particular country must be willing to accept if it is to remain a member of the Commonwealth'. The primary aim should be to persuade all countries to accept that the Head of State was the King's representative for both internal and external purposes. However, it was likely that India and/or Pakistan would reject the King's authority in internal affairs and the Eire precedent was awkward. It would then be better that, as well as accepting the King's jurisdiction in their external relations they accepted, as Eire had not, 'the Crown as the Supreme Head of the Commonwealth'. The Ministerial Committee welcomed both sets of suggestions.[34] While it approved the changes of 'usage', it recognized that the definition of the 'minimum formal ties' requiring acceptance by Commonwealth members was a matter on which the older Commonwealth countries must be consulted. Attlee was asked to take it up with the Prime Ministers of Canada, Australia, and New Zealand, with a view to its discussion at the forthcoming Commonwealth Conference in October.

[34] Minutes of second and third meetings of Cabinet Cttee on CR, 31 May and 27 July 1948, ibid.

In August Brook was despatched to Ottawa, Canberra, and Wellington with a personal message from the Prime Minister conveying the Cabinet Committee's provisional views on the future development of the constitutional relationship between the self-governing countries of the Commonwealth. The visits yielded clear approval by the old Dominions for the policy directions that had emerged in London.[35] All of the Prime Ministers were very ready to re-examine the Commonwealth relationship. Though they were uneasy about the consequences of the admission of three Asian Dominions lacking their common heritage and sentiment, they were agreed that the risk of serious loss to the Commonwealth by secession justified compromise in the constitutional field. They insisted that no compromise should be made that would impair the existing relations between Dominions and were opposed to the idea of framing any new 'articles of association' for the Commonwealth as a whole. The British ministers' rejection of any general 'dilution' of the Commonwealth bond and the concept of 'association' was wholly endorsed. Brook's discussions on the 'minimum tie' required of Commonwealth members mainly concerned India, and there was agreement that 'it would suffice if she accepted the King's jurisdiction in her external relations'. Republicanism was no insuperable barrier as long as the President was the King's representative in external relations (even if he were elected). Thus, the Eire precedent would be acceptable, but if India refused to follow it then she must become a foreign state. Similarly, if Eire repealed the External Relations Act she could not be regarded as a member of the Commonwealth. There was agreement that if a country did leave the Commonwealth but wished to remain in special association with it then the question should be examined sympathetically. But there was no interest in a prior examination of the question. Similarly, there was general endorsement of HMG's wait-and-see policy in regard to the Asian Dominions' attitude toward the Crown, and no disposition to take initiatives by suggesting possible changes to the Statute of Westminster.

Brook's report on his mission presented a statement of general principles, substantially agreed by Britain, Canada, Australia, and New Zealand, for discussion at the October meeting of

[35] Brook's notes on his discussions appear in CAB 21/1818.

Commonwealth Prime Ministers.[36] It included the previously proposed changes of usage in respect of 'Dominions', 'Dominion Status', 'Commonwealth Prime Ministers' and 'Commonwealth of Nations', which Canada, Australia, and New Zealand generally welcomed, though the latter regretted the lapse of 'British' in the title of the Commonwealth. Its most important provision was that the 'recognition of the Crown for external purposes only must be regarded as the minimum constitutional link'.

In the light of subsequent events the most remarkable omission from Brook's report is any reference to a formula based on the King as Supreme Head of the Commonwealth. In his May Report Brook had considered that while the new Dominions might reject the King's authority over internal affairs they might 'be encouraged to remain within the Commonwealth on the basis of recognising the Crown as the Supreme Head of the Commonwealth'. At the Ministerial Committee that month it was thought 'doubtful whether India would be prepared to recognise the Crown as the Supreme Head of the Commonwealth'. Ministers seem not to have pursued the point. On 13 August, at the beginning of the very first meeting of Brook's mission, the Canadian Prime Minister, Mr Mackenzie King, said that 'he disliked the suggestion . . . that India should be asked to recognise the Crown as the Supreme Head of the Commonwealth. He thought that this would imply that the Commonwealth was a single unit.'[37] This diverted Brook from the prospect of defining the Commonwealth in terms of its relation as a whole with the King. He subsequently confined himself to exploring the minimum basis of the allegiance for external affairs. The basis no sooner crystallized in his mind than its utility was destroyed.

On 8 September Mr J.A. Costello, Prime Minister of Eire, confirmed what had been the subject of speculation since his summer election victory and formation of an inter-party government: that Eire was about to repeal the External Relations Act. In reply to a question at a press conference in Ottawa he affirmed that this involved secession from the Commonwealth. At that moment Brook was on his way home. In his report a week later he wrote that

---

[36] 'Commonwealth Relationship: Consultations with Canada, Australia, and New Zealand', Report by Secretary to the Cabinet, 14 Sep. 1948, CAB 134/118.

[37] Brook's 'Note of Points Raised with Mr Mackenzie King', 13 Aug. 1948, CAB 21/1818.

he had 'no reason to believe that [Costello's] statement will alter the definite view expressed to me by the Prime Ministers of Canada, Australia, and New Zealand that if Eire should repeal this Act she can no longer be regarded as a member of the Commonwealth'. He therefore proceeded with his adumbration of principles for discussion by the Commonwealth Prime Ministers when they gathered in London from 11 October.

On 5 October Attlee asked the Lord Chancellor for a definitive statement of the legal implications of Eire's intended step. Lord Jowitt's advice of 9 October was that 'the repeal of Executive Authority (External Relations) Act, 1936, unless accompanied by declarations of the Eire Government or other circumstances putting some other complexion on the repeal, could only be construed as a categoric renunciation by Eire of further membership in the Commonwealth'.[38] The Solicitor-General and the legal departments of the Foreign, Home, and Commonwealth Relations Offices concurred in this opinion. Concurrence in Brook's principle that acceptance of the King's authority in external relations was necessary to membership of the Commonwealth must therefore mean acquiescence in the secession of Eire.

When Brook saw Dr H.V. Evatt, Australia's Minister for External Affairs, in Paris on 7 October he found that Evatt (who had been abroad during Brook's visit to Australia) was anxious that 'a determined effort should be made to get Mr Costello himself to come over to London for discussions on this constitutional issue while the other Commonwealth representatives are here'.[39] He recognized that Eire's repeal of the External Relations Act would carry her out of the Commonwealth and felt 'strenuous efforts should be made to find a basis on which Eire can be kept within the Commonwealth'. He envisaged that Mr Mackenzie King, Mr Peter Fraser (Prime Minister of New Zealand) and himself should meet Attlee the following week and seek 'a common line', which should then be put to Costello during the second week of the Conference. Mackenzie King fell ill and spent the period of the Conference in his suite at the Dorchester Hotel, receiving a steady stream of bedside visitors. On Tuesday the 12th he saw Noel-Baker:

Mr Mackenzie King then talked to me about the question of Eire and India

---

[38] Jowitt's minute for PM, 9 October 1948, CAB 134/118.
[39] Brook's report of conversation with Evatt on 7 Oct., ibid.

staying in the Commonwealth. He said that he thought it was eminently desirable that we should find some formula by which any nation who desired to remain in association with the Commonwealth should be able to do so. Changes were never made in the Commonwealth by Statute, but Statutes or Imperial Conference reports had sometimes described and confirmed changes which had already happened. He thought it might be possible to agree that any nation which in the past had owed, or which now was owing allegiance to the Crown, (including any non-self governing territories that might in future attain independent status) should remain a member of the Commonwealth so long as it desired to do so. In other words, while allegiance to the Crown should be a binding link between all members who desired it, it should not be insisted on for those who did not, provided they had once owed it.[40]

The same day Evatt wrote to Attlee that they should 'avoid at this stage formulating conditions which must be accepted in order that a particular state shall not cease to be a member of the Commonwealth'.[41] They should seek 'links that would be acceptable to all, including Ireland'. Evatt demanded a meeting between Commonwealth and Irish leaders. Faced with the dire consequences of the principle that Brook had espoused Commonwealth leaders were resiling.

The conditions of Commonwealth membership were never discussed in formal session at the Conference. Instead, exploratory discussions were held at Chequers, and in Paris between representatives of the Irish and Commonwealth governments. They revealed the boundless goodwill of the old Dominions towards Eire but an implacable Irish wish to break the formal link with the Crown and quit the Commonwealth. To a large degree the conciliatoriness of Evatt, Fraser, and Mr Lester Pearson, Canada's Foreign Minister, neglected their own governments' apprehensions of weakening the link with the Crown. Certainly, Attlee and his colleagues believed that the legal consequences of Eire's repeal of the External Relations Act should be enforced, that is the withdrawal of her trade preferences with the Commonwealth and the treatment of her citizens as aliens. The retention of Commonwealth privileges by Eire as a non-member might complicate negotiations with the Asian Dominions. Again, other foreign countries might

---

[40] Record of conversation between Secretary of State and Mackenzie King, 12 Oct. 1948, CAB 21/1818.

[41] Evatt to Attlee, 12 Oct. 1948, cited in O'Brien, 'Australia and the Repeal of the External Relations Act', unpublished paper of 20 Oct. 1983, 10.

claim any trading preferences and citizenship rights enjoyed by Eire. However, at a meeting held at Chequers on 17 October the Commonwealth and Eire representatives agreed that their countries should not become foreign, nor their citizens alien, in relation to each other.[42] Britain's acquiesence was based on a tenuous agreement that Ireland should apply for re-entry to the Commonwealth in six months' time. A Commonwealth without the King was thus contemplated, though briefly for the Irish *aide-mémoire* on the Chequers meeting ignored the question of re-entry. In consequence, on 12 November the Cabinet adopted a firm line in the draft that was prepared as a reply. When it was shown to Evatt he made a decisive intervention, arguing that even if Eire 'was not a member of the Commonwealth, she and the Commonwealth countries would not regard one another as "foreign" '.[43] Irish citizens resident in Commonwealth countries would be 'treated by law or practice not as "foreigners" or aliens but as entitled to rights and privileges of nationals or citizens of those nations'. When the Irish and old Dominion leaders accepted Evatt's formula Britain concurred, in Jowitt's words because 'if we persisted in the view that Eire must be regarded as a foreign country once the ERA was repealed, we should find ourselves alone in maintaining that view'.[44] Britain was left with explaining to bemused Asian Dominions or foreign nations the historic basis for Ireland's special treatment, so that it might not be cited as a precedent. Evatt had scarcely endeared himself to the British but his intervention had ensured that the old Dominions would be fully consulted in any negotiations over India's relationship with the Commonwealth.

In the course of 1948 first Burma and then Eire were lost to the Commonwealth. The loss occurred at a stage in its history when all of the members were required to be the King's men. The fact that in 1949 the Commonwealth was reconstructed to enable a republic to remain a member does suggest that if HMG's will had been sufficiently strong and urgent then the defections might never have

[42] Notes exchanged between PM of UK and PM of Eire on ministers' 17 Oct. meeting, cited ibid., 15.
[43] Cabinet memo. by Lord Chancellor and Secretary of State for CR, 17 Nov. 1948, CAB 129/31, cited ibid., 18.
[44] Ibid., 19.

occurred. Yet in view of the expert opinions of Professors Tinker and Mansergh on Burma and Ireland respectively that would be a misjudgement. Tinker argues convincingly that the accommodation of Burma in the Commonwealth was a 'dream' that 'never had much reality'.[45] Mansergh has said that, in retrospect, it is clear that Eire had really regarded herself as separate since 1937.[46] His considered judgement is that by 1948 Eire was looking to a future in Europe, the geographical area of which Ireland was a part, rather than to countries overseas where Irish emigrants had settled. Eire's relations with the Commonwealth had become, 'despite ties of kinship with the old dominions . . . an artifically imposed superstructure'.

It may have been as well that the Commonwealth was not hastily recast in 1947–8 to accommodate unwilling partners, for it would have been pointlessly weakened. As it was the tactic of treating the new Dominions as full partners in the Commonwealth was about to bear fruit. The leisure of a full year's reflection enabled India to perceive the advantages of the Commonwealth connection. In effect, the British game of wait-and-see induced Nehru to take an initiative. The problem for Attlee's Government became finding a means, acceptable to all parties, of satisfying Nehru's wish to remain in 'the Club'—and yet preserve the link with the Crown.

---

45 Tinker, *Burma*, ii, p. xxx.
46 Mansergh, *Commonwealth Experience*, ii, 144–5.

5

Nehru's Initiative

HAD Ireland's determination to formalize her republicanism not provoked a reconsideration of the allegiance test of Commonwealth membership, then in September 1948 India's attitude would surely have done so. At the end of the month Noel-Baker circulated to his colleagues on the Commonwealth Relations Committee some documents that had come in from the High Commission in Delhi. A 'reliable' source had reported the conclusions of a recent Congress Working Committee meeting:

The Working Committee was unanimous that India must be a sovereign independent state, i.e. she must leave the Commonwealth. This decision was taken because the Working Committee felt that they are pledged to the mass of the party to create an independent sovereign India, and that it would be politically impossible for the Congress to change from that violently reiterated position.[1]

However, the Committee wanted to retain the most cordial relations with the UK, Canada, Australia, and New Zealand. To that end, Nehru would explore 'the possibilities of treaties of alliance and friendship' with them in London. At the High Commission J.S.H. Shattock ascribed the decision to the UN's handling of the Kashmir dispute, the role of British officers of the Pakistan Army in Kashmir, and South Africa's treatment of Indians.

At the same time, Shattock interviewed V.P. Menon, who claimed that the report 'only represented half the facts':

There was another strong section of the Congress Party as well as senior Government of India officials who were in favour of retaining the Commonwealth connection. Their wish was to weave this connection round the British Nationality Act with its provisions for Commonwealth citizenship on the lines which Lord Mountbatten had proposed. Menon

---

[1] J.S.H. Shattock (UK High Commission, Delhi) to H.A.F. Rumbold (CRO), 14 Sept. 1948, encl. report on CWC meeting of 5 Sept. 1948, PREM 8/1008.

said that those who held this view hoped that Lord Mountbatten would be able to bring a good deal of influence to bear on Pandit Nehru (who was a bit afraid of the Indian Socialists in this regard) in favour of this course when the latter goes to London in October. The Working Committee . . . had given the Dominion Cabinet authority to come to a final decision on this question.[2]

Menon's comments are clarified by a cable that he sent to Mountbatten on 7 October, through the High Commission and the CRO rather than India's diplomatic channels.

I have had a long discussion with Sardar [Patel] regarding India's position in the Commonwealth. No decision on this question has been taken, and Panditji has been asked to sound opinion in England. Presumably he will discuss this question further with the Congress Party and the Cabinet on his return, and then come to a final decision. The view of the Congress Party is that, if the objectives resolution had not been passed by the Constituent Assembly, India today would have unhesitatingly agreed to remain a member of the Commonwealth without any reservation or conditions. In view of Panditji's leanings towards the Socialist Party, it would be difficult for him to try and rescind the objectives resolution as such. On the other hand, Sardar is quite sure that, if we could find a compromise on your common citizenship formula, there is every chance of its general acceptance by the Congress.

2. Panditji requires a lot of persuasion, but if you and Lady Mountbatten with your great personal influence on him can get him to accept the citizenship formula, then I am satisfied that I can persuade the Sardar to get it accepted by the Congress Party.[3]

Here, at a critical moment, is the revival of the Patel–Menon–Nehru–Mountbatten nexus that had produced the dual Dominions deal at Simla in May 1947. The English counterpart of the Viceregal Lodge *pourparlers* was to be discussions at Broadlands, where Nehru twice stayed with the Mountbattens in October.

The idea of a Commonwealth based on a 'common citizenship formula' was mooted by Nehru in a discussion with Mountbatten the day after he was sworn in as Viceroy, 24 March 1947:

Nehru said that he did not consider it possible, with the forces which were

---

[2] Acting UK High Commissioner to CRO, 14 September 1948, reporting Shattock-Menon meeting of same date, ibid.

[3] Acting UK High Commissioner to CRO, 7 Oct. 1948, ibid.

at work, that India could remain within The Commonwealth. But basically, he said, they did not want to break any threads, and he suggested 'some form of common nationality' (I feel that they are beginning to see that they cannot go out of the Commonwealth; but they cannot afford to say that they will stay in; they are groping for a formula).[4]

During a visit to Malaya the previous year Nehru had suggested a common nationality between India, Ceylon, Burma, Malaya, and Indonesia. 'The visit gave Nehru an opportunity to think further on the problems of Indians living outside India', writes B. N. Pandey. 'Should they return to India? Or should they be asked to renounce Indian citizenship for their country of adoption?'[5] Nehru advised the half million Indians in Malaya to adopt Malayan nationality until the time came for a common nationality. He responded to a suggestion of Aung San's for a conference of Asian countries and the Asian Relations Conference was in session during the first ten days of Mountbatten's viceroyalty. The migration and racial problems were on its agenda and the idea of common citizenship was much in the air. On 31 March Krishna Menon emphasized 'the Indian desire for common citizenship but not Dominion Status', for 'reciprocity'.[6]

Though Ceylon and Burma each had 750,000 Indian residents the problem of Indians overseas existed in its most acute form in South Africa, where they numbered 285,000.[7] The inferior status of South African Indians had been a running sore with generations of nationalists since the young Gandhi had made their cause his own. In 1946, when South Africa introduced a Land and Franchise Act that provided segregationist restrictions on housing, the Viceroy's Council took the matter to the United Nations. South African Indians launched a satyagraha defying the 'Ghetto Act'. After Nehru was sworn in as Minister for External Affairs and Commonwealth Relations he appointed his sister, Mrs Vijaya Lakshmi Pandit, as India's principal delegate to the United Nations. Mrs Pandit was disappointed when Britain and the old Dominions supported Smuts in his contention that the matter

---

[4] *TP*, x, 11.

[5] Pandey, *Nehru* (1976), 256. See also, Gopal, *Nehru*, i, 309–11.

[6] Campbell-Johnson, *Mission with Mountbatten*, 50.

[7] For the problem of overseas Indians generally, see Tinker, *Separate and Unequal: India and the Indians in the British Commonwealth, 1920–1950* (1976). See esp. 292–305, 313–15, and ch. 10.

was an internal one. However, in December 1946 the General Assembly (with only Australia of the Commonwealth members abstaining, the remainder opposing) voted 32 to 15 to require South Africa to treat Indians in conformity with international obligations and the UN Charter. In April 1947 Nehru called upon Smuts to give effect to the resolution and made future diplomatic and trading relations between India and South Africa dependent on his compliance.[8] Smuts resented the insistence by UN members upon the application of the Charter to South Africa when many of them were violating it in their own countries. His line towards India hardened, while his replacement by Dr D.F. Malan and the Nationalists in late 1948 would mean that there could be no prospect of agreement on citizenship matters in a Commonwealth that included India and South Africa. Moreover, their experience of the UN in 1946 led Indians to deduce that Britain and the old Dominions stood against them. Yet the vast preponderance of India's four million residents in overseas colonies were not in the old Dominions. For them a Commonwealth based on common nationality would be a boon.

In February 1947 a British Commonwealth Conference on Nationality and Citizenship met in London to consider a draft British Nationality Bill. The basic principle of the Bill was that citizens of Commonwealth countries would, by dint of that citizenship, become British subjects. A 'combined citizenship of the United Kingdom and the Colonies' would be the 'gateway' through which the common status of British subjects would be conferred on the people of both the United Kingdom and the Colonies.[9] The Home Office intended the Conference to encourage the development of reciprocal relationships equivalent to a combined nationality and citizenship for all: 'In order to give practical value to the common status it would be desirable that, as far as practicable, equal treatment under its domestic law should be accorded by each member of the Commonwealth to citizens of other parts when residing in its territory'.[10] With not only South Africa but also some other Commonwealth countries in mind, it was 'appreciated that this ideal could not in practice be fully realized'. Certainly, too,

[8] The Nehru–Smuts correspondence for April–August 1947 appears in file L/E/9/1405, IOL.

[9] Tinker, *Separate and Unequal*, 359.

[10] Ibid., 361.

while Britain left open the door to unrestricted entry by 'British subjects' from abroad, it was apparent that few other members of the Commonwealth were prepared to follow her lead. Nevertheless, here was Britain seeking, in Hugh Tinker's words, 'to broaden the conception of citizenship so that the Commonwealth became much more of a mutual, reciprocal association'.[11] The intention harmonized with the wish that Nehru explained to Mountbatten a month later to base the Commonwealth relationship on common citizenship.

At the beginning of May 1947 Mountbatten sought advice from Monckton on whether it was possible, as Krishna Menon envisaged, to retain the link between the Indian Union and the countries owing allegiance to the King 'by developing the idea of a "common citizenship" so as to provide that a citizen of the Indian Union would owe allegiance first of all to his own State and further to His Majesty as head of the association'.[12] Monckton found difficulty in locating the reciprocity that seemed necessary to such an arrangement: in what sense would a UK citizen owe allegiance to the Indian Union? And would the old Dominions admit Indians to common citizenship with them? Thus 'the idea of common citizenship and the allegiance which might be derived therefrom cannot be lightly accepted', though it was 'worthy of ample consideration'.

Once a transfer of power on the basis of Dominion status was agreed there was no early need for such consideration. At the beginning of 1948, however, the questions of citizenship and the Commonwealth claimed the attention of Sir B.N. Rau, Constitutional Adviser to the Constituent Assembly. He had just visited the USA, Canada, Eire, and Britain for discussions with constitutional experts. It was not intended that the Indian constitution should legislate on either the Commonwealth connection or citizenship, but in London Noel-Baker emphasized to Rau the complete independence that Commonwealth members enjoyed in their foreign relations, whilst Irish officials urged upon him the necessity of a Nationality Act.[13] During Rau's absence a draft of the British

---

[11] Ibid., 363.
[12] Monckton to Mountbatten, 4 May 1947, *TP*, x, 308; see also x, 169.
[13] Rau, *India's Constitution in the Making* (1960), 304, 312.

Nationality Bill was supported by the Indian Ministry of External Affairs without comment. On 24 January he wrote a paper on 'India and the Commonwealth'.[14]

Rau argued that much had happened since the 'independent sovereign republic' resolution had been passed and 'India now has new and vast problems requiring the whole of her attention and there are many who feel that this is no time for leaving the Commonwealth and venturing into the unknown'. India also now had experience of dominionhood. The 'conception of the Commonwealth has been steadily growing, and has now reached a stage where even Republics may well be given a place therein.' The 'Dominions' had 'become, to all intents and purposes, sovereign States and may well be called "Sovereignties" '. The Statute of Westminster's definition of Dominions would need to be changed to emphasize that they were 'united' by 'allegiance' not to the Crown but to 'common ideals and by common citizenship'. Steps might be taken 'to establish a Commonwealth citizenship' under His Majesty's protection, so that the Crown would continue as 'the symbol of its unity'.

Rau's paper was seen by Mountbatten, Nehru, and some others in January. Erskine Crum wrote a minute that insisted that allegiance to the Crown was basic to Commonwealth membership and that common citizenship could not replace it.[15] However, in addition to those Dominions 'which have common ties of blood, culture and religion with His Majesty and with the United Kingdom' and owed allegiance to the King, Crum envisaged a second category of members having no such ties of allegiance. The latter would be linked by 'common citizenship, with every citizen entitled to His Majesty's protection and with the Crown acting as a symbol of unity'. He suggested that Mountbatten meet with Campbell-Johnson, Brockman, and himself to discuss the next step. He sent a copy of his paper to V.P. Menon. On 21 February Menon discussed the Rau and Crum papers with Christie and Shattock.[16] Christie and Menon agreed that Crum's division of the Commonwealth between white and coloured races was abhorrent.

---

[14] The paper exists in successive drafts. The draft of 24 Jan. 1948 appears in the Gordon Walker Papers, Churchill College, Cambridge: GNWR 1/7. Cf. the later and more developed version in Rau, op. cit., 342–51.

[15] Crum's minute to the Governor-General, 6 Feb. 1948, GNWR 1/7.

[16] A.C. Symon (UK High Commission) to Carter, 4 Mar. 1948, ibid.

They concurred with Rau's view that the term 'Dominion' might lapse and that republicanism was not inconsistent with Commonwealth membership. The oath of allegiance to the King was a real difficulty. Furthermore, because the Kashmir issue had alienated many Indians from the Commonwealth the whole matter should be deferred as long as possible. On 23 February Monckton, who happened to be in Delhi, explained to a meeting of Mountbatten's staff that the British Nationality Bill made it possible 'to be a subject of the King without owing allegiance in the citizenship sense': that is, the subject derived his citizenship from his nationality.[17]

On 25 February Mountbatten completed an '*aide-mémoire* for Mr Gordon Walker', another fortuitous visitor.[18] Mountbatten found his constitutional position 'irksome at times'.[19] He could 'no longer step in between London and Delhi'. His only link now was with the King, 'who strictly separates his various sovereignties'. Gordon Walker's visit afforded 'the physical opportunity . . . for renewing informal and indirect diplomacy' on the Commonwealth issue.[20] Mountbatten discussed the *aide-mémoire*, 'India and the Commonwealth', with Gordon Walker and Rau on 26 February. The paper offered 'tentative suggestions as to how the structure of the Commonwealth could perhaps be altered, particularly in nomenclature, to allow Asian countries to remain more easily associated with it'.[21] Following Rau, it argued for the supersession of the word 'Dominion' by, say, 'Sovereignty', the advantage of substituting the term 'Commonwealth citizen' for 'British subject' and that there was 'room for a "Republic" within the Commonwealth'. It would leave unstated the formal link with the Crown in any revised Commonwealth arrangements and, again following Rau, explore 'a new conception . . . based on common citizenship with every Commonwealth citizen entitled to His Majesty's protection, and the Crown continuing to be the symbol of the Commonwealth's unity'. On the day of this meeting India's draft constitution was published, reiterating the 'independent sovereign republic' objective in its preamble but noting that the question of India's relation to the Commonwealth remained to be decided.

[17] Campbell-Johnson, op. cit., 289.
[18] Ibid., 289–91.   [19] Ibid., 287.   [20] Ibid., 290.
[21] 'Aide Memoire for Mr Gordon Walker from the Governor-General of India: "India and the Commonwealth" ', 25 Feb. 1948, GNWR 1/7.

Mountbatten followed up the meeting with a flattering letter to Gordon Walker:

No visit has ever been so welcome to me personally, to my Government, and indeed to the whole of India, as yours, for as you know I consider it to have been literally providential at this critical moment.

I believe that you have it in your power to save India for the Commonwealth and to keep both India and Pakistan within the Anglo-US line up if you can only persuade the Prime Minister and Noel-Baker to follow the line we agreed upon.[22]

On 5 March Gordon Walker replied from London that he was 'wholeheartedly in agreement' with the object of keeping India in the Commonwealth and had not 'left anything undone that I could properly do'.[23] Mountbatten pursued him with some impatience for news of HMG's reactions. On his return home Gordon Walker had told Attlee of the Delhi discussion and shown him the memorandum.[24] He was instructed to reply 'in a rather non-committal way'.[25] This was largely because Attlee had now taken the step of writing personally and at length to Nehru. He approved the legal evaluation of the 'Commonwealth citizenship' concept but declined 'to fish for an official request from India' to consider it.

The personal appeal that Attlee sent to Nehru on 11 March was an impressive attempt to retain India's membership of the Commonwealth through the Crown link. He had shown it in advance to only the King and Cripps:

My dear Nehru,

I have observed that the Indian Constituent Assembly has made great progress in formulating a constitution for India. The question will naturally arise as to the relationship between India and the British Commonwealth. I believe that the association of a number of Nations in the Commonwealth is not only a great advantage to every one of the constituent States, but is an important factor in building up a peaceful world. . . . The British Commonwealth as we know it today has evolved not by design or by the application of theories of the interrelation of States,

---

[22] Mountbatten to Gordon Walker, 27 Feb. 1948, ibid. See also Brockman to Gordon Walker, 7 Mar. 1948, ibid.

[23] Ibid.

[24] Gordon Walker to Mountbatten, 16 Mar. 1948, ibid.

[25] Minute by Gordon Walker, 16 Mar. 1948, ibid.

but from the application of democratic principles of self government and from the practical needs of the age. . . . The advent into the Commonwealth of countries such as India and Ceylon opens a new era. I have myself always regarded the Commonwealth and Empire as a collection of nations all moving to a common goal of self government and equal status, though necessarily at a different rate in accordance with their individual histories and internal conditions. It has been a matter of pride to me that during my Premiership in Great Britain the family circle should have been enlarged by the coming of age, so to speak, of the nations in Asia. The British Commonwealth of Nations is now in effect the Commonwealth of British and Asiatic nations. It may well be that the title should be changed, but it is my hope that the reality may remain. . . . I have examined the question of what are the links which bind together the various peoples of the Commonwealth. They are mostly intangible. In some instances a common racial background, in others historical association, in others common economic interests, but more generally they are, I think, rather moral than economic. Adherence to certain absolute values, faith in democratic institutions, belief in the rule of law and acceptance of the need for toleration. All these things make up together a 'way of life' which with many local differences yet give a general sense of community.

But apart from these intangibles there is only one link, the Crown. The common allegiance to the Crown is the link within which all kinds of association for mutual advantage are possible; without it they are more difficult to establish. If one seeks to go beyond this and to draft any form of constitutional relationship one finds oneself in very great difficulties.

The point, therefore, which I would like you to consider is whether there is any real objection to the continuance of India in the British Commonwealth owing to the common allegiance to the Crown.[26]

Nehru replied on 18 April:

My Dear Attlee,

. . . The question you have raised is important and vital for the future of India and will have to be decided ultimately by the Constituent Assembly.

2. I am, therefore, not attempting an answer at this stage. You will appreciate that strong views are held by various groups and individuals on this subject. For my part I have deliberately tried to delay any decision so that we might be able to consider the question as dispassionately as possible and without the heavy legacy of the past.

3. I agree with you in much that you say and I can assure you that it is my desire and the desire of many of my colleagues that the association of India with the United Kingdom and the British Commonwealth of Nations

[26] PREM 8/820.

should be close and intimate. I am more interested in real friendship and co-operation between these countries than merely in a formal link which does not carry with it that friendly co-operation. The problem before us, therefore, is this close psychological as well as other relationships. I am myself not clear in my own mind what the best way would be to ensure this. I have been hoping that the course of events would help in clearing the atmosphere to enable us to decide the question dispassionately and objectively.

4. If anyone had asked this question of us about a year ago, I have little doubt what the answer would have been, and this answer would have been almost unanimous. The mere fact that another opinion is held now by many persons indicates the change that has come over the situation. This change has undoubtedly been due to the change in British policy in regard to India and more particularly to the presence and activities of our present Governor-General. Indeed it is remarkable what Lord Mountbatten, and may I add Lady Mountbatten also, have done to remove many of the old causes of distrust and bitterness between India and England. I have often wondered what the history of India would have been if they had come a year earlier. I imagine it would have been very different and that we might well have avoided many of the perils and disasters that we have had to face. It is with exceeding regret that we shall part with Lord and Lady Mountbatten when they go away in June next.

5. You are aware that the Constituent Assembly of India has been drafting a constitution and has now reached a stage when the final draft will be considered. Right at the beginning of its existence the Constituent Assembly laid down certain objectives. It stated that the constitution was going to be for an Independent Sovereign Republic. Whether we use those exact words or not will be decided later; but in any event the constitution as drafted had to follow this direction. Even then, however, we made it clear that the question of India's relation with the United Kingdom and the British Commonwealth will be considered separately. We were anxious not to come to any hurried decision and we hoped that the lapse of time would make it easier to decide. That decision was bound to be influenced by the events which preceded it.[27]

On 14 May Attlee acknowledged Nehru's inability to give 'any definite answer at the present time' and intimated that his own purpose had been to offer assurance that the Commonwealth was 'a very comprehensive and flexible association'.[28] He sought to keep open 'an informal exchange' to avoid the 'rigid positions' that emerged 'once these matters get into the hands of the constitutional

---

[27] Ibid.   [28] Ibid.

lawyers'. The correspondence consolidated a link between Prime Ministers that was to be fruitful when they met at the London conference.

The fact that the correspondence extended over two months is explained largely by its strictly personal character. Attlee's letter was conveyed by the Head of Chancery, and the subsequent exchange through Krishna Menon by hand. The High Commission in Delhi was denied sight or copy of Attlee's letter, which was not officially recorded. Mountbatten complained to Ismay of being bypassed:

As you know, I am doing my best, behind the scenes, to see that the Indian leaders fully realise the advantages which will accrue to their country by continued association with the Commonwealth after the new Constitution comes in. I had been under the impression that I was ploughing a lonely furrow in this, as no word had come through from London for some time. Then suddenly a few days ago Nehru astounded me by showing me a copy of a letter he had received over a month previously from Attlee on the same subject. . . . Of course I realize the constitutional snags to my having been sent a copy. . . . Nehru has shown me his reply—not too discouraging and Patel has said that as soon as he is fit again (he has been *hors de combat* after a heart attack) he will see to it that India remains in!!![29]

Ismay explained that no one at the CRO had been consulted and only Carter had seen Attlee's letter after it had been sent.[30]

While Attlee looked forward to a London meeting with Nehru later in the year the Indian initiative on the basis of citizenship continued to develop. In mid-March Rau told Shone that while India was not about to reach a decision on the Commonwealth the 'nexus' of the new relationship was the evolution of a 'common citizenship'.[31] He raised with Shone and Gordon Walker the question of changing the term 'British subject' in the British Nationality Bill.[32] On 30 March Krishna Menon wrote to Attlee that 'The Government of India request that the use of this term may be reconsidered with a view to replacing it by some such term as Citizen of the Commonwealth or Commonwealth Citizen'.[33] Parliamentary Counsel advised that

[29] Mountbatten to Ismay, 20 Apr. 1948, Ismay Papers, III/7/30a.
[30] Ismay to Mountbatten, 29 Apr. 1948, ibid., III/7/35.
[31] Tinker, *Separate and Unequal*, 372.
[32] Ibid.   [33] PREM 8/812.

'British subject' could not be abandoned entirely but that 'citizen of the British Commonwealth of Nations' might be inserted as an alternative.[34] Gordon Walker was enthusiastic for the change, which was 'perhaps a question of saving the Commonwealth'.[35] Both he and Noel-Baker chose the shorter 'Commonwealth citizen', and the latter advised Attlee that this concession to India 'may well have a really important effect on their readiness to remain inside the British Commonwealth'.[36] In April the Dominions were sounded and the alternative nomenclature to describe citizenship was adopted. The alternative terms 'British subject' and 'Commonwealth citizen' were incorporated in the Nationality Act when it came into operation on 1 January 1949.[37]

Rau enlarged his January paper on 'India and the Commonwealth' for an address in New Delhi in April.[38] This public advocacy by the Constitutional Adviser to the Constituent Assembly of Commonwealth membership on the basis of common citizenship must surely indicate the direction of official policy, though Rau insisted that the opinions were 'entirely personal'. At an International Conference of the Legal Profession at the Hague in August he spoke on 'Citizenship in the Commonwealth of Nations'.[39] He praised the Nationality Act and its potentialities, hoping that the Commonwealth would strive for the ideal of 'a common citizenship with no arbitrary discrimination between the citizens of one unit and those of another'.

Rau was now developing his ideas in one direction that alarmed Gordon Walker. He envisaged the possibility of the British Nationality Bill being extended to provide Commonwealth citizenship not only to the nationals of members but also to those of 'associate states'.[40] Members but not associates would owe allegiance to the Crown, so that instead of Commonwealth citizens being united by a common allegiance they would be divided as nationals of two classes of states. Rau's thought was moving towards Stent's concept of a British Commonwealth and

---

[34] Noel-Baker to Attlee, 9 Apr. 1948, ibid.
[35] Cited in Tinker, *Separate and Unequal*, 373.
[36] Noel-Baker to Attlee, 9 Apr. 1948, loc. cit.
[37] See Tinker, *Separate and Unequal*, 374–82.
[38] Address to Indian Council of World Affairs, in Ministry of External Affairs, GOI, File 85-4/48-OS III, 1948, NAI. This is essentially the version that appears in Rau, op. cit., 342–51.
[39] Ibid., 334–41.   [40] Ibid., 339.

Associated States. Gordon Walker had noted in his diary for 1 June that 'things are not going so well', for the Cabinet's Commonwealth Relations Committee had the previous day asked the Official Committee to examine the British and Associated Nations concept.[41] It had also questioned dropping the word 'British' from the title of the Commonwealth as the Officials had proposed. HMG and Rau seemed thus to be converging towards a 'two-tier Commonwealth'. Gordon Walker went to see Mountbatten and sent him a note on 'Changes in the Conception of the Commonwealth', with a request that he should draw 'these ideas to the attention of people of importance in India'.[42]

Gordon Walker argued for adopting the title 'Commonwealth' without the adjective 'British', which would be in line with the acceptance of the term 'Commonwealth citizen'. Emphasis should be placed upon 'common citizenship', which would preserve the link with the Crown if the notion of 'association' were dropped. The Crown would provide continuity and 'The King may well come to be conceived of as head of the Commonwealth as well as King of each Commonwealth nation'. Some new royal style, 'Supreme Head of the Commonwealth' and King of the several member nations, might develop. If the title were changed it was 'essential to preserve the unity of the Crown and . . . at all costs . . . something of the effect of "Supreme Head" ' must be retained. There was nothing new in any of Gordon Walker's points, which had appeared in the Official Committee's third report of 21 May. He was later to claim that the idea of the Crown's acceptance as Supreme Head of the Commonwealth was first expressed in his 20 July note for Mountbatten.[43] It was, in fact, prominent earlier in the Official Committee's thinking as expressed by Brook.

Mountbatten arranged for Brockman to write to Rau (and send a copy to Menon) on the lines suggested by Gordon Walker.[44] However, Brockman's letter made no mention of the 'Supreme Head of the Commonwealth' idea. It warned of the dangers of the

[41] Diary fragment for 1 June 1948, GNWR 1/7; minutes of second meeting of CR Cttee of Cabinet, 31 May 1948, CAB 134/118. See also Gordon Walker's 'Note on Stent's Memorandum', 15 Mar. 1948, GNWR 1/7.

[42] Gordon Walker to Mountbatten, 20 July 1948, encl. 'Change in the Conception of the Commonwealth', 20 July 1948, GNWR 1/7.

[43] Gordon Walker, *The Commonwealth* (1962), 183.

[44] Mountbatten to Gordon Walker, 22 July 1948; Brockman to Gordon Walker, 27 July 1948, encl. Brockman to Rau, 27 July 1948; GNWR 1/7.

Associated Nations concept producing two levels of members, 'respectively of white and coloured nations'. It alluded to the move to refer simply to the 'Commonwealth'. It gave credit to Rau for the 'original suggestion of common citizenship', which would be added to 'the link of the Crown' to produce 'a dual link throughout the Commonwealth'. Some members might emphasize the Crown link, others common citizenship. Changes 'in the King's title and position in the Commonwealth' were left for future consideration. The 'main thing' was 'Commonwealth unity', which 'thought in Whitehall' envisaged being best accomplished without the categorization of British and non-British members. It can not have been coincidental that Brockman's letter was sent on the very day that the Cabinet Committee rejected the idea of Associated Nations. Menon's cable to Mountbatten in early October, indicating Congress support for Commonwealth membership on the basis of common citizenship, was thus the consequence of an Indian initiative nurtured and tended by the Governor-General himself and the Under-Secretary of State whom he inspired.

But if common citizenship was the form of the Indian initiative, what substance did V.P. Menon and the Congress expect of the Commonwealth relationship? In April 1947 Nehru had been so adamant, saying that 'Under no conceivable circumstances is India going to remain in the British Commonwealth, whatever the consequences. This is not a question for me to decide or for any few of us to decide. Any attempt to remain in the Commonwealth will sweep away those who propose it and might bring about major trouble in India.'[45] It is arguable that Nehru calculated at that time upon Pakistan's collapse, and that its survival made India's withdrawal from the Commonwealth unwise. It is said that Nehru was shown and expressed full agreement with a pro-Commonwealth argument that Sir Tej Sapru expressed in a letter to the Governor of Bombay in April 1948:

If you cut off connection altogether with England and Pakistan continues to be like a dominion and if trouble arises in future between Hindustan and Pakistan, why should you blame the British if they openly render military help to Pakistan? The relations between the two dominions of Hindustan

[45] Nehru to Baldev Singh, 14 Apr. 1947, Gopal (ed.), *Selected Works of Jawaharlal Nehru* (1984), ii, 370–1.

and Pakistan are by no means very pleasant at present. They may easily become worse. . . . I am, therefore, writing to you frankly that whatever form of government may be established you must not go out of the British Commonwealth of Nations at least for some time to come.[46]

Professor Mansergh believes that the argument 'may well have been decisive'.[47] Mountbatten had used it with success in April 1947 when he was working through Krishna Menon and Baldev Singh to persuade Nehru to accept dominionhood. The Kashmir war rammed the point home and in October 1948 Liaquat was to urge the need for the Commonwealth to go beyond mere consultation on foreign policy and tackle the Kashmir problem. The importance of India's presence to ensure that he did not get his way can scarcely be underestimated. Krishna Menon questioned Nehru about the point in December 1948 but received no reply.[48]

It must also be said, as Nehru had acknowledged to Attlee, that at the level of personal relationships British diplomacy had transformed Indian attitudes towards an enduring connection with Britain. Indian leaders were unanimous in ascribing much of the credit for the change to the Mountbattens. At the end of their fifteen months in India Nehru wrote to Cripps that they 'left us in quite a blaze of popularity—a remarkable feat'.[49] Patel and Rajaji were laudatory. Moon's judgement was that the Mountbattens were 'wonderfully popular. No sane man should belittle their achievement.'[50] Mountbatten's contrivance of the Dominion status medium for the transfer of power was worked through such intermediaries as Krishna Menon, V.P. Menon and Baldev Singh, who thereby felt a responsibility for its operation. Short viewed the latter two, together with the Mountbattens, as the key workers for India's retention in the Commonwealth.[51] Such open relationships as those disclosed by Cripps's personal correspondence with Indians—Nehru, Patel, Rajaji, Prasad, Sudhir Ghosh, Birla, Krishna—also nourished goodwill. Although from November 1947 he was

[46] Sapru to Governor of Bombay and to Rajaji, 19 Apr. 1948, cited in Mansergh, *Commonwealth Experience*, ii, 148.
[47] Ibid., 147.
[48] Menon to Nehru, 27 Dec. 1948, cited in Brecher, 'India's Decision to Remain in the Commonwealth', *Journal of Commonwealth and Comparative Politics*, 12 (1975), 62–90, p. 75; Nehru to Menon, 12 Jan. 1949, Das, *Patel's Correspondence*, viii, 1–2.
[49] Nehru to Cripps, 1 July 1948, CAB 127/143.
[50] Moon to Short, 4 Mar. 1948, Short Papers, 189/22.
[51] Short to H.V. Hodson, 5 Apr. 1948, ibid., 21.

Chancellor of the Exchequer tending a very sick economy, Cripps always found time for his Indian correspondence. Though Attlee did not at first include him in the Commonwealth Relations Committee, once it began to meet he was an indispensable member. He was also active in India's interest on the Commonwealth Affairs Committee. Attlee was himself patience personified as he nurtured relations with the new Dominion, ever accessible to Krishna Menon. By September 1948 Krishna, the one-time rabid anti-imperialist, was an Anglophile. V.P. Menon was 'astonished' at his 'remarkable change in attitude to the British'.[52] He was 'one of the UK's strongest protagonists and favoured the continuance of the Commonwealth connection'. He had told V.P. Menon that the British were 'the very quintessence of all that a nation should be' and he had the highest admiration for Attlee and Bevin.

Personal relationships helped Britain to weather the diplomatic storms that blew up over Kashmir, the officers in the Pakistan Army, and civil rights in South Africa, but ultimately national interests must be decisive. There were large areas of mutuality. Keynes's adage that the massive debtor is master of his creditor is apposite. India had a vested interest in the value of sterling. The Beaverbrook press was to editorialize unworthily under the headline, 'Why did India want to stay in?'

. . . the Empire connection suits the Indians. Analyse what it means to them. Take first the Sterling Balances—about £700 million—which Great Britain is said to owe for defending India against the Japs. The debt, of course, is grossly inflated, as vast sums were made by Indian war-profiteers which will burden the British taxpayer for years and years . . . Sir Stafford Cripps, who loves India, has accepted the sterling debts at their inflated face value. So now valuable exports that could be earning dollars in Canada go to India in repayment of sterling debts. But suppose India had left the Empire. Then there would have been a still stronger case than now exists for revising these debts. Or they might even have been frozen until the dollar problem is solved. Mr Nehru could not afford that. The whole Indian economy might collapse if the support of the Sterling Debts were withdrawn.[53]

Both sides in fact benefited from the sterling area, which while not coterminous with the Commonwealth was most likely to retain

---

[52] Shattock to Rumbold, 14 Sept. 1948, loc. cit.
[53] *Daily Express*, 28 Apr. 1949.

India if she remained in the Commonwealth. At Independence the balances stood at £1,160m., reduced to £960m. for India in July 1948 by offsets for military stores left behind and provisions for the payment of pensioners of the Raj.[54] For 1947 £35m. was released, of which £15m. was expected to be spent in dollars, the rest on sterling imports from the UK and Australia.[55] In consequence of sterling's collapse during the August 1947 convertibility crisis sterling and dollar releases were negotiated periodically. In January 1948 the agreed release for six months was £18m. (£10m. of it in dollars). When India exceeded her dollar quota she was treated gently. In a memorandum of June 1948 Cripps quoted from an official study: 'It should be remembered that the attempt to impose excessive economy upon some Dominions might set up strong pressures towards their leaving the sterling area'.[56] In July 1948 a three-year agreement was reached. There would be no releases for a year but £40m. would be made available in each of the next two years, and anticipatory drawings might be made if necessary. A dollar ration was prescribed. Nehru wrote to Cripps that many in his Cabinet were 'not at all happy' at the size of sterling releases but he was cheered by hopes of further advances in case of difficulty in the third year.[57] The Cabinet accepted Britain's terms 'after careful consideration of all the factors'. He believed that the cordial spirit of the sterling negotiations would 'result in promoting further good-will between India and England'. During a severe rice shortage in September the British Cabinet accepted Cripps's advice to make 'every effort' to supply India from non-dollar sources and to press Australia to accelerate shipments of wheat and flour; but India was also allowed to draw upon dollar area imports.[58] Towards the end of the year Britain's gold and dollar trading deficit rose sharply, mainly because of heavy drawings by India and seasonal factors.[59]

[54] See the recent analyses of Tomlinson, 'Indo-British Relations in the Post-Colonial Era: The Sterling Balances Negotiations, 1947–49', *Journal of Imperial and Commonwealth History*, 13 (1985), 142–62; A.I. Singh, 'Economic Consequences of India's Position in the Commonwealth: The Official British Thinking in 1949', *Indo-British Review*, 9 (1984), 106–11; and P.S. Gupta, 'Imperialism and the Labour Government of 1945–51', in Winter (ed.), *The Working Class in Modern British History* (1983), 99–124.
[55] CM 70(47)7, 7 Aug. 1947, CAB 128/10.
[56] Memo. of 23 June 1948, CP(48)161, CAB 129/28.
[57] Nehru to Cripps, 3 July 1948, CAB 127/143.
[58] CM 59(48)2, 10 Sept. 1948, CAB 128/13.
[59] CM 79(48)6, 9 Dec. 1948, ibid.

Patel wrote to Cripps, 'We have all realized how helpful your attitude was in regard to the Sterling Balances and are grateful for your assistance'.[60] In December 1947 Prasad had expressed gratitude to Cripps for Britain's willingness to make agricultural machinery available and help India grow more food.[61] Within the sterling area India walked in locked step with Britain. Dollar earnings from say, Malayan rubber, might serve India's need for hard currency. At loggerheads, Britain and India might resort to extreme measures: from the one side the balances might be blocked; from the other the sterling pensions might be stopped, or British private investments (estimated at between £150m. and £600m.) might be confiscated. If India cut its link with sterling Britain's Indian imports of tea and raw materials would have to be purchased with scarce dollars; and whereas India might obtain elsewhere the commodities that it bought from Britain the same was not true of scarce capital goods.[62]

Beyond currency conventions lay trading preferences. The *Daily Express* continued its diatribe:

After sterling debts, what next? Why, Imperial Preferences. Valuable as these are for India today, they will be much more precious in a year or two when world primary producers are competing vigorously for the profitable British market.

Mr Nehru and his wealthy manufacturer and landowner supporters look ahead to the time when the Imperial Preferences alone will make it worth while for India to stay in the Empire.[63]

Again there was impressive mutuality.[64] In 1948 51 per cent of India's exports went to the Commonwealth, with Britain taking 45 per cent of the Commonwealth total. Thus almost a quarter of India's exports were to Britain, which accorded tariff preferences to more than half of them. In 1946 India was Britain's largest market and in 1948 took 6 per cent (worth £96.5m.) of her total exports.

---

[60] Patel to Cripps, 14 Sept. 1948, CAB 127/113.

[61] Prasad to Cripps, 8 Dec. 1947, ibid.

[62] Tomlinson, op. cit., 155. Despite such short-term advantages to Britain of India's membership of the sterling area Tomlinson finds 'a strong flavour of uninterestedness on London's part' (p. 158). He contrasts it with London's interest in both pre-war India and the post-war development of the Colonies.

[63] Loc. cit.

[64] See Tomlinson, op. cit.; A.I. Singh, op. cit.; Murti, *India in the Commonwealth* (1953), 60–63.

About 30 per cent of them enjoyed preferences averaging 12–15 per cent (most notably cotton piece goods, cycles, motor vehicles, chemicals, and electrical equipment). In the post-war sellers' market for industrial products this was to India's advantage. In 1948 almost half of India's total imports came from the Commonwealth. Britain's reciprocal advantage was apparent not only in trade preferences but from the favourable treatment that resident companies and individuals enjoyed. Invisible earnings from this source were put at £20m. in 1948. Maurice Zinkin's unofficial estimate of Britain's earnings from shipping for the Indian trade in 1948 was £40–50m.[65] The figure was probably 'on the high side' but the returns may well have exceeded the total dollar earnings of all Malayan commodities.

In February 1948 General Bucher and H.M. Patel led a supply mission to London, seeking defence supplies and services—stores and equipment for the army and the police, petroleum products, technical personnel for ordnance factories, scientific advice in research and development. At Mountbatten's instance Attlee saw the mission together with Krishna and gave it his blessing.[66] In 1948–9 India spent R53,966,000 in England for defence services.[67] The Defence Minister, Baldev Singh, whom Major Short knew as 'a firm believer in the Commonwealth and in India staying in it', told the Congress Working Committee in September 1948 that for defence 'the only possible tie for India was with the UK'.[68] An appreciation of 'Economic Co-operation within the Commonwealth' that the Ministry of External Affairs made in August found no reason for India to leave the Commonwealth.[69] As Nehru was to tell the Constituent Assembly, while there may be sentiment in favour of 'complete separation from Britain . . . the fact is that in industrial and other matters we need considerable help'.[70]

Yet the main reason for India's attraction to the Commonwealth in 1948 was the world-wide challenge of Communism and the

65 Zinkin to C.L. Bruce, 14 Apr. 1949, CAB 127/154.

66 PREM 8/822.

67 Murti, op. cit., 63.

68 Short to A.V. Alexander, 11 Apr. 1948, Alexander Papers; encl. to Shattock to Rumbold, 14 Sept. 1948, CAB 134/118.

69 Ministry of External Affairs and Commonwealth Relations, GOI, File 9 (52)-UN I/48, NAI.

70 'On Commonwealth: 1948', n.d., unsigned, but evidently notes on Nehru's address to CA in Nov./Dec. 1948, AICC Papers, File 8 (part 2), 1948.

closing of ranks in the West to face it. To an unusual degree India's foreign policy was the work of its Prime Minister. Until Independence Nehru's essential concern was anti-colonialism, spiced with a dash of theoretical Marxism. His colours as an anti-imperialist looking forward to a free Asia under Indian inspiration or leadership were flown in February 1947 when Delhi played host to the impressive conference of Asian nations. Britain's rapid decolonization of the subcontinent, Ceylon, and Burma somewhat weakened the perfidious Albion emphasis of his anti-imperialism though he remained a critic of the Malayan remnants of the Empire, of British neutrality in Indo-China, and sympathy and moral support for the Dutch in Indonesia. In large measure Bevin's continuing defence of the European empires in South East Asia flowed from his need for a European alliance against the USSR. America's announcement of Marshall Aid to Europe in July 1947 was followed in October by the establishment of the Communist Information Bureau in Belgrade to co-ordinate the activities of the Communist parties in Europe generally.

The European events that followed Bevin's realization of Western Union early in 1948 alienated the sympathies of Indian freedom fighters from the Cominform. On 25 February the Communists seized power in Czechoslovakia, just two weeks after India had named Czechoslovakia as her nominee on the Security Council's commission on her dispute with Pakistan. Diplomacy in Europe and Asia was evidently of a piece. Mrs Pandit found her ambassadorship to Moscow 'extremely irksome' and told Noel-Baker of 'her complete disillusionment with the Soviet Union, the sharp change in the treatment which they had given her after February last'.[71] Russia refused to recognize Ceylon as independent of Britain, opposing her entry to the UN, and Nehru observed that Russia believed 'that we still continue to be camp-followers of the British'.[72] In June, when Russia blockaded Berlin, Bevin called all High Commissioners to his room and appealed for aeroplanes from the Dominions to help with the airlift. The Russians, he said grimly, 'think our Government is weak but this time we're sticking. . . . No one has stood up since the war to Russia: we are

[71] Noel-Baker's record of conversation with Mrs Pandit, beginning of October 1948, CAB 21/1808. See also, Pandit, *The Scope of Happiness: A Personal Memoir* (1979), 236–45.
[72] Nehru to Menon, cited in Gopal, *Nehru*, ii, 45.

going to stand up now. . . . We must stick in Berlin. Otherwise there will be a complete collapse in W[estern] Europe.'[73] The airlift is said to have been first suggested by Noel-Baker, and the echo of India's airborne rescue of Srinagar from invasion was clear.[74] India sent no planes to Berlin but it is apparent from Nehru's comments to a senior British diplomat that he profoundly disapproved of Russian methods.[75]

For Nehru the way to fight Communism in Asia was by recognizing the legitimacy of nationalist values and raising living standards. Yet in 1948 the difficulty of relying wholly upon such means became patent. In February 1948 Calcutta was host to a Conference of the World Federation of Democratic Youth, which British Intelligence believed was related to Cominform and intended to stimulate the Communist insurrections that now broke out in South East Asia.[76] Scholars dispute the linkage but certainly the Calcutta conference and the almost simultaneous Congress of the Indian Communist Party were occasions for the propagation of Soviet doctrine. Communist insurrections occurred in Burma (March), Malaya (June), the Philippines (August), and Indonesia (September). The long French war against the Democratic Republic of Vietnam had begun in 1946. The British were concerned at the implications of the looming Communist takeover in China for Hong Kong and, with their large Chinese minorities, Malaya and Singapore. V.P. Menon's cable to Mountbatten on the eve of the Commonwealth Conference concluded:

One last word. We are finding the resistance of the Communists in Warangal and Nalgonda more determined than even I had anticipated. In Panditji's absence I intend to take all powers to liquidate them as effectively and rapidly as possible. There is also Communist infiltration from Burma into Assam. In this case I propose to ask for a meeting of the Defence Committee of the Cabinet on October 13th, and will recommend that special powers should be taken by Government to deal with this menace.[77]

[73] Gordon Walker's diary fragment, 28 June 1948, GNWR 1/7.

[74] Harris, *Attlee*, 312.

[75] Strang's report, 27 Feb. 1949, CP(49)67; Lord Strang, *Home and Abroad* (1956), 242.

[76] For the beginnings of the Cold War in Asia, see Nagai and Iriye, *The Origins of the Cold War in Asia* (1977), esp. chs. by D.C. Watt, 'Britain and the Cold War in the Far East, 1945–58', and Tanigawa Yoshihiko, 'The Cominform and Southeast Asia'; D.C. Watt, *Succeeding John Bull: America in Britain's Place, 1900–1975* (1984).

[77] Loc. cit.

Next month three battalions of Indian infantry and two of Hyderabad's State forces were proving insufficient to clear Nalgonda and Warangal districts of Communists.[78] At the end of the year Nehru wrote to Cripps that 'Communist subversive propaganda has been in evidence in India too during this year and has given us some trouble'.[79] Nye reported that harsh measures had been taken and that there were thousands of Communists in gaol.[80]

In September 1948 Madam Pandit told the CWC that

> close and friendly relations must be maintained with the UK. . . . It was impossible for India to go into the Russian camp; the Americans would use dollars and demand too much of a *quid pro quo*; consequently the UK and Commonwealth countries . . . who were reasonable and with whom strong ties already existed were the only group with which India could be closely associated.[81]

At the start of the London conference Noel-Baker learnt from Bajpai that Nehru had very recently 'begun to see that the Commonwealth and Western Union might form a middle Bloc, both geographically and politically, between the USA and Russia, and that it might be used to preserve the peace'.[82] Bajpai hoped that the conference 'would confirm Pandit Nehru in this view'. Like his sister Nehru was mistrustful of the Americans. He had been bitterly disappointed with the United States' treatment of his Kashmir reference to the UN. In February Mountbatten reported that 'high circles in India' believed that President Truman was regretting the bitterness which his actions at the UN over the partition of Palestine had caused among the Arab and Muslim nations of the Middle East, and was anxiously looking for a means to placate them in Kashmir.[83] Nehru thought it 'astonishing how naïve the Americans are in their foreign policy' and suspected them of expansionism by dollar diplomacy.

By personal relations and mutual economic interests carefully nourished, and by considerations of *realpolitik*, India was brought to the brink of a new Commonwealth by October 1948. Nehru's visit

---

[78] US Chargé in India to Secretary of State, 29 Nov. 1948, *FRUS*, 1948, v, 464–5.
[79] Nehru to Cripps, 17/18 Dec. 1948, CAB 127/143.
[80] Nye to Cripps, 20 Dec. 1948, ibid.
[81] Shattock to Rumbold, 14 Sept. 1948, loc. cit. Mrs Pandit was referring to Canada, Australia, and New Zealand.
[82] Noel-Baker note on conversation with Bajpai, 13 Oct. 1948, PREM 8/1008.
[83] Mountbatten to Gordon Walker, 27 Feb. 1948, GNWR 1/7.

to London would be important. This was his first Commonwealth Prime Ministers' Conference, indeed his first exposure to Europe since the brief abortive London talks of December 1946. The Conference would have an importance beyond its severely practical agenda items: defence, security, and economic development.[84] Attlee would rise to the 'historic occasion' of the first attendance of the South Asian Dominions, now united with the old Dominions 'by a common faith in democracy and freedom' for 'the establishment of peace and the building up of the prosperity of our peoples'.[85] Nehru, now a world statesman, could scarcely be immune to the appeal at that stage of the Cold War. Yet a formula to unite the old and new Dominions and Britain remained to be found.

Nehru arrived in London on Wednesday 6 October and spent the weekend (9–10th) with the Mountbattens at Broadlands. Cripps joined them on the Sunday morning and left after tea. Bajpai told Noel-Baker 'as top secret . . . what Pandit Nehru had said' to him when he returned to London:

India had now accepted the common citizenship plan of our British Nationality Act. Common citizenship implied allegiance to the King; an elected President of India would therefore owe such allegiance, and it would be as a man owing such allegiance that he would fulfil the functions, both internal and external, now carried out by the Governor-General.[86]

Attlee saw Nehru, together with Lord Jowitt, on the Thursday and noted:

It was obvious that Mr Nehru is extremely keen to continue in association, but is hampered by previous declarations as to the objective of India being a free sovereign independent republic. We explored the question of citizenship, and the Lord Chancellor pointed out the position under the recent Act. There was general agreement that this provided a useful link. We further discussed the point that the President of the Republic might also be The King's representative. The Lord Chancellor put up the suggestion that he might be a member of the Privy Council which would be an additional link. We also explored the possibility of having a Privy Council

---

[84] For preparations on these items, see CAB 21/1805–8, 1811.

[85] Attlee's broadcast of 11 Oct. 1948, Attlee Papers, 74/25.

[86] Record of conversation between Secretary of State and Bajpai, 13 Oct. 1948, PREM 8/1008.

in India, and also of continuing the jurisdiction of the Judicial Committee of the Privy Council. Mr Nehru is going to Paris and will see Sir B. Rau with a view to his coming over for talks on these constitutional points with the Lord Chancellor. I regarded the results of the meeting as most encouraging.[87]

A week later Rau had returned from Paris, where the UN was in session, and joined a committee appointed and chaired by the Lord Chancellor to evaluate common citizenship as a basis of Commonwealth membership.

Nehru's initiative had thus led Attlee to set in train a juristic analysis of the Commonwealth relationship. A major British concern was that any change occasioned by India's intended republicanism should preserve the Commonwealth's status in international law. The validity of Commonwealth trade preferences rested upon their immunity to challenges under the Most Favoured Nation convention. An MFN clause was commonly included in treaties between foreign nations, so that each of the signatories automatically received the benefit of any more favourable treatment that the other might extend to a third nation. As Commonwealth nations were not foreign to each other their preferences could not be claimed by third parties. Jowitt's committee believed that a sound basis for resisting an MFN challenge would be provided as between Britain and India if the British Nationality Act were complemented by a reciprocal Indian act.[88] However, in the old Dominions the rights of Commonwealth citizens were so limited (indeed South Africa denied the franchise to resident Indians) that the committee was 'not confident' that a similar basis existed. The only *watertight* legal foundation was that India's new constitution should remain silent upon the Independence Act's conferment of Dominion status, while both Britain and India reaffirmed India's recognition of the King's sovereignty. Rau referred the conclusion to Nehru and reported back: such an affirmation was 'politically impossible' for India.[89] The committee now looked for 'any device by which the association of the Crown and the link of the Crown

[87] Memo. by PM on meeting with PM of India and Lord Chancellor, 14 Oct. 1948, CAB 127/115.

[88] Note of discussion on 21 Oct. of Lord Chancellor's cttee on Indian constitutional issues, ibid. The cttee comprised Rau, Laithwaite, the Solicitor-General, and two Law Officers.

[89] Minute by Laithwaite on further discussions of the cttee on 21 Oct. 1948, ibid.

with India could be maintained'. It took up the possibilities previously approved by Brook, finding 'a sufficient link' in the Irish precedent of the King accrediting India's ambassadors and attraction in 'The King as Head of the Commonwealth'. The latter basis would be strengthened if the King performed functions such as convening Commonwealth conferences or conferring Commonwealth honours. What seemed quite clear was that unless India affirmed 'an element of allegiance' no legal support could be provided by claiming 'an element of allegiance to The King through the link of Commonwealth citizenship'.

These unpromising conclusions were discussed at Broadlands, where Nehru was again a weekend guest (23–24 October), and Cripps a Sunday tripper. Cripps doodled with draft points that might be aggregated as a basis for the membership of the Indian republic. On the Monday Rau explored the main points with Jowitt.[90] India would enact the reciprocal of the British Nationality Act. India's position on allegiance was that under her constitution the King would 'not exercise any of the functions of sovereignty' but his sovereignty would not be extinguished. Rau was proposing, *ex silentio*, the subtle concept of 'dormant sovereignty', which, as it was not expunged, was in theory capable of revival. He then drew the inference that the path to India's republicanism was the Independence Act and the King's non-exercise of his powers. Cripps had suggested that India might acknowledge the King as the 'Fount of Honour' in the Commonwealth, and Jowitt confirmed that Commonwealth honours might give useful 'signs of life' to the King's dormant sovereignty. A further point was that India's Nationality Act might profitably affirm India's membership. This was to build upon a thought that Mackenzie King had put to both Nehru and Jowitt from his sick bed. He had noted: 'I gave [Nehru] my views on the emphasis being placed on Community of Free Nations, rather than having emphasis on the Crown which would almost certainly be drawn into controversy if it were made the main issue. He saw the point at once and said he regarded it as quite important.'[91] Jowitt soon wrote to Mackenzie King: 'I like your suggestion of describing the "Club" as "the Commonwealth of Free Nations". I put this to the Indians.'[92]

---

[90] Laithwaite's note of meeting between Jowitt and Rau, on 25 Oct. 1948, ibid.

[91] Cited by Eayrs, *In Defence of Canada: Peacemaking and Deterrence* (1972), 239.

[92] Jowitt to King, 26 Oct. 1948, ibid., 238.

As secretary of Jowitt's committee Laithwaite had been impressed by the legal weakness of the citizenship basis of the Commonwealth relationship and he felt that the Cripps–Nehru–Rau–Jowitt discussions had added insufficient substance to it.[93] On Tuesday 26 October his minister, Noel-Baker, wrote to Attlee, 'uneasy lest there should be any misunderstanding in the minds of Indians as to how far we can go to meet them over their remaining in the Commonwealth'.[94] He wanted the points discussed to be evaluated by Jowitt and the Law Officers before they were reported to Cabinet. Nehru had a rough note of the points with him when he saw Attlee that day, just before he left London, and intimated that he would inform him of 'the exact proposals' that he would put to his Government.[95] Attlee adumbrated the points at a Cabinet meeting on the Thursday, and Jowitt and Shawcross were asked to evaluate them.[96]

Nehru's 'Ten Points' reached Attlee through Krishna Menon after the Cabinet meeting.[97] They were much as expected, opening with a confirmation that the constitution would declare India to be a sovereign independent republic. It would provide for the repeal of the Independence Act only in so far as it was inconsistent with the constitution; the British and Indian Prime Ministers would announce the changes in the same terms; and the waiver by the King of his sovereignty in favour of the Indian people would be assumed to be the constitutional position. The King was accepted as 'the fountain of Commonwealth honour'. The relevant provisions of the British Nationality Act would be enacted 'on a reciprocal basis'; the Indian Government might use the services of any other Commonwealth government in foreign states where it was not represented; and the President would act on the King's behalf to fulfil the obligations of the Crown towards non-Indian Commonwealth citizens in India. Cripps had explored the latter point with Nehru at Broadlands in an attempt to make the President, in some sense, 'the Agent of the Crown'.[98] In subsequent

---

[93] Laithwaite to Brook, 26 Oct. 1948, CAB 21/2048.

[94] Noel-Baker's minute to Attlee on 'Indian Constitutional Position', 26 Oct. 1948, CAB 127/115.

[95] Menon to Attlee, 28 Oct. 1948, PREM 8/1008.

[96] CM 67(48)3, 28 Oct. 1948, ibid.

[97] Encl., d. 25 Oct. 1948, to Menon to Attlee, 28 Oct. 1948, loc. cit.

[98] Cripps to Noel-Baker, 1 Nov. 1948, CAB 127/115.

legislation on treaties with other countries Commonwealth nations and citizens would not be treated as foreign, and in commercial treaties it would be made clear that in the application of the MFN clauses Commonwealth countries were not foreign. In essence, Rau's theories on dormant sovereignty, the historic British source of the constitution, and Commonwealth citizenship provided the basis of the Points, with specific provisions added to give some 'life' to the King's position and to discourage any MFN challenge. The Points closed with an expression of 'sincere desire to continue the Commonwealth association' and an intimation that Nehru would discuss them with his colleagues and communicate them to the British Prime Minister in an official proposal.

A week later Brook told Attlee that the lawyers' provisional view was that the Points did 'not afford a sufficient basis for a satisfactory constitutional link' and he wished to give Nehru a 'preliminary warning'.[99] Brook and Noel-Baker were anxious about Nehru's possible embarrassment for he would inevitably need to refer to the subject in discussions with colleagues or in speeches.[100] They also advised consulting the Commonwealth governments. Attlee proposed to wait for the Law Officers' Opinion and consult Cabinet. The Opinion (d. 3 November) was unequivocal.[101] There was 'no doubt' that a 'sovereign democratic republic' declaration in the constitution would 'extinguish His Majesty's sovereignty in India'. Rau's dormant sovereignty was 'as subtle as it is novel . . . but in the end we find ourselves with regret quite unable to agree with it'. The tie between India and the Commonwealth would thus be broken unless sufficient evidence of its preservation could be mustered. Evidence for a plausible case in international law could be supplied by the Commonwealth Prime Ministers declaring that they regarded themselves as 'still bound in a special form of association' and by common Commonwealth citizenship. However, there was no '*real* common citizenship', for though UK law conferred rights of entry and the franchise on Commonwealth citizens from India such rights were not conceded in other Commonwealth countries. Other minor links included in the Points did not affect the question. In consequence the lawyers felt insufficient

[99] Brook's minute for PM, 6 Nov. 1948, PREM 8/1008.
[100] Noel-Baker's minute for PM, 9 Nov. 1948, ibid.
[101] Opinion of the Lord Chancellor and Law Officers on 28 Oct. statement of Indian PM, 3 Nov. 1948, annex B to CP (48)254, ibid.

confidence that the Points would answer an MFN claim to 'satisfy Parliament or public opinion'.

Brook now advised Attlee that in its discussion on the Opinion Cabinet should consider 'what other basis might be put forward for India's continuing membership of the Commonwealth'.[102] He reverted to the previously discarded possibilities of India recognizing the King as either having '*some* jurisdiction in respect of India's external affairs' or being the ' "Head" of the Commonwealth'. The latter, he recalled, had been 'dropped some little time ago, because Mr Mackenzie King objected to its implication that the Commonwealth is a unit' but in the last resort he might relent if it were the only way of keeping India in the Commonwealth. The former had been dismissed because it was thought the Constituent Assembly would reject it, but perhaps Nehru could get acceptance for 'the least possible degree of recognition', that the King should continue to accredit India's ambassadors to foreign countries. Cripps had been adamant that 'obviously to satisfy the Indian point of view, there can be no subordination of the President to the Crown, as there is in the Irish Foreign Relations Act of the Crown to the Eire Government!'[103]

On Friday, 12 November the Cabinet lifted the question to the political plane.[104] It contemplated that in due course HMG must simply treat republican India as a member of the Commonwealth and 'take the risk' of an MFN challenge. The interim should be used 'to elaborate the conception of a new form of constitutional relationship'. Before taking such a decision the other Commonwealth members must be consulted and the whole question discussed with the Opposition. It was agreed that Nye should be sent a copy of the Opinion and convey its substance to Nehru personally.

The old Dominions had been left almost in the dark since Brook's August visits to them. They were at once disturbed at the change of direction that Nehru had initiated. On Wednesday morning, 17 November, Jowitt, Noel-Baker, Brook, and Laithwaite discussed the Opinion with Evatt, Fraser, and Lester Pearson in Paris.[105]

[102] Brook's minute to PM, 11 Nov. 1948, ibid.

[103] Cripps to Noel-Baker, 1 Nov. 1948, CAB 127/115.

[104] CM 71(48)2, 12 Nov. 1948.

[105] Note of a discussion with representatives of Canada, Australia, and New Zealand, at the Hôtel Vendôme, Paris, at 10 a.m. on 17 Nov. 1948, CP (48)286, PREM 8/1008.

Evatt, now President of the UN General Assembly, had misunderstood Nehru's position when he had met him in London on 13 October, believing that India was 'ready to accept' allegiance in 'the external field'. The Dominion representatives were in agreement on the need for 'some substantial link with the Crown', the absence of which would be difficult to justify in their parliaments. At Evatt's suggestion Bajpai was brought into discussions with the group that evening, but Brook could not attend.[106]

Bajpai denied any knowledge that Nehru had ever intended to retain 'a link through The King in the external field' and thought 'there must have been some misunderstanding'. The discussion of the King's relations with the Commonwealth rambled around, with Pearson illuminating the role of 'The King as a symbol of association' who had delegated all of his powers in Canada to the Governor-General. Fraser even suggested that it might be possible 'in the light of the Canadian precedent . . . to bring in The King perhaps as Head of the British Commonwealth, as the connecting link between India and the Commonwealth'. It was ironical that at this point Canada, whose Prime Minister's objection to the Head of the Commonwealth formula had caused it to be dropped in August, should have emerged as providing the precedent for an Indian link through 'The King as a symbol of the association'. Had Brook been present the point might have been seized and referred to India. Instead, largely under Evatt's influence, the discussion moved to the prospect of a permanent delegation of the King's powers to the President. In the end Bajpai prepared a cable to Nehru, which the meeting approved, emphasizing the Dominion representatives' insistence on a link with the King and suggesting 'that as symbol of Commonwealth association authority to appoint Heads of Missions abroad should derive from The King', who would delegate it permanently to the President.

Bajpai's cable was the first indication that Nehru received of the inadequacy of his Ten Points. Noel-Baker's absences in Paris had delayed the drafting of cables to Nye, their approval by Attlee, and Nye's acquiescence in the difficult role expected of him. Attlee and Cripps balked at letting Nehru see the Law Officers' Opinion. The cable that Nehru received from Attlee on 19 November briefly stated the Points' 'insufficiency from the purely legal point of view'

---

[106] Note of discussion in Evatt's room at 6 p.m. on 17 Nov. 1948, ibid.

and that the matter was under 'urgent consideration'.[107] Two days later he received a long cable from Attlee, explaining that the Points would not enable an MFN claim to be resisted and that Nye would convey details of the Opinion to him.[108] It reiterated Britain's wish for India to remain in the Commonwealth and alluded to the old Dominions' concern for a Crown link. It particularly requested a reaction to the 'principle underlying' the link that Bajpai had suggested.

Nehru's reaction resembled that of the British Cabinet on 12 November. Cripps was probably in large measure influential in the belief of both Nehru and HMG that political realities were more important than legal niceties. As early as May 1947 he had observed that 'almost anything' could be improvised to keep India in the Commonwealth.[109] Even Jowitt had expressed the 'general view that whilst legal difficulty undoubtedly existed it was important that mere technicalities should not be allowed to override the broader political considerations involved'.[110] The problem with such reasoning was that it failed to take the views of the old Dominions into account. Nehru agreed to consider the link with the King and send on his views. On 28 November he did write to Krishna Menon that there was no chance of the Congress Parliamentary Party accepting a shred of allegiance:

The very point the United Kingdom wishes to emphasize for legal or sentimental reasons is objected to here. Most people are prepared to accept the common citizenship idea plus a declaration that we are in the Commonwealth. If you go beyond this there is difficulty. . . . Our people want to make it perfectly clear they are making a new start and that, as the Constitution will itself declare, sovereignty resides in the people and in no one else in any shape or form.[111]

Krishna did not convey these observations to British ministers. Nor did Nehru put them to Nye, who was told on 4 December that

[107] PM to UK High Commissioner for Nehru, 18 Nov. 1948, ibid.

[108] PM to UK High Commissioner for Nehru, 20 Nov. 1948, ibid.

[109] Marginal notes on Monckton to Ismay, 2 May 1947, *TP*, x, 367.

[110] Nehru's paraphrase in UK High Commissioner to CRO, 19 Nov. 1948, PREM 8/1008. Brook had minuted Jowitt's having 'suggested more than once that, when the strictly legal position has been ascertained and stated, the political question remains' (to PM, 11 Nov. 1948, ibid.).

[111] Nehru to Menon, 28 Nov. 1948, cited in Gopal, *Nehru*, ii, 49–50.

HMG would much welcome an indication of 'how Nehru's mind is moving on the question generally and of his reaction to Prime Minister's message'.[112] Krishna, who felt that recently he had been rather left out of things, was dilatory in his handling of a slightly revised version of Nehru's points that were sent to him on 2 December.[113]

Krishna discussed Nehru's revise, known as the 'Eight Points', with Attlee on 7 December. As instructed by Nehru he stated that the issue was not one of 'legal formalities and arguments' but 'essentially a political problem . . . based upon our mutual desires and interests'. India wished to meet any legal difficulties as they arose, meanwhile proceeding on the basis of Commonwealth citizenship, an express assertion of her Commonwealth membership, and India's desire for the 'Commonwealth association and what is practical and adequate at present'. Nehru did not envisage the Commonwealth as a 'Super-state, but the voluntary association of free and equal nations which it has always maintained itself to be'.

Menon did not send on the Eight Points to Attlee until 11 December. He confessed to being 'rather distressed about the delay' and 'not feeling up to handling it as one sometimes does'.[114] He requested that a general response should be available to Nehru before the Congress Party meeting scheduled for the 16th. Nehru had told Nye that 'he would have to carry them with him on the major policy to be adopted'.[115] Krishna intimated that Congress would not discuss the details of policy 'but the issue will be raised and it would both be wrong and tactless for Panditji to evade it or be unprepared to give a lead'. Whilst the Eight Points added nothing to the substance of Points already evaluated, Attlee must now, in the light of Nehru's reticence on the Crown link, ascertain the views of his colleagues and the old Dominions on the question of principle.

On 15 December the Commonwealth Relations Committee of Officials observed at once that 'the other Commonwealth countries would agree that, without any recognition of the Crown, India

---

[112] CRO to UK High Commissioner, 4 Dec. 1948, PREM 8/1008.
[113] Menon to Attlee encl. *aide mémoire* and Nehru to Attlee, all d. 11 Dec. 1948, ibid.
[114] Menon to Attlee, 13 Dec. 1948, ibid.
[115] UK High Commissioner to CRO, 19 Nov. 1948, ibid.

cannot be accepted as a *member* of the Commonwealth'.[116] Armed
with this advice Attlee, Cripps, Jowitt, Noel-Baker, Brook, and
Laithwaite met Pearson, Evatt, and Fraser that night.[117] Attlee
argued that 'at the present time' (he had the spread of Communism
in mind) the practical case for keeping India in the Commonwealth
was compelling. Nehru had made 'great efforts' and a 'rebuff'
might alienate him. Evatt agreed on the strength of the case but
insisted that 'there should be some substantial recognition of the
Crown'. He wanted to press Nehru for a specific answer on the
question of delegation of the King's powers and to pursue other
possible links with the Crown. With Pearson and Fraser he
favoured a 'special association' if such overtures failed. Indeed,
though the meeting skirted briefly around such possibilities as a
Commonwealth honours system, and the King functioning as
'First Citizen' or 'Head of the Commonwealth', it retreated to the
exploration of a new form of 'association'. Soon after midnight
Attlee sent a cable that was bound to offend Nehru:

> I have had an opportunity tonight to discuss with Mr Fraser, Dr Evatt and
> Mr Pearson your message of 11th December.
>   Your proposals in their present form do not seem to us to be satisfactory
> as a basis for continuing the full degree of association within the
> Commonwealth through the nexus of the Crown. We hope that you may
> be able to give this matter further consideration. If, however, you are
> unable after such reconsideration to alter your position in this matter, we
> nevertheless earnestly trust that a close commonwealth association can still
> be maintained. . . . We must, however, have time in which to work out
> some of the main implications of this form of commonwealth association.[118]

The cable arrived just after Nehru had extracted the following
resolution from the Congress Subjects Committee at Jaipur:

> In view of the attainment of complete independence and the establishment
> of a Republic of India which will symbolize that independence and give to
> India status among the nations of the world that is her rightful due, her
> present association with the United Kingdom and the Commonwealth of
> Nations will necessarily have to change. India, however, desires to main-
> tain all such links with other countries as do not come in the way of her
> freedom of action and independence, and the Congress would welcome her

[116] Report of Official Cttee, 15 Dec. 1948, ibid.
[117] Note of discussion of 15 Dec. 1948, ibid.
[118] PM to Nye (personal) for Nehru, 16 Dec. 1948, ibid.

free association with independent nations of the Commonwealth for their common weal and the promotion of world peace.[119]

Nehru wrote in chagrin to Cripps:

I have had a message from Attlee informing me that our proposals about India continuing in the Commonwealth are not considered sufficient. These proposals were based on the talks we had in London and were fully in accord with them. I have had a hard time getting people to agree to them here. Only yesterday we got the Subjects Committee of the Congress to agree generally to the line of approach we were taking up. I do not know quite what the position is now. I am afraid we cannot go much further.[120]

The rebuff rankled with him and he followed with a long acrimonious letter:

These proposals were based on our talks in London and largely on the draft that you produced. On this basis I have been trying to do my utmost, since my return from England, to cultivate public opinion. I have met several kinds of opinion and I have gone dead against the prevailing current opinion in India. Yet I have persisted because I thought this was the right course. . . . The Congress has adopted it giving us a free hand, within certain limiting factors, to work out this association with the Commonwealth. We have done that, but I do not see what step I can take now, because I can not go beyond what we agreed to in London. I have been left high and dry. . . . I am disturbed that matters should take a wrong turn and come in the way of that close co-operation between India and UK which I had looked forward to.[121]

A week later Krishna appealed to Cripps:

The situation all round is bad and something has to be done. I should tell you that on the Commonwealth [Nehru's] feeling is that Attlee has terminated the course we were pursuing and that he has been under a misapprehension as to the basic agreements and desires.[122]

Nehru had every reason to complain.

Nehru had left the Commonwealth Conference 'so glad' that he had attended.[123] His relations with Mountbatten, Attlee, and

---

[119] Congress Party Resolution, 16 Dec. 1948, CAB 21/1824.
[120] Nehru to Cripps, 17 Dec. 1948, CAB 127/143.
[121] Nehru to Cripps, 17/18 Dec. 1948, ibid.
[122] Menon to Cripps, 23 Dec. 1948, ibid.
[123] Nehru to Cripps, 27 Oct. 1948, ibid.

Cripps had seemed warm and constructive. One of the grand old men of the Commonwealth, Mackenzie King, had shown him and his sister 'real friendship, even affection'.[124] From India *The Times* reported gratification that the Asian Prime Ministers had played an important role in proceedings.[125] Gordon Walker noted that Nehru had been 'dominant'.[126] The *Hindustan Times* found the final communiqué 'stimulating' and welcomed the 'new concept of Commonwealth', for a 'community of outlook' on world problems had appeared, together with refreshing changes in nomenclature.[127] The word 'British' as a prefix to 'Commonwealth' had been dropped and 'Dominion' and 'His Majesty's Government' had been avoided. Nine Indian members of a Commonwealth Parliamentary Conference that met simultaneously with the Prime Ministers' Conference had gone home 'to work for the dropping of the idea of "Sovereign Independent Republic" '.[128]

Nehru's advocacy upon his return to India is reflected in a secret note on foreign policy and an account of his secret meeting with the Constituent Assembly. The former argues:

. . . India can not remain in isolation from the rest of the world. It is to the advantage of India, as it will be to the advantage of other countries, to have closer contacts and associations. This may help us in many ways, and this may also help the cause of world peace. . . . The old world in which we have lived so long is rapidly changing before our eyes. India is changing. We can not therefore think in terms of the past, even of the immediate past, for if we do we shall forget the present and we shall not be prepared for the future. Therefore all questions have to be considered in the light of this new world that is growing up and the changing conditions that we are in. In these conditions we should seek co-operation wherever we can have it, while maintaining our freedom and dignity.[129]

The best available association, he told the Constituent Assembly, was with the Commonwealth:

Provided our independence was guaranteed, internally and externally, it

[124] Cited in Eayrs, op. cit., 239.

[125] *The Times*, 28 Oct. 1948.

[126] Diary fragment, 16 Oct. 1948, GNWR 1/7.

[127] Cited in *The Times*, 28 Oct. 1948. The 'Final Communique' of 22 Oct., which Gordon Walker drafted, appears in GNWR 1/7. It concluded: 'This blending of the West and the East in the lofty task of building a lasting peace on the basis of freedom justice and economic prosperity provides a new hope for harassed mankind.'

[128] Noel-Baker minute to PM, 29 Oct. 1948, CAB 127/115.

[129] 'Note on Foreign Policy', 2 Dec. 1948, File 8 (pt. 2) 1948, AICC Papers.

would be advantageous for us to maintain some connection with the Commonwealth. . . . Complete isolationism is impossible. . . . A link with UK and Commonwealth has greater advantages for us than joining any group. . . . The Socialist Party is talking of India's becoming the leader of a neutral group of nations. Even so this is the only way to it. India is the natural leader of Asia. But isolation does not bring it into leadership of such countries. . . .[130]

The 'old world' of colonialism was passing; in the new world of the Cold War isolation was hazardous. The only alternative to the Commonwealth connection was a relationship with the USA, involving 'a certain subservience to the US policy . . . a certain dependence'. The Commonwealth 'gentlemen's agreement does not bind [us] in any way'.

Yet at the end of the year the rejection of his initiative drew from Nehru a return to the old ambivalence towards Britain. His anti-imperialism peppers his letters to Cripps:

You mention the Communist advances in Asia. We are anxious about them also. But one of the chief obstacles is the Indonesian problem. The Dutch attitude there has done more to weaken the position of the UK and USA than any Communist action. Marshall aid for rehabilitation goes to the Dutch in Java and the French in Indo-China. I am afraid there is little realization in Western Europe or America of how their policies are undermining their position in Asia.[131]

And:

Unless the USA and the UK come to the decision that Colonialism in South East Asia must end their prestige will go down, and in a moment of real crisis in South East Asia they will have few friends.[132]

Clearly Nehru needed to be handled with care. Cripps knew him well enough to chide and coax:

Haven't we taken every step in our power to end colonialism in South East Asia? And hasn't that helped stay the Communist advance? You must be fair Jawaharlal, and not take the attitude that any stick will do to beat the British with![133]

As for the Commonwealth:

[130] 'On Commonwealth', 1948, ibid.
[131] Nehru to Cripps, 17 Dec. 1948, CAB 127/143.
[132] Nehru to Cripps, 17/18 Dec. 1948, ibid.
[133] Cripps to Nehru, 7 Jan. 1948, ibid.

[We] are determined to find a solution that is satisfactory to all of us—if
that be humanly possible—and we must make it possible. I entirely understand your difficulties and I know you appreciate that we have some too!
. . . We are *all* working at it with a will to succeed and a very intense desire
to see India a full member of the Commonwealth however that may have to
be constituted.

Somewhat mollified Nehru did not pursue his criticism of Britain's
policy in South East Asia, agreed that she had 'acted generously
and with vision' in India, Burma, and Ceylon, and was 'anxious to
settle the Commonwealth issue as soon as possible'.[134] Yet speed
was scarcely possible and in the months that were to elapse before
negotiations were renewed he remained puzzled by the inconsis-
tencies in the treatment of his initiative.

To write, as Cripps did, of HMG's 'difficulties' was to understate
the problem. The policy cupboard was bare. Each apparent
solution had foundered on legal or political objections. The old
Dominions' August requirement that India accept allegiance to the
King in her external affairs offended her republican sentiments.
There was insufficient common citizenship in the Dominions to
provide a sound basis for the Commonwealth in international law,
however it was embellished by other points indicative of a
continuing relationship. In any event, the old Dominions insisted
upon the Crown link, though they were prepared to strip it down to
India's acceptance of the permanent delegation to her President of
the King's power to appoint her ambassadors. As Nehru had
not responded to the point Attlee raised it with Krishna on
22 December.[135] Such a delegation might even be made to the
Governor-General and then transferred to the President under
India's new constitution. Nye was asked to press the idea of delegation upon Nehru at the end of December.[136] However when it was
referred to Parliamentary Counsel for evaluation it was found to
raise 'substantial difficulties'.[137] Though the King could make a
delegation to the Governor-General, once the new constitution
came into effect the King's sovereignty in India, and thus the

[134] Nehru to Cripps, 17 Jan. 1948, ibid.
[135] Note of meeting of 22 Dec. 1948 at 10 Downing Street between PM, Cripps,
Gordon Walker, and Menon, PREM 8/1008.
[136] CRO to UK High Commissioner, 24 Dec. 1948, ibid.
[137] Gordon Walker minute to PM, 31 Dec. 1948, ibid.

delegation, would be extinguished. Nor could the delegation await the passing of the constitution, for the King would then have no powers over India nor any ministers there to provide the advice necessary to a delegation. The idea was thus insufficient in itself to supply the necessary link with the Crown. This all seemed too much for Nye (though he was a qualified barrister): 'It looks as though earlier on we were prepared if not to back the solution at least to think it worthy of consideration whereas now we see difficulties. . . . Perhaps there is a subtle point here which I have missed.'[138] He was told to let the idea 'recede into the background'.[139] HMG was clutching at straws, for whatever the legal position Nehru wrote firmly to Menon that 'No type or form of delegation is going to be accepted here'.[140]

Attlee insisted to Menon that in the absence of a Crown link, 'something by way of association would have to be examined but this would involve a different relationship from membership'.[141] Of course the official and ministerial committees had discarded 'association' months ago and Attlee's return to it in December signified desperation. On 16 December, together with Cripps, Jowitt, and Noel-Baker, he had seen the Opposition leaders: Churchill, Eden, Stanley, Maxwell-Fyfe, and Salisbury.[142] Immediately after the Commonwealth Conference Churchill had observed the changes to traditional terminology and asked whether the Commonwealth was being allowed to dwindle away.[143] He questioned whether a republic might yet retain the commercial and political advantages of membership. When Attlee now urged the need to find 'some form of association' for India he 'at once went off the deep end with his usual attitude to Indian matters, and suggested that India should now be a foreign power: if we wanted anything from them we could make a treaty'. His colleagues saw difficulty in any form of 'association' answering the MFN problem. Attlee argued that international law was evolving to accommodate to the emergence of groupings of states. Stanley, a former Secretary of State for the Colonies, argued that the best alternative to

[138] Nye to Laithwaite (personal), 31 Dec. 1948, ibid.
[139] Laithwaite to Nye (personal), 3 Jan. 1949, ibid.
[140] Nehru to Menon, 12 Jan. 1949, Das, op. cit., viii, 1–2.
[141] Note of 22 Dec. meeting, loc. cit.
[142] Attlee's note on meeting with Opposition leaders, 16 Dec. 1948, PREM 8/1008.
[143] *Commons Debates*, 28 Oct. 1948, cols. 242–53.

Commonwealth membership would be a comprehensive treaty. Salisbury doubted whether India shared sufficient of the common outlook of the Commonwealth to be a satisfactory member (to which Attlee replied by reference to the spread of European ideas in India). Attlee did win the somewhat grudging assent of the Opposition leaders to the exploration of the idea of association. But Menon instantly repudiated 'association' for it implied 'two circles of members, and this was not at all what India wanted. India did not want to get into the same position as Ireland. It wanted to be clearly in or out.'[144] India would scarcely accept a place in an outer circle of the Commonwealth if Pakistan were an inner circle member.

Besides the difficulties of finding a formula for India's relationship with the Commonwealth there also re-emerged in December the old Foreign Office doubts about India's suitability as a member. The Foreign Office had been disappointed that diplomatic relations with South Asia had fallen to the CRO. Sir Orme Sargent was due to retire at the end of January 1949 and he now made a determined final effort to secure the subcontinent as a Foreign Office province. A letter was sent at PUS level requesting that the FO should have the right to communicate direct with Commonwealth governments in matters of foreign affairs.[145] The CRO was brought in question as a substantial department of state. In mid-December, too, Bevin sent to Attlee a copy of an FO memorandum, 'India and the Commonwealth', on 'the problem in so far as it concerns them'.[146] The paper considered the pros and cons of India's secession and membership. The case was slanted by the general observations that while India's present rulers were

as satisfactory from our point as any that are likely to achieve power. . . . India even under her present direction, is not a fully satisfactory member of the Commonwealth. Her rulers are not animated by the same sentiments of kinship and loyalty as are those of the older Dominions; they have so far shown little sign of adopting a viewpoint parallel to that of the United Kingdom in world affairs, and their successors might be even less inclined to do so; the effect of their policy is to obtain the maximum advantage from the Commonwealth relationship, while accepting the minimum obligations in return; and they do not conform to those standards, e.g. as regards the exchange of information, and co-operation

---

[144] Note of 22 Dec. meeting at Downing Street, loc. cit.
[145] Garner, *Commonwealth Office*, 301.
[146] FO Memorandum, 24 Nov. 1948, PREM 8/1008.

in trade and defence, which have hitherto been expected in the case of other members of the Commonwealth.

Clearly, a CRO–FO battle remained to be joined early in the new year. As yet Bevin had not 'had time to form a definite view'.[147] Would there be a replay of the Attlee–Bevin conflict of winter 1946? If so, India's future relations with Britain and the Commonwealth would, in equal degree, depend upon its outcome.

[147] Bevin to Attlee, 15 Dec. 1948, ibid.

6

The Apotheosis of Administration

THE Foreign Office request to assume direct relations with Commonwealth governments came to a new Permanent Under-Secretary at the CRO, Sir Percivale Liesching. A fierce battle raged between the senior officials of the departments for several weeks until Attlee himself ruled in favour of the status quo. Liesching's appointment from 1 January 1949 marked the end of the absurd division of the CRO into Divisions A (formerly Dominions Office) and B (formerly India Office). Gordon Walker had discussions on amalgamation with Mountbatten in mid-1948 and then wrote to him, 'I feel very strongly that we could handle the India problem better if (a) we had a single office here, and (b) as a general rule Indian problems were handled by men who did not have to deal with India in the past'.[1] When Carter left the Office it became possible to achieve both of these ends. Noel-Baker faced the difficult task of removing the unfortunate Machtig, a shy, autocratic, obstinate, aloof bachelor with no interest in India. The approval of both Bridges (as Head of the Civil Service) and Attlee was required before Machtig retired in December 1948. Bridges proposed Liesching as PUS and he integrated the divisions of the CRO within months. He was said to be 'the most able officer of his generation' in the Dominions Office.[2] He had opened up the High Commissions in Canada, South Africa, and Australia. He had been out of sympathy with Machtig and transferred from the DO. By 1948 he had become PUS to the Ministry of Food. In the reorganization Laithwaite was posted as Britain's first Ambassador to Ireland.

During 1948 the relatively junior Patrick Gordon Walker had, initially as Mountbatten's instrument in informal diplomacy, come

---

[1] Gordon Walker to Mountbatten, 20 July 1948, GNWR 1/7. Mountbatten, too, felt 'extremely strongly' about this, encouraged Gordon Walker to 'go on pressing hard' and undertook to raise it with Cripps (Mountbatten to Gordon Walker, 22 July 1948, ibid.).

[2] Garner, *Commonwealth Office*, 290.

to play an important role. He was, as Liesching was to be, impatient of Noel-Baker's preoccupation with the Kashmir problem, for his 'desire to execute an exercise in abstract peace-making came near to wrecking the Commonwealth'.[3] He had been a History Tutor at Christ Church, Oxford, before the war and cared deeply for the ideal of a Commonwealth of peoples. Attlee recognized his potentialities and took the unusual step of requiring his attendance at all of the meetings of the Commonwealth Prime Ministers in October. He handled publicity for them and enjoyed wide discretion over the contents of communiqués for the press. He was encouraged by Attlee's appreciation of his grasp of the Indian problem and made himself the central strategist in the administrative and diplomatic manœuvres that were devised to solve it. Attlee must have groaned under the Indian burden as the new year opened. After eighteen months of official and ministerial committees, recondite reports, Brook's August mission, the October conference, informal discussions with the Indians, old Dominions, and the Opposition, the prospect was for more of the same.

On New Year's Eve Gordon Walker contrived a fresh start in a minute on 'The Link with India'.[4] He argued the need to accept that no Crown link of the Dominion type was likely to be acceptable to India, though it should continue to be sought. He adverted to the possibility of the King acting as Head of the Commonwealth for such purposes as conferring honours or calling conferences, but that would not produce a direct Indian link with the Crown. He rejected both 'association' as unwanted by India and 'tricky' to define and a treaty as a 'confession of failure'. His main constructive proposal resembles, and probably drew upon, suggestions made in October by Mackenzie King and in November by Leopold Amery. King had argued for 'the emphasis being placed on Community of Free Nations, rather than . . . upon the Crown', for 'describing the "Club" as "the Commonwealth of Free Nations" '.[5] Amery envisaged India declaring its 'free association with the Commonwealth and with the Crown as the historic symbol of that association'.[6] Gordon Walker now believed that if no Crown

---

[3] Gordon Walker's Diary fragment, 21 Apr. 1948, cited in Pelling, *The Labour Governments, 1945-51* (1984), 162.

[4] Gordon Walker's minute for PM, 31 Dec. 1948, PREM 8/1008.

[5] Cited in Eayrs, *In Defence of Canada*, 238-9.

[6] Amery to Attlee, 30 Nov. 1948, Attlee Papers, 76/238-41. For Amery, see also Hall,

link were achievable then planning should 'start again from the fact that India wants to be in the Commonwealth and all its other members want to accept her into membership'. This common will and intent was at least 'a *real* link to start from'. Then one of two alternative steps might be taken. First, 'embellishments' might be aggregated (citizenship, honours, etc.) to illustrate the real link, though argument about the status of the Crown might be thereby provoked. Second, the problem might be faced of 'fitting an open Republic into the Commonwealth' beside the 'Crown Dominions', thereby scrapping the common link with the Crown and accommodating a republic as a willing member through reciprocal declarations by India and the Dominions. It seemed quite possible that the Dominions would accept such a situation rather than drive India from the Commonwealth by demanding the Crown link. The approach required evaluation as a defence against challenge under international law; but in practice potential challengers might be intimidated and deterred by the strength of such a Commonwealth.

A similar approach appeared a few days later when Cripps asked George Blaker, his secretary at the time of the Cabinet Mission, for a note on the Commonwealth problem.[7] Blaker argued that the 'real' link was a 'fundamental community of outlook' and a desire to remain in the Commonwealth. The common outlook was a striving for a 'spiritual' or democratic rather than 'materialist' or Communist way of life. Republicanism was not inconsistent with it nor monarchy intrinsic to it. The King might remain for the Dominions severally but become 'President of the Commonwealth collectively'. Blaker rejected both a two-tier scheme (which involved 'discrimination') and a treaty relationship (as 'a failure to adjust outward mechanisms to fit the inward reality'). Cripps sent the note to Attlee, adding that 'it puts the basic conception at which we should aim very well'. On 4 January, when at Attlee's behest Gordon Walker saw Krishna Menon, he found him prepared to conjure with the King's title to give it application to the Commonwealth as a whole but not to India individually.[8] Menon was receptive to Gordon Walker's suggestion of the title 'Head of the

Commonwealth: A History of the British Commonwealth of Nations (1971), 841 n., 851 n., 852, 858 n., 864; Rau, *India's Constitution*, 358–9.

[7] Cripps to Attlee, 6 Jan. 1948 and encl. by Blaker, 'India and the Commonwealth', 5 Jan. 1948, PREM 8/1008.

[8] Gordon Walker's minute for PM, 5 Jan. 1948, ibid.

Commonwealth', with the King being the 'fount of Honour' for the award of honours.

The Commonwealth Relations Committee discussed the problem on 7 January.[9] It was a formidable gathering: Attlee, Bevin, Cripps, Jowitt, Noel-Baker, Addison, Shawcross, Gordon Walker, Creech Jones, Liesching, and Laithwaite. Gordon Walker noted in his diary that he had written all of the papers before this 'most important meeting'.[10] Attlee indicated that India seemed unlikely to accept a direct link with the Crown or any form of association short of full membership of the Commonwealth. She certainly wanted full membership and she might be prepared to recognize the Crown as the fountain of honour for the Commonwealth generally. The alternative courses available were therefore to seek close treaty relations with India as a foreign country, or to modify the Commonwealth to retain India as a republic. The alternatives divided ministers both at the meeting and for several weeks to come.

The discussion of 7 January opened with Bevin asserting that in foreign affairs HMG was likely to be embarrassed by India's attitude as a member of the Commonwealth and by her efforts to influence British policy 'in her own narrower interests'. Against this it was argued that temporary disagreements and specific foreign issues must not be over-emphasized. They were indeed an argument for 'more intimate co-operation and consultation' within the Commonwealth rather than a decisive argument for acquiescing in India's departure from it: 'Such a development would be a disastrous blow to the prestige and influence of the Commonwealth and would gravely affect the economic position of the United Kingdom and the sterling area generally'. This view was shared by the old Dominions, while 'Colonial peoples would be gravely affected by the failure of the Commonwealth to adjust itself to meet the susceptibilities of a non-European people'. Under attacks from his colleagues, including 'a child's guide lecture on the Commonwealth' by Noel-Baker, 'Bevin warmed up and began to help'.[11]

[9] Minutes of Cabinet Cttee on CR, 7 Jan. 1949, CAB 134/119.
[10] Gordon Walker Diary fragment, 7 Jan. 1949, GNWR 1/7.
[11] This paragraph and the next draw on both the official minutes and Gordon Walker's diary as quoted in his *The Cabinet* (1970), 135.

Towards the end of the meeting Attlee asked Gordon Walker to speak, for his minute, 'The Link with India', was on the table:

. . . I gave my views strongly. The Crown link with India is out. Let's fit in India as a Republic, based on the reality of a common act of will. Then let's add embellishments, which could become valuable—though they are dangerous if we try to *constitute* the link out of them.

Shawcross attacked this on the ground that unless we had the common crown or common nationality it would not stand up under international law. Cripps and the Prime Minister in effect said that law must be made for people and international law must adjust itself.

The drift of the meeting was summed up thus: 'The basic reality of the situation was that India and the older members of the Commonwealth were determined to maintain a long-standing association: the cardinal facts of the relationship were their common history and their common will to remain in association with each other'. It was suggested that one answer to the legal difficulty might be to establish a Commonwealth conference as an entity, with the King as its President issuing invitations to its meetings. Gordon Walker's approach seemed to prevail. The Official Committee was to be asked to submit proposals on the basis of the suggestions thrown out in the discussion.

Brook was again dominant in the Official Committee.[12] It soon revealed that the Commonwealth could not be based upon a conference convened by the King, who could only act on ministerial advice and whose dignity would be impaired if an invitation were refused. Moreover, member nations would never agree on formal rules of procedure and functions, and there would be no clear legal distinction between a Commonwealth conference and a meeting of foreign states. Brook undertook to prepare a paper proposing 'a new form of Commonwealth relationship based on a common will to maintain the existing membership'. It would include a declaration whereby members would subscribe to 'an authoritative definition of the essential meaning of the Commonwealth relationship'. He produced the following recasting of the Statute of Westminister's formula:

The members of the British Commonwealth of Nations are:-
(i)   independent sovereign states which owe, or have owed, allegiance to the British Crown;

[12] Minutes of Official Cttee on CR, 11 Jan. 1949, CAB 134/119.

(ii) equal in status and in no way subordinate one to another in any aspect of their domestic or external affairs nor foreign in relation one to another;

(iii) freely associated as members of the Commonwealth and united (some by their allegiance to the Crown, and all) by their acceptance of the principle of consultation on all matters of common concern and by the rights of common citizenship which the nationals of each enjoy in the territories of the others.[13]

Gordon Walker, who had noted his determination to 'get my hands on this', objected that the formula would provoke controversy. Reciprocal declarations by India and the other members would be preferable.[14] India should simply confirm her membership as a republic and the others should affirm the continuing relationship. Brook and his committee adopted Gordon Walker's proposal.

Ministerial meetings crucial to India's membership of the Commonwealth were held on Tuesday and Wednesday, 8–9 February. Gordon Walker's diary contains a perceptive account of them.[15] It differs significantly from the ostensible extract that he subsequently published and merits quotation:

Norman Brook played a considerable part: he and I absolutely agree. So does Liesching. We had a paper before us which largely embodied my ideas. Its whole basis was to fit India in openly as a Republic. I was the first to put this forward as an official idea. Its particular proposal is to base membership on simple declarations (a) by India, (b) by all other CW countries. This was not in the original draft, but was put in after a paper I wrote. Another idea that I have put forward only verbally was adopted during the discussion, namely that we should send emissaries to the Commonwealth countries—Liesching suggested that we should approach all bar India simultaneously. These were the main ideas. Noel-Baker played very little part indeed: though he did once or twice argue in favour of keeping India in.

It was unusual that I should be invited to attend. At the first meeting the Prime Minister asked me to speak. I said that I had no doubt India should be fitted in: we must give time a chance. There had been a rapid development of feeling towards Britain; recently even Congress had voted for association. I thought it would strengthen not weaken the Crown to keep it only where it had reality: we should keep as many royal embellishments as possible as the feeling for royalty might grow. I favoured the two

---

[13] First draft of Fifth Report of Official Cttee, 17 January 1948, CAB 134/119.
[14] Gordon Walker's minute to Liesching, 20 Jan. 1949, GNWR 1/7.
[15] Gordon Walker's Diary fragment, 10 Feb. 1949, ibid. Cf. his *The Cabinet*, 136–7.

declarations, rather than an attempt to redefine the Commonwealth. We needed two things: to limit the Commonwealth to those who had been in it; and to base it on a declared act of will.

The legal experts warned of the hazards of abandoning the legal basis. Jowitt 'wobbled' (in Gordon Walker's account), saying that he and Shawcross believed that an international court would reject the affirmation that members were 'not foreign in relation one to another'. 'Shawcross', noted Gordon Walker, 'was good. He over-pressed the legal arguments but admitted their subordination to political ones. He had a clear preference for a "compact Commonwealth" bound by the legal reality of allegiance to the Crown.' Ministers generally felt that the legal aspect was 'subordinate in importance to the far-reaching political issues'.[16] International law was capable of development in response to changes in political relationships. Foreign countries might not press their legal rights if their treaties with Commonwealth countries as a whole were beneficial. The Lord Chancellor and the Law Officers were to be asked to propose, with the help of the Board of Trade, an appreciation of the risks and costs of successful challenges under the Most Favoured Nation Convention.

The meetings were chaired effectively by Attlee and guided by Brook, as Gordon Walker observes with satisfaction:

Norman Brook played a part that an official really should not but he was good and met the hostile arguments. The Prime Minister was most impressive. He fully realizes the difficulties of the King, Opposition, other Commonwealth countries. He does not rush. But he moves the argument steadily forward (in fact allowing it to repeat itself too much). He wants India in; realizes the value of time; but also the need to press forward now. The issue is India in or out? Can a republic be fitted in? The value even of stupid and repetitive discussion is clear. It allows a gradual shaping of policy. At the end it was decided to get a working party [of officials] to look into the effects of India leaving the Commonwealth, with or without a treaty, or keeping her in: in terms of most-favoured nation clauses and citizenship. The basic paper is to be prepared in terms to send to Dominions. On my suggestion they are also to work out a timetable. We should take the next step in 2 or 3 weeks. I am convinced that we shall succeed if we act boldly and speedily—with a clear lead we will carry the Commonwealth. We can outface the opposition. I think we will in fact send

---

[16] Minutes of Cabinet Cttee on CR, Feb. 1949, CAB 134/119.

emissaries around in about a month and have a Prime Ministers' meeting by April. India will accept the proposals.[17]

The most remarkable feature of the success of the Gordon Walker–Brook–Attlee line in early February is that it prevailed over vigorous opposition from Bevin and the Foreign Office.

At the 7 January meeting it had seemed that while Bevin argued the Foreign Office brief he had been overborne by his colleagues. Gordon Walker recorded his

saying in effect that the Commonwealth ought to be dissolved. His officials had been at him: they are sore at Indian and Australian resentment over our attitude towards the Dutch aggression in Indonesia and over Evatt's escapades. At the bottom of their hearts they think they could run foreign policy better than we can run Commonwealth relations: they want ambassadors under direct instructions.[18]

The Indonesian issue rankled with the Foreign Office. What India and Australia saw as a regional conflict between Dutch imperialism and Indonesian nationalism had wider Cold War implications for Britain. For reasons of European security the Labour Government had helped the Dutch to rehabilitate their rule over Indonesia. British troops were withdrawn in 1946 when the Dutch and the republicans achieved a truce but in consequence of 'police actions' in 1948 Australia and India took the dispute to the Security Council. Anxious for Dutch co-operation in Western Union, Bevin pursued negotiations behind the scenes to bring about a liberal settlement, whereas India and Australia supported a Security Council resolution demanding the release of republican prisoners. Bevin discussed Indonesian affairs with Nehru in October and they corresponded in December.[19] Next month Nehru called a conference on Indonesia in Delhi. Australia attended but Britain was not invited. Evatt was a particular irritant to the British, not only over Ireland and Indonesia but also in his naïve misreading of Soviet intentions in his attempted mediation over Berlin and Greece.[20] Again, Australia's High Commissioner, Mr J.A. Beasley, had struck a new note of aggressiveness in London. At the October conference he had made 'an extraordinary personal attack on Attlee'.[21]

[17] Diary, loc. cit.   [18] Ibid.
[19] Record of Bevin's conversation with Nehru, 27 Oct. 1948, FO 800/470; Bullock, *Bevin*, 611 n. 2., 630–31.   [20] Ibid., 676.
[21] Gordon Walker's Diary, 24 Oct. 1948, GNWR 1/7.

Gordon Walker noted that Australia had then 'succeeded in justifying and deepening the dislike everyone seems to feel for her'. The Foreign Office was disappointed at Bevin's apparent capitulation on the Commonwealth in January. It reacted vigorously against the strategy adopted in Brook's paper. Sargent attacked its assumption of the desirability of redefining the Commonwealth to retain India.[22] He pressed for a prior examination of the political issues, along the lines of the Foreign Office's own recent memorandum on pros and cons:

... signs are not wanting that Indian policy is diverging from our own; witness Pandit Nehru's anti-Colonial pronouncement in the Assembly, his recent calling (without prior consultation with any members of the Commonwealth) of a Conference on Indonesia which was by implication directed against the Western Powers with rights in Asia, and the tone of his declarations at that Conference. This divergence may lead to a direct conflict of interests; and, so long as India remains in association with the Commonwealth, we may at any time find ourselves in a position, particularly in Asian affairs, where we must either pursue a course we consider wrong in deference to Indian views, or risk open disagreement which will weaken the Commonwealth association and be detrimental to Commonwealth prestige.

We shall in fact be exposing ourselves to constant pressure by India under the open or implied threat that she will break her association with the Commonwealth unless we conform to her ideas. The temptation on India to use this pressure will be the greater in that she will already have succeeded in inducing us to dilute the Commonwealth relationship in order to retain her association.

Brook and his committee declined, in the absence of ministerial instructions, to examine the wider questions of policy.[23] But they did propose to Attlee that an official appreciation of economic, financial, and defence, as well as political issues should be prepared for use by the emissaries in their consultations with the Dominions.

At the meetings of 8–9 February Bevin's return to the Foreign Office line provoked a major debate on policy, as Gordon Walker reported:

Bevin was extremely defeatist. Under Orme Sargent's influence he argued repeatedly that it was not worth keeping India in; it was not going to be committed to us but we to it; it would pursue its own foreign policy etc. All

---

[22] Sargent to Brook, 31 Jan. 1949, CAB 134/119.
[23] Minutes of Official Cttee on CR, 3 Feb. 1949, ibid.

these arguments would lead to the breakdown even of the old Commonwealth—and this Bevin once or twice said. From time to time he warmed up and made positive suggestions—not very good ones ('a Commonwealth' for 'the Commonwealth'). But his role was almost wholly negative.[24]

Against his arguments the 'central fact' to receive assent was India's expressed wish to remain, to rebuff which would not only be 'a grave failure of statesmanship' but might 'set in train forces which would have a corroding and disintegrating effect upon the cohesion of the remaining members of the Commonwealth'.[25] The Commonwealth's prestige and international influence would be diminished and the forces opposed to Communist aggression would be assumed to have suffered a setback. An affronted India might try to set up an Asiatic bloc hostile to the Western powers. The Commonwealth would feel itself obliged to support Pakistan (as a member) in her differences with India. As Australia and New Zealand realized, relations with new nations in South East Asia would be affected. While it was agreed that no decision on the question of India as a republic remaining in the Commonwealth could be made until other members had been consulted, the drift in favour of that policy was unmistakeable. As the Brook committee had suggested officials would prepare an objective appreciation of the implications of the alternative answers to the policy question. The Official Committee would also prepare a statement of the arguments for and against its proposed redefinition of the Commonwealth.

Within weeks Bevin underwent a remarkable conversion. When ministers next met, on 1 March, to consider the documents prepared by the officials, he said that the

successful conclusion of an Atlantic Pact would have the effect of drawing India closer to the Commonwealth. Confidence in the United Nations had been gravely shaken and there was a general tendency for countries of like mind to group together; in India's case, this tendency was likely to be strengthened by the increasing hostility of Communist propaganda towards her. In his view, every effort ought to be made to retain India within the Commonwealth; it would be right to incur substantial risks in order to avoid the dangers to our position in South-East Asia which would result from her secession.[26]

[24] Diary, 10 Feb. 1949, GNWR 1/7.
[25] Minutes of Cabinet Cttee on CR, 8 Feb. 1949, CAB 134/119.
[26] Minutes of Cabinet Cttee on CR, 1 Mar. 1949, ibid.

At a later meeting he said that 'he very much hoped that means would be found to retain India within the Commonwealth. Her departure would greatly jeopardise the British position in South-East Asia and the Far East, and weaken our power to exercise any effective influence on the course of events in that region.'[27] The achievement of America's commitment to the defence of Western Europe under the Atlantic Pact (4 April) made British sensitivity to the South East Asian interests of her European allies less important. America's anti-imperialism in the region also harmonized with India's, as, to a lesser degree, did its anti-Communism. Bevin's conversion therefore owed something to developments in Cold War diplomacy early in 1949. However, it may have been worked more directly by a long report that Sargent's successor produced on 27 February, after a six-week tour of South East Asia and the Far East.

Sir William Strang's tour covered the central and eastern parts of the sea-girt periphery that skirts the heartland of Europe and Asia.[28] Following Halford Mackinder geopoliticians called it 'Rimland'. As the heartland was largely under Soviet control Strang argued that it was necessary to deny Rimland, from Oslo to Tokyo, to Communism:

In all this, the Indian sub-continent has a special importance. It lies at a place about half-way round the periphery. If India tends to look eastwards, Pakistan looks both east and west. The sub-continent should not be regarded in isolation as a separate section. India in particular has an important role to play in peripheral politics—as a Great Asian Power; as a possible member of the Commonwealth; as a country with whom the United Kingdom now has an opportunity to develop relations on a new basis; as a country with political, cultural and economic interests in South East Asia, which we should try to carry with us in the framing of policies and the development of action in that region. The Delhi Conferences on Indonesia and Burma may be pointers to the future. . . . [We have] a part to play in this area which can be played by no other Power though we clearly cannot play it alone. It can be best played by a combination of British experience and United States resources.

In Malaya Malcolm MacDonald emphasized the need to look at South East Asia as a whole, as the Communists did. Many Foreign

---

[27] Minutes of Cabinet Cttee on CR, 22 Apr. 1949, ibid.
[28] 'Sir William Strang's Tour of South East Asia and the Far East, from 12 Jan. to 21 Feb.', 27 Feb. 1949, circulated by Bevin as CP(49)67, 3 Mar. 1949. See also Strang's *Home and Abroad*, ch. 8.

and Colonial servants told Strang of the need for 'not merely a United Kingdom policy but a Commonwealth policy; and that policy should, so far as possible, be concerted with the United States'.[29]

Bevin must also have been influenced by the fact that the expert analyses clearly revealed the desirability of holding an Indian republic to the Commonwealth. In response to Foreign Office prompting, he had requested the preparation of an offical analysis of the arguments on the question of policy. A working party drawn from the FO, CRO, CO, Treasury, Board of Trade, Home Office, and Ministry of Defence had prepared a long document on the respective implications of India's membership and secession. Brook advised Attlee that

most of the arguments in it against retaining India within the Common-wealth are included at the suggestion of the Foreign Office. . . . But broadly speaking . . . the only arguments [against] . . . are the political considerations put forward by the Foreign Office; all the economic consid-erations tend in favour . . . and the balance of the argument clearly tilts that way.[30]

The Chiefs of Staff were quite clear that 'Our strategic require-ments cannot be met unless India is friendly both to the Common-wealth as a whole and to Pakistan. The best way of ensuring this is for India to remain a member of the Commonwealth.'[31] If India became a foreign state she 'might then drift towards Russia'. Ministers deemed the opinion of Jowitt and the Law Officers 'unduly pessimistic' towards the prospect of defeating an MFN challenge to the Commonwealth trade with a republican India.[32]

---

[29] Ibid., 240.

[30] Brook's minute to Attlee, 28 Feb. 1949, CAB 21/1824; 'India's Future Relations with the Commonwealth: Implications for Commonwealth Countries', 24 Feb. 1949 (CR(49)5), CAB 134/119. For the arguments favouring India's membership as a republic, see 'Document on Constitutional Questions: Report by Official Committee', 23 Feb. 1949 (CR(49)5), ibid., which was based upon the Official Committee's Fifth Report. For a recent discussion see Singh, 'Keeping India in the Commonwealth: British Political and Military Aims, 1947–1949', *Journal of Contemporary History*, 20 (1985), 469–81.

[31] 'Military Implications of India's Possible Future Status: Appreciation by the Chiefs of Staff Committee', Feb. 1949, Appx to CR(49)6, loc. cit.

[32] Minutes of Cabinet Cttee on CR, 4 Mar. 1949, CAB 134/119; 'The Commonwealth Relationship: Most Favoured Nation Questions', 25 Feb. 1949, CR(49)7, ibid.

Attlee, Bevin, Cripps, and Noel-Baker chose the emissaries to the Dominions. Brook would go to Canada, Liesching to South Africa, Listowel to Australia and New Zealand, and Gordon Walker to Ceylon, Pakistan, and India. On 1 March the King was told of the strategy. On 3 March Attlee simply informed the full Cabinet of the intended dispatch of the emissaries, preparatory to a spring conference of Prime Ministers. The Cabinet generally endorsed the view that Brook suggested to Attlee:

. . . that the political advantages of retaining India within the Commonwealth—especially at the present time when the whole of South East Asia is overshadowed by the threat of Communist encroachment—are so great that Commonwealth countries would be justified in making *some* concessions from their traditional point of view about the Commonwealth connection, and taking *some* risks, with a view to keeping India with them.[33]

Next the Opposition leaders were put in the picture. The press, however, was told that the emissaries were being sent out to discuss business arising from the October Prime Ministers' Conference. Finally, instructions to the emissaries were approved by the Ministerial Committee.[34] As Gordon Walker was to proceed to India after the other visits were completed, he would require further instructions at a later stage.

As personal representatives of the Prime Minister the emissaries received precise instructions.[35] They were to explain to the respective Prime Ministers the reasons for proposing a special conference in April to discuss India's future relations with the Commonwealth and to inform them of the general state of discussions with India and the result's of HMG's deliberations to date.

You will begin by outlining the great political advantages of retaining India within the Commonwealth. . . . You should, in particular, stress the advantages of keeping India within the Commonwealth at a time when the Commonwealth influence is more than ever needed throughout South East Asia in combating the encroachment of Communism from the north and east. . . . You may also refer . . . to the important practical difficulties

[33] Brook's *aide mémoire* of 2 Mar. for Attlee's oral statement to Cabinet next day, CAB 21/1824. See CM(49)17, 3 Mar. 1949.

[34] Minutes of Cabinet Cttee on CR, 4 Mar. 1949, CAB 134/119.

[35] Directive annexed to minutes of 4 Mar., ibid. This was drafted by Brook (Brook's minute to PM, 3 Mar. 1949, CAB 21/1820).

which would arise—political, economic, financial and military—if India left the Commonwealth while Pakistan and Ceylon remained within it. The conclusion to which all of these considerations point is that all the countries of the Commonwealth—including India herself—have a substantial interest in India remaining a fully co-operative member of the Commonwealth.

Whilst every effort should be made to find a substantial Crown link acceptable to India and as HMG alone may not be able to persuade India of its desirability, India may be influenced by the expression of the common desire of all members of a conference. If no such link were found then Commonwealth governments must decide whether 'the constitutional basis of the Commonwealth connection should be so adapted as to . . . include a republican India which owes no allegiance to the Crown'. Emissaries were authorized to say that the King and the Opposition leaders concurred with the attempt to retain India in the Commonwealth.

Brook's mission to Canada brought no surprises. In interviews with Mackenzie King, now retired, Louis St Laurent, who had succeeded him as Prime Minister, the Governor-General, Vincent Massey, and Lester Pearson, he found virtual unaniminity.[36] Canada did not want its own link with the Crown weakened and favoured attempts to persuade India to retain her allegiance. If they failed she would support attempts to find an alternative substantial link but, in the end, Canada would accept a republican India as clearly preferable to her expulsion (which Mackenzie King thought would prompt Russia to argue that members of the Commonwealth were not free). Canada disliked the idea of a public redefinition of the Commonwealth and, in particular, mention of common citizenship, which implied a commitment to extend special rights to Commonwealth citizens. The Canadian leaders repeatedly emphasized the overriding political advantages of India's membership. An External Affairs Department memorandum submitted to Cabinet on 17 March argued that 'There is obvious value in India's continued membership in the Commonwealth, from a political and strategic point of view, particularly in view of the present international situation. This is of importance not only in terms of the Soviet menace but also as providing an important link between the peoples

[36] Brook's cables on the mission appear in CAB 21/1821.

of Asia and the Western Countries.'[37] That day the full Cabinet ratified the policy that Brook had foreshadowed. St Laurent decided to send Pearson as his representative to the Prime Ministers' Conference and to go over himself only if discussions there revealed the necessity. He would inform Nehru of the great importance to Canada of the Crown link and of finding an acceptable means of retaining India within the Commonwealth.

When Ben Chifley learned of Listowel's mission to Australia he 'spoke most strongly about need for political and strategic reasons to keep India within Commonwealth by hook or by crook and felt confident that it would be possible to devise some solution to achieve this object'.[38] HMG felt some anxiety about the disruptive potentialities of the self-important antics of the mercurial Dr Evatt. Impressed by the 'almost desperate' financial and economic position of Britain, Evatt assumed that by dint of their geography and capacity Australia and New Zealand should take the lead in speaking for the Commonwealth in South East Asia and the Pacific.[39] In August 1947 he had ruffled Indian representatives to a Canberra conference on the Japanese peace treaty by claiming such a status.[40] He was a fervent advocate of the South Asian dominions remaining in the Commonwealth and, in mid-1948, claimed that Australia's 'representation contributed largely to the decision that they, as well as Ceylon, should retain their membership'.[41] He lamented the loss of Burma. When Brook visited Australia in August 1948 he crossed Evatt in transit to London, which Evatt saw as a deliberate manœuvre to eliminate him from discussions. At the end of February 1949 he was in Delhi *en route* to London and care was taken to consult him in both locations. Nye was enjoined to discourage Evatt from opening an independent line of diplomacy with Nehru.[42] Upon his arrival in Delhi he was presented with a note from Nye asking him to defer discussion of the constitutional question with Nehru. After a discussion with Nehru Evatt cabled Chifley:

[37] Cited in Eayrs, op. cit., 247.

[38] UK High Commissioner to CRO, 27 Feb. 1949, CAB 21/1820.

[39] Australian House of Representatives Debates, 17 June 1948, p. 2204.

[40] B. Rama Rau's report to Nehru, 6 Sep. 1947, Ministry of External Affairs, GOI, File 60-FEA/47 Secret, NAI.

[41] Australian House of Representatives Debates, 17 June 1948, p. 2205.

[42] Liesching to Nye (personal), 26 and 28 Feb. 1949, CAB 21/1820.

I hope you will request Attlee that such emissaries and legal officers like Jowitt should see me in London well before any mission otherwise there might be a repetition of the Irish impasse where but for the intervention of Australia and New Zealand in London, Ireland would probably have been formally declared a foreign country. That undesirable result was fortunately avoided. Similarly, in the case of India, too, I believe active assistance and drafting very earliest stage is essential so that important objective of continuing India in the British Commonwealth can be achieved. Nehru is very anxious for practical suggestions from me and is giving me documentation to look over. If we can give him a hand and at the same time maintain the association of the British Commonwealth it will be a great stride towards peace in Asia.[43]

When he saw Nye he criticized the scheme for emissaries and a conference.[44]

In London Evatt saw Noel-Baker and Gordon Walker on 7 March and urged them 'not [to] seek to settle any line' in advance of the conference, for Nehru would feel that there was 'an attempt to "gang-up" against him'.[45] In the light of criticism by R.G. Menzies, leader of the Opposition, of the Australian Labour Government's unconcern with the continuance of the British Commonwealth of Nations, he urged the retention of the word 'British' in the title. Evatt 'did not want to have to make a new Commonwealth in order to keep India inside' and thought Nehru and Bajpai could be brought to accept more than had seemed possible in October 1948. He revealed his ignorance of Indian feeling by urging that India should be pressed to speak of herself as a 'Union' rather than a 'republic' and to accept the King's prerogative powers in external affairs. HMG was fortunate that Listowel was able to deal with Chifley uncluttered by his presence, and that his preoccupation with the United Nations prevented his attendance at the April conference.[46]

Australian opinion at large favoured close links with India. Towards the end of the war a member of the External Affairs Department spoke in Delhi of the rosy prospects of trade between

[43] Evatt to Chifley, 1 Mar. 1949, Evatt Collection, Flinders University.
[44] Nye to Liesching (personal), 1 Mar. 1949, CAB 21/1820.
[45] Noel-Baker's record of conversation with Evatt, 7 Mar. 1949, CAB 127/115.
[46] For Evatt's expansion of his ideas on the new Commonwealth, see: 'Towards a Greater British Commonwealth', BBC broadcast, 6 Sep. 1948; statement in Fremantle, 13 Jan. 1949 (both in Evatt collection); 'The British Commonwealth of Nations: Principles of Future Development', *The Times*, 12 Mar. 1949.

the two countries.[47] He identified wheat as having outstanding potentiality as an Australian export and jute as an import. In the second half of 1948 Australia exported £A10m. worth of wheat to India and imported fibres and textiles worth £A8.6m. In the full year 1947–8 Australia's exports and imports for India balanced at £A26.7m. In 1946, Sir Bertram Stevens, a former Premier of New South Wales, made a study of Australian–Indian relations for the Australian Institute of International Affairs, indicating opportunities for co-operation between the two expanding industrial nations.[48] In December 1948 he wrote three articles for the *Hindu*, emphasizing Australia's goodwill towards India and the importance of their co-operation for the future of South East Asia. India was 'destined to be the strongest power in Asia' and a stabilizing force.[49] Australia should help provide machinery and equipment for her economic development. The *Hindu* wrote of the benefits of Australia's remoteness from Europe and her Labour Government, which enabled her to pursue 'a policy which is independent of that pursued by the Western Powers with colonial possessions in the East'.[50] India and Australia had consistently supported Indonesia and they had the common aim of peace and prosperity for Asia. The Australian press linked Listowel's visit with an attempt to consolidate collective strength in Asia, just as the Atlantic Pact would achieve that goal in Europe. It expected the Commonwealth Prime Ministers' Conference to consider 'the new outlook in Asia, as affected by the spread of Communism, the persistent terrorist outrages in Malaya, the complete chaos in Burma, and the dubious trends implicit in Pandit Nehru's announcement of a republican policy for India'.[51]

Chifley told Listowel that every effort should be made to persuade India to retain the Crown link but, in the probable event of failure, he would welcome India as a 'Sovereign Republic'.[52] India was 'a bulwark against Communism in Asia' and a 'member whose loss would weaken Commonwealth structure'. India's foreign

[47] Critchley, 'Prospects of Trade between India and Australia', address to Indian Council of World Affairs, New Delhi, 9 Dec. 1944, *India Quarterly* (1945), 46–56.
[48] Stevens, *New Horizons* (1946).
[49] Cited in the *Hindu*, 14 Dec. 1948.
[50] Ibid.
[51] Melbourne *Age*, 11 Mar. 1949.
[52] Listowel to CRO, 15 Mar. 1949, CAB 21/1821.

policy would be favourable to Commonwealth interests and her opposition to colonialism accorded with Australia's policy. Republicanism did not matter so long as the real basis of mutual confidence and consultation remained. Opposition attacks were inevitable but he would not take Menzies into his confidence. He valued Australia's Indian trade and did not believe that preferences would be challenged. In any event the risk must be taken, for 'he regarded political considerations as outweighing economic considerations in this issue'.[53] As the Defence Minister was to tell Listowel, 'it was vital for Australia to have a powerful friend in Asia' and 'the only country which could fill this role was India'.[54] Chifley agreed with South Africa and Canada in the rejection of reciprocal citizenship rights with India, but he valued Australia's relations with India above her Commonwealth link with either of them. Unlike St Laurent he felt no need to consult his Cabinet during Listowel's visit.

Prior to leaving for the Prime Ministers' Conference Chifley did bring the matter before Cabinet.[55] It 'agreed that it is desirable that the association of India with the British Commonwealth of Nations be maintained and that the matter be left with the Prime Minister to deal with on his visit to London'. The Cabinet had been presented with a persuasive memorandum on the subject, which emphasized Australia's interest in preserving its own link with the Crown whilst arguing that 'India is more important to Australia, economically and strategically, than some members of the British Commonwealth who are prepared to accept the present constitutional framework' (notably South Africa and Canada).[56] Australia's interests pointed to a flexible policy. The memorandum saw the association in the Commonwealth of Australia, New Zealand, India, Pakistan, Ceylon, and Britain (for Malaya, etc.) as obviating the need for a regional agreement in Asia. As for the Most Favoured Nation problem, a challenge should be met by an appeal 'to the historical position and gradual evolution of the Commonwealth' (a defence that Mackenzie King thought fully adequate). Like Canada, Australia would avoid any redefinition of the Commonwealth

---

[53] Listowel to CRO, 16 Mar. 1949, ibid.

[54] Ibid.

[55] Cabinet minutes, 7 Apr. 1949, Agenda no. 1586, A2700, vol. 38, Australian Archives.

[56] 'India and the Commonwealth', 7 Apr. 1949, ibid.

(which might only prejudice its position) and restrict any announcement to 'short statements of an actually recognised position . . . stressing historical and evolutionary factors rather than legal concepts'. Again like Canada, Australia could not, without risk to its longstanding immigration policy, accept the notion of common citizenship.

In New Zealand Listowel found Fraser doubtful whether the retention of India was worth the sacrifice of a Commonwealth based on common allegiance to the Crown.[57] He was apprehensive of his Opposition and emphasized the importance of kinship to New Zealand. He regarded Australia's concern for a Regional Pacific Pact as 'too Asian' and preferred a close association with British foreign policy in the Far East and the Pacific. It was 'better to have our British peoples prepared to stick together and cut our losses than to have a flabby Commonwealth with no clear guiding principle'.[58] Nehru renounced any form of military co-operation, and association with India would weaken the Commonwealth as a mutual support system. Listowel viewed Fraser's stance primarily as a criticism of Britain's failure to press Nehru for concessions. In the absence of instructions to represent HMG's view he simply allowed Fraser to develop his case. He was disturbed that Fraser would assume that his own views prevailed and he cabled home to suggest that they were at odds with HMG's understanding of 'the inexorable exigencies of the situation'.[59] The British High Commissioner was critical of Listowel's handling of the interview:

. . . Fraser's exuberant and non-stop declamation was not countered by any correspondingly determined advocacy of the documents' point of view. It was a striking exhibition of how the ascendancy of personality affects the course and outcome of negotiation. . . . The point is . . . that if we were expected to fight for the case expounded in the documents, the case has so far . . . gone more or less by default.[60]

A strong cable was drafted for Attlee to send to Fraser, arguing that in the end India must be accepted as a republic.[61] However, it was never sent, perhaps because there was support for New Zealand's viewpoint in cables from Liesching and Gordon Walker.

[57] Listowel to CRO, 21 Mar. 1949, CAB 21/1821.
[58] Listowel to CRO, 22 Mar. 1949, ibid.
[59] Listowel to CRO, 24 Mar. 1949, ibid.
[60] Patrick Duff to Liesching, 25 Mar. 1949 (personal and top secret), ibid.
[61] Draft telegram from Attlee to Fraser, ibid.

When Liesching arrived in South Africa the High Commissioner arranged for him to see Smuts prior to meeting the Prime Minister, Dr Malan. Smuts had guessed the purpose of Liesching's mission and expressed 'concern at the special difficulties' for South Africa of India remaining in the Commonwealth as a republic.[62] He felt that 'the strong cohesive character of the old Dominions association' would be impaired by the admission of 'peoples of such differing background and origin'. India's full membership would be 'an unnatural development'. He would prefer India, Pakistan, and Ceylon to have treaty relationships with the Commonwealth. He would also oppose India's membership as a republic for 'local' reasons, for it would precipitate the emergence of a South African republic. Malan's Nationalists would claim the approval by Britain of their aim of republicanism within the Commonwealth. In consequence, English-speaking South Africans would feel let down by Britain and be unable to offer effective resistance to Afrikaner isolationism. Liberal Europeans in South Africa would be discouraged and 'consider that the United Kingdom had indirectly but powerfully assisted those in South Africa who preached race hatred'. The Nationalists would be strengthened and the British connection weakened.

Malan favoured sustaining the existing membership of the Commonwealth as 'an effective part of the Democratic and anti-Communist world' but he seemed drawn to the alternative of a treaty relationship with a republican India.[63] As an Indian nationalist Nehru would most fear European Russian interference, whether or not India remained in the Commonwealth. Malan most feared India exacting conditions from within the Commonwealth by a call to 'help our people to obtain full rights in all parts of the Commonwealth or we will leave it'. His stand was clear: '. . . no concessions to Indians in South Africa could be made either in respect of immigration or of civil disabilities. He could see no matters on which the Government of the Union and India could co-operate except joint opposition to the advance of Communism.' A few days later when Malan had read the official British documents and discussed them with his Cabinet he was struck by Britain's

[62] Liesching to CRO, 14 Mar. 1949, ibid. For Smuts' criticism of republican membership, see: *Cape Times,* 29 Apr. 1949; South African House of Assembly Debates, 11 May 1949, cols. 5565–75.

[63] Liesching to CRO, 14 Mar. 1949, CAB 21/1821.

apparent willingness to accept India as a republic.[64] His political opponents in general saw that the Nationalists sensed 'a great victory' in respect of their own goal of republicanism and, thereby, in their aim of curtailing the civil liberties of non-Europeans.[65] However, Liesching had left feeling that South Africa was likely to welcome India's withdrawal as removing a source of embarrassment.

As Brook acknowledged, Gordon Walker was assigned 'the most complicated task'.[66] He visited Pakistan first. Liaquat undertook to use all his influence to persuade India to accept the Crown link.[67] However, if that failed and India as a republic remained a full member of the Commonwealth, then Pakistan would also become a republic. It would be impossible to convince Pakistanis to retain the Crown link if it offered no advantages above those enjoyed by republican members. (Liaquat had already pressed HMG on the point in January in relation to Eire's position.)[68] Zafrulla revealed more of the Pakistani mind. He favoured 'a Commonwealth linked by the Crown' and saw 'no really satisfactory alternative to the Crown as a symbol of unity'.[69] To admit a republic 'might be the first step in the dissolution of the Commonwealth'. He had prevented the insertion of the term 'republic' in Pakistan's draft constitution. Consistently with Pakistan's calls for Commonwealth intervention over Kashmir he clearly thought 'the Commonwealth should and would grow closer together'. It was symptomatic that Liaquat was disturbed by press reports that the London conference was to consider the danger of Communism and regional defence.[70] For though she was closest of all Commonwealth countries to Russia, Pakistan was really most fearful of India, and her main interest in the Commonwealth had always been as a check on Indian aggression. For Pakistan a Commonwealth growing 'closer together' meant primarily its willingness to settle disputes between its members. As a prominent Pakistani stated a few months later, 'It is not sufficient to say: ''The Commonwealth affords protection

[64] UK High Commissioner for Liesching, 4 Apr. 1949, ibid.
[65] Ibid.
[66] Brook's minute to PM, 3 Mar. 1949, CAB 21/1820.
[67] Gordon Walker to CRO, 12 Mar. 1949, CAB 21/1821.
[68] UK High Commission in Pakistan to CRO, 19 Jan. 1949, CAB 134/119.
[69] Gordon Walker to CRO, 14 Mar. 1949, CAB 21/1821.
[70] Gordon Walker to CRO, 16 Mar. 1949, ibid.

against the naughty boy from outside, even though it does not afford protection against the naughty boy inside" '.[71] Here, concluded Pakistanis aggrieved over the Punjab massacres and the fate of Junagadh, Hyderabad, and Kashmir, was 'an illogical and generally a most unsatisfactory situation'.

Gordon Walker found that attitudes in Ceylon resembled those in Pakistan. Senanayake intended to spend a day in Karachi in discussion with Liaquat 'as Pakistan and Ceylon have obvious problems in common if India becomes a Republic or leaves the Commonwealth'.[72] Senanayake felt that Nehru's position was weak, that he was run by Congress, that India was unstable, and 'might be as mischievous in South East Asia as Russia'. His Foreign Minister, Mr K. Vaithianathan, said that 'Ceylon's real interest in the Commonwealth was to have the United Kingdom's support as a counterweight to India'.[73] There seemed little danger that Ceylon would follow India into republicanism in the short term. Senanayake's instinct was to withhold Commonwealth membership from an Indian republic, for no one would know what 'obligations' such membership would involve, especially with regard to respecting Ceylon's independence.[74] For Ceylon and Pakistan, as for New Zealand, the loss of the Crown link seemed like a step towards disintegration, a portent of the weakening of the Commonwealth as a mutual support system.

For over two months after Attlee's 16 December cable rejected his Eight Points, Nehru was left uncertain of HMG's next move. On 20 February he wrote to Mountbatten, 'I have done my best in the matter. Somehow matters have come to a standstill. I do not quite know where we are.'[75] Three days later Nye went to see him, aware that 'in certain responsible circles in Delhi it was felt that whilst six months ago we had been very anxious for India to remain in the Commonwealth, recently it was thought that our enthusiasm had waned'.[76] Nye corrected this misreading of the hiatus, which was in

---

[71] Hasan, *Pakistan and the Commonwealth* (1950), p. 11. This was originally prepared as a paper for a Commonwealth Relations Conference in Canada in September 1949.
[72] Gordon Walker to CRO, 21 Mar. 1949 (1), CAB 21/1821.
[73] Gordon Walker to CRO, 21 Mar. 1949 (2), ibid.
[74] Gordon Walker to CRO, 25 Mar. 1949, ibid.
[75] Cited in Gopal, *Nehru*, ii, 51.
[76] UK High Commissioner to CRO, 23 Feb. 1949, CAB 21/1824.

fact a time of intensive analysis at the London end. He reminded Nehru that the problem was now narrowed down to the position of the King, which was not merely a legal matter but vital to the people of Britain and the old Dominions. Nehru felt that at the London conference he had been misled, mainly by Cripps's confidence, into an assumption that his own initiative afforded a sufficient basis for reconstructing the Commonwealth. He had suffered personal disappointment and embarrassment in his Cabinet and in the Congress Party. His unofficial correspondence with Cripps had left him 'muddled' over the state of play and feeling that 'we have been rather tiresome over the whole business'. Two days later, Nye was instructed to deliver an oral message from Attlee emphasizing the attention that the matter had been receiving, together with a cable that informed him of the scheme for emissaries and a Prime Ministers' Conference.[77] Nehru seemed 'very pleased' with the choice of Gordon Walker to visit India but found it 'difficult to understand' why he was first to spend a fortnight in Pakistan and Ceylon.[78] In mid-March Nehru was at a loss to know what more he could say at the Conference and expected it to be 'inconclusive'. He was nonplussed by a long letter that Attlee sent him on 20 March.[79] It seemed 'surprisingly naïve', and he could not see 'what we are going to discuss in London if this is the approach of the United Kingdom Prime Minister'.[80]

Attlee's 'long screed' calls to mind his letter of March 1948. It was similarly 'unofficial' and 'very personal'. It was an impassioned plea for the consideration of the continuing value of kingship in the traditions of India as well as the Commonwealth. It was no doubt occasioned by the cables of his emissaries (especially in New Zealand, South Africa, Pakistan, and Ceylon), which had indicated significant preferences for insisting upon the link with the Crown.

Hitherto the link has been The King. I say The King rather than the Crown. King George has often stressed this point to me. The Crown is an abstract symbol connoting authority, often connected in the minds of some with an external power. But the real link is a person, The King. At the head of the Commonwealth is a family. This family does in a very real sense

---

[77] CRO to UK High Commissioner, 25 Feb. 1949, CAB 21/1820.

[78] UK High Commissioner to CRO, 1 Mar. 1949, ibid.; Nehru to Patel, 14 Mar. 1949, Das, *Patel's Correspondence*, viii, 2–3.

[79] Attlee to Nehru, 20 Mar. 1949, CAB 127/344.

[80] Nehru to Patel, 26 Mar. 1949, Das, op. cit., viii, 3.

symbolise the family nature of the Commonwealth. I think this is important in these days when there is in many parts of the world an over-emphasis on the State. We are fortunate in having a Royal Family that does inspire affection not only among those who know them but among millions who have not seen them in person. People see in the Royal Family a projection of the family life which they hold dear. The family is the basic unit of society. It is something universal, transcending creeds and races. . . .

The existence . . . of a King and Royal Family provides a mystique which is appreciated by a very wide range of people, and a mystique is a valuable point of unity and stability. Their very remoteness from the play of politics and the clash of creeds make them a unifying influence. They are above the battle. . . .

. . . I am deeply concerned with two things; the peace of the world, to which I believe that the Commonwealth can make a great contribution, and the peace, prosperity and stability of India and the well being of the Indian people.

Nehru waited until 1 April to reply, firmly and finally rejecting any recognition of the Crown in the Indian constitution. 'For a whole generation now we have built up a certain tradition and a certain way of thinking. Our draft constitution is based on this. Any attempt to change it during its final stages would lead to an uproar and would create enormous difficulties.'[81] However, he had by then had long talks with Gordon Walker, explored various possibilities, and was 'anxious to find a solution which would be satisfactory to all the parties concerned'.[82] In fact, a breakthrough had been achieved.

Attlee's instructions to Gordon Walker for his critical mission to India were framed by Brook, and approved by Noel-Baker and the Commonwealth Relations Committee, in the light of reports of the discussions with the other Prime Ministers.[83] As it was clear that India's refusal to accept a Crown link would divide the Commonwealth, Gordon Walker was required to convince Nehru of the 'real difficulties' faced by other members.[84] He must emphasize Britain's anxiety for India's membership, not only because it served the self-interest of both countries but also because it was

[81] Nehru to Attlee, 1 Apr. 1949, CAB 127/344.
[82] Ibid.
[83] Minutes of Cabinet Cttee on CR, 24 Mar. 1949, CAB 134/119.
[84] Attlee to Gordon Walker, 25 Mar. 1949, CAB 21/1821.

of 'substantial importance to the resistance of Communist encroachments and the preservation of world peace that the Commonwealth should be seen to stand firm and unimpaired in the present crisis of world relationships'. The Crown was the one common feature of the Commonwealth relationship. For members it was 'the symbol of their long historical development and of their present association as free and independent peoples'. Any break in continuity would sharpen demands for the definition of procedures and obligations, which would be difficult to meet without dissension. These were no mere 'legal niceties'. In descending order of value, the links open to discussion were some recognition of the King in the Indian constitution, the delegation of powers by the King to each incoming President, an Indian declaration that she remained in the Commonwealth and recognized 'the King as the Head of the Commonwealth', reciprocal citizenship, recognition of the King as the fountain of Commonwealth honours, the establishment of a Commonwealth arbitral tribunal, and the appointment of Prime Ministers to the Privy Council. While the Commonwealth Prime Ministers would agree that either of the first two links was sufficient, they would probably not feel any of the others to be adequate in itself. On no account was Gordon Walker to imply that a solution was possible without a link with the Crown.

In a preliminary talk with Bajpai on 27 March, the evening of his arrival in Delhi, Gordon Walker learnt that Nehru underestimated the value of the Crown to members of the Commonwealth.[85] Gordon Walker spent much of a ninety-minute interview with Nehru on 28 March overcoming Nehru's resistance on this point. Nehru reiterated his puzzlement that in October 1948 and for some months afterwards 'no one had talked to him about the Crown with such emphasis'. At a second interview, on 30 March, he still harked back to the autumn discussions and his Eight Points.

At Gordon Walker's first interview with him Nehru alluded to Attlee's personal letter and emphasized that 'it was quite impossible to make room for a King in the Constitution'.[86] That would cause 'division and controversy'. At the second interview he explained the impossibility of the delegation approach, for the constitution was absolutely and radically republican:

85 Gordon Walker to CRO, 28 Mar. 1949, ibid.
86 Ibid.

It categorically declared that all the President's powers flowed from the people. There was strong feeling in India against any powers being derived from outside. He spent some time describing the internal political difficulties in India. Both the Communists and the communalists were increasingly inclined to resort to terrorism and violence. . . . Moreover the Socialists though democratic and anti-Communist have very strong republican views and would eagerly raise slogans such as 'India has been sold'. They would have a considerable following if the constitution were altered or anything done in violation of its spirit.[87]

Nehru had gone on record against any sort of delegation when he had discussed the Eight Points with Congress MPs. It was not 'practical politics' to recognize the King as the source of any of the President's powers. Clearly, neither of the two approaches that seemed to afford a sufficient Crown link could be pursued. Yet Nehru remained adamant in his wish to have India in the Commonwealth, 'particularly because the Commonwealth was a factor for world peace'.

The problem, as Bajpai had told Gordon Walker on 27 March, was to find some way of linking India with the Crown that would avoid 'a serious split in the Congress'. Bajpai's 'own idea', which he had not then discussed with Nehru, was that India 'might recognise the King as head of the Commonwealth'. At Gordon Walker's second interview with Nehru Bajpai was present and 'Nehru himself threw out a suggestion that India might perhaps recognise King as head or symbol of unity of the Commonwealth as a whole. I said that this might well be a fruitful line of approach and I hoped he would seriously consider it.' Here was Nehru's first constructive suggestion on the link with the Crown and it is reasonable to suppose that Bajpai had put it to him. When Gordon Walker saw Krishna Menon on the morning of 1 April, the latter was thinking of the Crown as the Head of the Commonwealth.[88] That afternoon he and Bajpai were present at Gordon Walker's final interview with Nehru, who 'for the first time brought up the idea of a solution by way of mutual declarations'.[89] Gordon Walker 'assumed that he meant a declaration enshrining some agreed solution of the problem of finding a link through the Crown between a republican India and the Commonwealth'. That evening Bajpai told him that

---

[87] Gordon Walker to CRO, 30 Mar. 1949, ibid.
[88] Gordon Walker to CRO, 1 Apr. (19.00 hours) 1949, ibid.
[89] Gordon Walker to CRO, 1 Apr. (20.30 hours) 1949, ibid.

his own mind was 'turning on a declaration of the type of the Balfour Declaration' and that he had 'briefly discussed it with Nehru'.[90] It would refer to the Crown as 'the symbol of unity' in the Commonwealth and to the common ideals of its members (justice, liberty, etc.).

It seems that Jowitt saw Gordon Walker's report of Nehru's proposed 'Head of Commonwealth' formula as soon as it reached London on 30 March. The next day, he asked Rau to call and to comment on a draft declaration, claiming it as entirely his own and unseen by his colleagues.[91] The nub of it was its third paragraph, in which India stated that 'She, as a member of that Commonwealth, recognises the position of the King as the (fountain) head of the Commonwealth of which she freely elects to become a member'. Rau thought it the best formula he had seen, for as a result of attending meetings of the Congress Party he was convinced that whatever Nehru's own views he would find it 'politically impossible' to recognize the King's sovereignty over India. Jowitt commended it to the Commonwealth Relations Committee. At his instance, Rau sent it to Nehru (through Bajpai) with the hope that Nehru 'with his gift for phrasing might be able to suggest something, particularly as regards third para of statement, which without being too definite might satisfy sentiment'.[92]

When Gordon Walker reviewed 'Tactics on India' in a Cabinet Committee memorandum on 6 April, he indicated that:

The main Indian suggestion will almost certainly be some mention of India's acceptance of the King, not as territorial King of any country in the Commonwealth, but as being in some way personally pre-eminent in the Commonwealth and the symbol of its unity. . . . Bajpai will press it strongly on Nehru and he feels the urge of unconcealed pride of authorship in the idea.[93]

Still, Gordon Walker by no means recognized the idea as a breakthrough. He was only 'a little more optimistic' than he had been prior to his mission to South Asia. Certainly Nehru no longer had 'an absolute objection' to a direct Crown link and would accept it as 'a mark of membership of a club to which he wants to belong'. But

---

90 Gordon Walker to CRO, 2 Apr. 1949, ibid.
91 Memo. by Lord Chancellor, 4 Apr. 1949 (CR(49)11), CAB 134/119.
92 Rau to Nehru, 2 Apr. 1949, Das, op. cit., viii, 8–10.
93 CR(49)12, CAB 134/119.

he still feared the political repercussions, 'that the Socialists would win increased popular backing and that a large dissident group in Congress might join them on this issue'. He twice told Gordon Walker that he might be able to use his prestige to get a direct Crown link adopted. Patel had said that India would 'go to the utmost consistent with its constitution to find a solution', for it was 'essential for world peace and to resist Communism that India should be a member of the Commonwealth'.[94] Rajaji believed that Nehru and Patel 'could get anything through that they wished' but would 'flinch' at accepting a direct Crown link, because 'the political difficulties were too great'.[95] Gordon Walker therefore believed that there could be no direct link between India and the Crown. The change that encouraged him was that India was no longer pressing for Commonwealth membership as 'a Republic without the Crown link' but was seeking 'ways and means of linking a Republic through the Crown to the rest of the Commonwealth'. The great danger was that the 'Head of Commonwealth' and 'symbol of unity' approach would be insufficient to satisfy other members. Pakistan, Ceylon, South Africa, and New Zealand all saw the absence of common allegiance as a step towards disintegration. The emissaries' reports had revealed 'an unsuspected solidarity' of the Commonwealth on the desirability of the bond of allegiance. Gordon Walker's gloomy conclusion was that 'agreement on a deliberate delay . . . is likely to be the best outcome of the Conference'. In two years' time Indian opinion would probably be more favourable to a Crown link.

When the Commonwealth Relations Committee met on 8 April it decided that if Nehru could not be persuaded to accept the 'normal Crown relationship' then

. . . the second stage of the discussions would be to seek some other link through the Crown which would be acceptable to India and to other Commonwealth Governments; and it might be appropriate at that stage to indicate the United Kingdom Government's view that the most helpful suggestion hitherto put forward under this head was that India should recognise the King, not as King of India, but as head of the Commonwealth and as the symbol of the free association of Commonwealth peoples.[96]

[94] Gordon Walker to CRO, 1 Apr. (12.35 hours) 1949, CAB 21/1821.
[95] Gordon Walker to CRO, 1 Apr. (12.10 hours) 1949, ibid.
[96] Minutes of Cabinet Cttee on CR, 8 Apr. 1949, CAB 134/119.

Ministers decided that agreement should be sought on a joint declaration of members recognizing the King as 'head of the Commonwealth and symbol of their free association as independent nations within the Commonwealth', whose sovereignty resided in or was derived from the King. As India might reject the latter point, Canada and South Africa might oppose the 'head of Commonwealth' point, and some members might insist on stating their allegiance, a joint declaration might be unobtainable. In that case reciprocal declarations might be proposed, with India's statement of adherence being welcomed by the rest of the Commonwealth. A further meeting on 12 April was told that Krishna Menon had intimated that Nehru might himself propose a declaration.[97] It decided, too, that the postponement by agreement of any decision at the conference carried serious political risks, practical difficulties, and the danger of the Crown becoming an election issue in several member countries.

Nehru discussed the forthcoming conference with the CWC on 10 April and probably secured their acquiescence in his taking an initiative with a declaration.[98] On 14 April he sent to Patel 'merely our latest drafts': suggested points of agreement among members of the Commonwealth and a common declaration, adapting the language of the Balfour declaration, of their acceptance of the King as 'the symbol of this free association'.[99] The idea of common citizenship was prominent in the drafts. Though they made no mention of the King as head of the Commonwealth the drafts were probably Bajpai's, for the ideas and approach were his, and he accompained Nehru to London. On Thursday, 21 April, the day after he arrived for the conference, Nehru gave copies of a statement of India's position to Attlee and Pearson.[100] At 10 a.m. next morning Attlee gave the Commonwealth Relations Committee an account of his private discussions with the Commonwealth ministers individually since their arrival.[101] It was agreed that immediately after his opening remarks defining the problem for the conference Attlee should invite Nehru 'to state the Indian position'.

On the eve of the conference Attlee might feel well pleased.

97 Ibid.
98 UK High Commissioner to CRO, 14 Apr. 1949, CAB 21/1821.
99 Nehru to Patel, 14 Apr. 1948, and encl., Das, op. cit., viii, 10–11.
100 Eayrs, op. cit., 249; Nehru to Patel, 23 Apr. 1949, Das, op. cit., viii, 12–13.
101 Minutes of Cabinet Cttee on CR, 22 Apr. 1949, CAB 134/119.

Nehru could scarcely feel that the Commonwealth had 'ganged-up' against him. Instead, Nehru's co-operation had been won and he would make the running. The problem would be to move other members towards a compromise. Attlee found Malan to be anxious mainly about the problem of Indians in South Africa, indeed about the colonization of the East Coast of Africa by Indians.[102] Neither he nor Pearson liked the term 'Head of Commonwealth'. Senanayake preferred to have India in the Commonwealth and thus under constraint, but feared the implications of republican membership for the future. Both he and Liaquat were anxious about 'defensive arrangements' in view of Nehru's known aversion to international alignments. Similarly, New Zealand wanted a definition of principles to clarify obligations. Yet Attlee knew that to each of these problems there was a ready answer. South Africa might fear for its immigration policy but Canada and Australia had problems similar in kind if not in degree, while acceptance of India as a republic held great attractions as a precedent to the Nationalists. As for collective security, a fresh scrutiny of the possibilities of a treaty relationship revealed that an act of faith in India's growing co-operation in the Commonwealth was a superior policy to leaving India isolated and exposed to Russian influences.[103] It was clear that in essentials Canada and Australia were at one with Britain. Attlee's painstaking preparation for the conference would enable him to achieve his object in a mere twelve hours of formal discussion.

---

[102] Attlee's memoranda on meetings with Malan, Pearson, and Senanayake, 21 Apr. 1949, CAB 21/1819.

[103] 'Treaty Relations with India: Report by Official Working Party', 11 Apr. 1949, CR(49)17, CAB 134/119. See also 'Notes by the Foreign Office on an Eventual Treaty between the United Kingdom and India', 6 April 1949; Noel-Baker's minute for PM on 'India's Foreign Policy and her relation to the Commonwealth', 20 Apr. 1949; CAB 21/1821.

7

The New Commonwealth

ON Friday, 22 April, when Attlee invited him to state India's position to the Dominions' ministers, Nehru suggested that India's association with the Commonwealth might be based on Commonwealth citizenship, a declaration of her continuing membership, and acceptance of 'the King as the symbol' of members' free association.[1] In the light of these suggestions and the expression by other members of their wish to retain allegiance to the Crown, Attlee agreed to put up written proposals to the Monday afternoon session. On the Friday afternoon, Attlee, Cripps (who attended the conference) and Nehru drafted two declarations, the first proclaiming the allegiance of the other members, the second emphasizing India's acceptance of the 'King, Head of the Commonwealth', as the symbol of the free association. Nehru advised Patel that he would have preferred to avoid the phrase 'Head of Commonwealth' but Attlee and Cripps had insisted upon its necessity.[2] The formula was consistent with Bajpai's mid-April drafting, which limited any functions performed by the King to his role as the symbol of the Commonwealth association. Patel approved of it as not derogating from India's sovereign republican status.[3] He was critical, however, of the implication of the two declarations that there were two classes of members, with India a 'mere associate'. During informal discussions other members, notably Pearson, made the same point, so that in the draft that Attlee presented on the Monday afternoon the two declarations had been amalgamated. Malan objected that 'Head of Commonwealth' implied the existence of a ' "super-State" infringing the sovereign rights of the individual Parliaments', and Pearson agreed. The difficulty was eventually overcome by referring to the King as 'the symbol of the free association' and 'as such the Head of the Commonwealth', and by including, at Malan's insistence, an

[1] Minutes of Meetings of Prime Ministers, 22–7 April 1949, CAB 133/89.
[2] Nehru to Patel, 23 Apr. 1949, Das, *Patel's Correspondence*, viii, 12–13.
[3] Patel to Nehru, 23 Apr. 1949, ibid., 15–16.

explanation in the conference minutes that the new terminology did not alter existing relations within the Commonwealth or imply that the King exercised any constitutional function as its Head.

There was only muted objection to India's membership as a republic. At the outset Malan spoke strongly in favour of it as a natural result of historical development. Some observers found this affirmation a sensation, others an irony, but it was of course the product of a shrewd assessment of the National Party's own interests. To some it also seemed strange that two of the newest members, Pakistan and Ceylon, were those most disturbed by the break in India's allegiance; but again, their real concern was for mutual support. Menon felt that Pakistan was trying to push India out, Nehru that Pakistan's 'intrusions' were the only exceptions to the 'good temper' of the proceedings.[4] At the outset Liaquat argued that each member should know 'to what extent she could rely on assistance from others in the event of aggression. The real test of Commonwealth solidarity was the assurance of mutual help in time of trouble'. He later sought the inclusion of 'mutual assistance' as proof of the value of the Commonwealth. This drew a sharp riposte from Nehru, who objected to stating political purposes in a constitutional document and demanded, with success, the replacement of the word 'security' by 'liberty' (together with 'peace' and 'progress') in the objects of the Commonwealth. On 27 April, after agreement had been reached on the declaration, Fraser asked the conference to reaffirm its unity of purpose in international relations, in peace and war. He was supported by Liaquat but Nehru felt provoked. It was not enough, he argued, to build up a Commonwealth defence bloc to check Communism: 'The problem was to capture the minds and imagination of these [Asian] peoples'. The conditions that encouraged Communism must be removed. With a long and (for Pearson) 'impressive dialectical statement' he won Chifley's ready assent—'military strength was not an effective weapon against Communist encroachment'.[5] He achieved Commonwealth membership with non-alignment unsullied.

Nehru also secured, despite Australian and New Zealand opposition, agreement that in *future* the association would be called the 'Commonwealth of Nations', though the declaration correctly

[4] For Menon, see Brecher, 'India's Decision to Remain in the Commonwealth', 77; Nehru to Patel, 27 Apr. 1949, Das, op. cit., viii, 23-4.
[5] For Pearson, see Gopal, *Nehru*, ii, 53.

added the adjective 'British' when it referred to the status quo. The vision of a reciprocal Commonwealth citizenship was, under pressure, dropped from the declaration, surviving only in a milk-and-water minute providing that members would take steps to ensure that nationals of other members were not treated as foreign. In another minute, members agreed that India's trade would not be treated as trade with a foreign country. The Declaration itself was released for publication on the morning of 28 April:

The Governments of the United Kingdom, Canada, Australia, New Zealand, South Africa, India, Pakistan and Ceylon, whose countries are united as Members of the British Commonwealth of Nations and owe a common allegiance to the Crown, which is also the symbol of their free association, have considered the impending constitutional changes in India.

The Government of India have informed the other Governments of the Commonwealth of the intention of the Indian people that under the new constitution which is about to be adopted India shall become a sovereign independent republic. The Government of India however declared and affirmed India's desire to continue her full membership of the Commonwealth of Nations and her acceptance of the King as the symbol of the free association of its independent member nations and as such the Head of the Commonwealth.

The Governments of the other countries of the Commonwealth, the basis of whose membership of the Commonwealth is not hereby changed, accept and recognize India's continuing membership in accordance with the terms of this declaration.

Accordingly, the United Kingdom, Canada, Australia, New Zealand, South Africa, India, Pakistan and Ceylon hereby declare that they remain united as free and equal members of the Commonwealth of Nations, freely co-operating in the pursuit of peace, liberty and progress.

The new Commonwealth was born.

In the weeks following the triumphant London Declaration the Labour Government basked in the warmth of press and public approval. Congratulatory letters circulated among the principals in the saga. One of the best informed was Ismay's letter to Attlee:

Now that 'the Captains and the Kings' have departed for their homes I feel less guilty about adding to your reading matter: but I can no longer resist the pleasure of sending you my warmest congratulations on the outcome of the Prime Ministers' Conference. It was a wonderful personal triumph for you—as was the original decision to appoint a definite date for the handing over of power in India, and to send Dickie as Viceroy. You have, if I may be so bold as to say so, ridden an absolutely consistent and far seeing line on India from the very outset: whereas I am ashamed to admit that I have wobbled badly at various junctures, and lost faith at moments.[6]

Ismay excused his wobbles as occasioned by the miseries that attended the partition and the disputes over Kashmir and Hyderabad, when he felt India to be unworthy of Commonwealth membership. At that time, as Ismay knew, Attlee's staff complained 'that he is really more interested in the Indian problem than in anything else'.[7] *The Times* applauded Attlee's 'great achievement' of 'far and away the most civilized grouping of sovereign States which the world has known'.[8] The *Guardian* and the *Telegraph* were remarkably in harmony as they rhapsodized upon self-governing India's remaining in the Commonwealth as a partner.[9] While the *Economist* carped at the Declaration's avoidance of 'the difficult subjects—common citizenship, common defence arrangements, imperial preference, the settlement of the existing disputes within the Commonwealth', it gave Attlee due credit.[10] The Declaration was generally recognized as the culmination of his crusade for a multi-racial Commonwealth of equal partners, 'co-operating in the pursuit of peace, liberty and progress'. In June 1949 the chairman of the Labour Party's Annual Conference claimed, with justice, 'the Government's handling of the Indian problem as the greatest of its many contributions to world progress'.[11]

Characteristically, Attlee acknowledged Ismay's congratulations as if he had acted merely as a good Prime Ministers' Conference chairman: 'My job was really to prevent any clashes or any introduction of awkward topics such as the Indians in South Africa'.[12] But as he observed in his memoirs the real work had been done in advance.[13] It was a major administrative achievement, a team effort certainly, but he had chosen the team. In his letter to Ismay he noted: 'I am afraid that in this instance as in so many

[6] Ismay to Attlee, 6 May 1949, Attlee Papers, 82/265–7.
[7] Sir G. Abell to Ismay, 20 Aug. 1947, Ismay Papers, III/7/67/30a.
[8] *The Times*, 28 Apr. and 2 May 1949.
[9] *Guardian* and *Daily Telegraph*, 28 Apr. 1949.
[10] *Economist*, 30 Apr. 1949.
[11] Jim Griffiths, cited in Harris, *Attlee*, 430.
[12] Attlee to Ismay, 7 May 1949, Ismay Papers, III/7/53.
[13] ATLE 1/13, Churchill College, Cambridge.

others one tends to get the credit that should be given to many others. You and Dickie made possible this result by creating the atmosphere of goodwill.'

Mountbatten's official biographer makes a larger claim for him: 'Mountbatten . . . believed that his overriding priority was to keep India in the Commonwealth. It is reasonably certain that but for him this would not have happened.'[14] It is doubtful whether Mountbatten as Viceroy was necessary to India's initial dominion-hood. The historical context, and especially the contribution of Jinnah and the Muslim League to it, provided the conditions necessary to the transfer of power to Dominions. It is also questionable whether as Governor-General Mountbatten was essential to the retention of India as a republic to the Commonwealth. His main role, apart from creating goodwill, was to influence in India's favour British policy towards the Kashmir dispute. On the other hand, at several stages his judgements and actions revealed a bias that could only alienate Pakistan from the Commonwealth, provoking a pro-Pakistan thrust from other Britishers (such as Noel-Baker and Grafftey-Smith) to redress the balance.

Both Attlee and Mountbatten were quick to acknowledge Cripps's part in the achievement. The former wrote that he was being 'given credit which should properly be shared by others, notably yourself', for he was 'most conscious and appreciative' of Cripps's work on the Indian problem over many -years.[15] Mountbatten thought that 'few people know better than me how much of this success is due personally to you'.[16] Malcolm MacDonald was certain that Cripps's correspondence with Nehru had 'an immensely good influence in maintaining understanding and a sense of partnership between Britain and India'.[17] The *Observer* believed that the London settlement would have been 'impossible but for two men', Attlee and Cripps, whose integrity Nehru trusted.[18] In November 1948 Noel-Baker told Gordon Walker that Cripps was 'more Indian than the Indians'.[19] However, Cripps was over-confident of his ability to accommodate

---

[14] Ziegler, *Mountbatten*, 469.
[15] Attlee to Cripps, 30 Apr. 1949, CAB 127/85.
[16] Mountbatten to Cripps, 28 Apr. 1949, CAB 127/139.
[17] MacDonald to Cripps, 13 Mar. 1949, CAB 127/143.
[18] *Observer*, 1 May 1949.
[19] Gordon Walker's Diary fragment, 11 Nov. 1948, GNWR 1/7.

Britain to Nehru's requirements. Relations between their countries sometimes suffered from Cripps's well-meaning interventions, as they did in winter 1948–9.

Attlee also wrote to Gordon Walker, 'you know how much the success achieved is due to others, notably to yourself'.[20] Geoffrey Crowther, editor of the *Economist*, congratulated Gordon Walker on the adoption of 'your idea of making H. M. Head of the Commonwealth. I regard this historic decision as primarily your work, and no doubt the fact will be duly disclosed by that ultimate judge of statesmanship, the "future historian".'[21] To a degree, Gordon Walker was to be his own historian. In *The Commonwealth* (1962) he claimed to have suggested the Head of Commonwealth formula first, in July 1948, and to have elaborated it later in an official paper.[22] In reality the formula was embedded in the Statute of Westminster and it had been plucked out by Shawcross in April 1947 and Brook in May 1948. What mattered was not discovering the formula but reconciling India and the old Dominions to it. A clearer statement of Gordon Walker's large contribution appears in a diary entry that he made during his mission to Karachi in mid-March 1949:

This position we are now in has been to a quite considerable extent influenced by me. I was the first to say, and write, that we must face the question of a Republican India: I propounded the 'act of will' as the basis for membership, which is now in the documents: I proposed the initial declaration by India and by all the others, instead of a new definition of the Commonwealth. I also suggested the sending of emissaries. I have undoubtedly been given the most difficult job, India, Pakistan & Ceylon.[23]

Gordon Walker received his deserved reward within a year, when Attlee took the remarkable step of making him Secretary of State for Commonwealth Relations. The inevitably uncelebrated sheet-anchor in the administrative achievement of the new Commonwealth, Norman Brook, was later to become Head of the Civil Service.

Labour's policy for a new Commonwealth in South Asia was not achieved without dissension in the Cabinet. A reviewer of Lord

[20] Attlee to Gordon Walker, 30 Apr. 1949, ibid.
[21] Crowther to Gordon Walker, 29 Apr. 1949, ibid.
[22] *The Commonwealth*, 183.
[23] Entry of 14 Mar. 1949, GNWR 1/8.

Bullock's monumental study, *Ernest Bevin: Foreign Secretary* (1983), observes that 'We skip over the Far East and the evolving Empire/Commonwealth a little too lightly. It is not altogether possible to reconcile Bevin's sentiments about withdrawal from India with the general impression that the Foreign Secretary was a devoted Commonwealth man.'[24]

There were, indeed, sharp conflicts between Attlee and Bevin, first in winter 1946 over the time-limit for withdrawal, secondly in winter 1948 over retaining a republican India to the Commonwealth. After the first Bevin was silenced (for relations with the new Dominions became the province of the CRO), until the reference of Kashmir to the UN opened the subcontinent to Foreign Office influence throughout 1948. After the second, Bevin became constructively involved (notably with the Colombo Plan) in the development of the new Commonwealth as a bulwark against Communism in South East Asia.

The constant element in Bevin's outlook was his preoccupation with Cold War diplomacy. From 1945 to 1948 he was engaged preeminently in securing Western Europe against the Soviets and, largely as a corollary, in consolidating the British Empire in the Middle East. He read policies for India in the light of their implications for these concerns. He wished, indeed, to develop the Middle East as a replacement for the lost Indian Empire, as a source of both prosperous trade and investments and a vast army.[25] In such power play, Pakistan was essentially a Muslim power, to be handled as a Middle Eastern pawn. Located, as he said, at 'the middle of the planet', Pakistan should take the lead in an Arab bloc as against the Soviets.[26] Such perspectives were shared by Mudie, and in January 1949 Liaquat expounded his own 'pet idea of an anti-Communist *bloc* from Turkey to Pakistan'.[27]

On the other hand India seemed an uncertain ally. It was all very well for Cripps and Nehru, both theoretical Marxists in the 1930s, to harmonize their antipathies to Communist methods and colonialist practice alike. For Bevin the colonialists in South East Asia were allies in Europe and the Communists enemies. While Cripps would

[24] Keith Robbins, *History*, 70 (1985), 183.
[25] See esp. Louis, *The British Empire in the Middle East*, passim.
[26] Dalton's Diary, 15 Oct. 1948, cited in P.S. Gupta, *Imperialism and the British Labour Movement*, 299.
[27] Strang's Report of 27 Feb. 1949, loc. cit.

abandon Hong Kong to Communist China Bevin would make it 'a Berlin of the East'.[28] What changed Bevin's estimation of a new South Asian Commonwealth was the extension of the Cold War to Asia. Though that began for Britain with the Malayan insurgency of mid-1948, a Foreign Office policy to combat Communism in Asia as a whole only emerged with Strang's report and elevation as PUS in February 1949. As India could play a crucial role in that policy, in March 1949 Bevin became an advocate of the new Commonwealth.

It is difficult to know whether British apprehensions of India or Pakistan finding Russia a congenial ally during the early post-war years were justified. Prior to Independence Russia had favoured Congress nationalism, deprecating Muslim separatism as imperialist inspired. There is no evidence of Soviet encouragement of Pakistan's occasional intimations that she might seek refuge in Russian support against British Indophilia. Russia's attitude to Independent India seems to have been obtuse. She could not reconcile India's professions of freedom with the accreditation of ambassadors by George VI or the governorship of his first cousin.[29] When India was opposed to Russia at the UN over such issues as Greece, Korea, and the non-permanent members of the Security Council, Russia readily consigned her to the Anglo-American bloc. The only clear Russian initiative towards the subcontinent during our period was its invitation of Liaquat to Moscow in June 1949, which, despite Liaquat's acceptance, was never followed up.[30] It may be that the success of Britain's new Commonwealth diplomacy in the Cold War world discouraged Russia from any early intervention in South Asia.

Britain's new Commonwealth diplomacy did not achieve an alliance with India and Pakistan for the defence of the Indian Ocean area. In the light of Nehru's attachment to non-alignment the hopes of the Chiefs of Staff seem Panglossian. By mid-April 1949 the Foreign Office had recognized that the political co-operation of South Asia could not be an immediate objective. The first step must be economic co-operation, with a view to stability on the subcontinent. On the eve of the Prime Ministers' Conference Bevin sent

---

[28] Bevin in Apr. 1949, cited in Bullock, *Bevin*, 673; for Cripps in May 1949, see D.C. Watt in Nagai and Iriye, *The Origins of the Cold War in Asia*, 99.

[29] Mrs Pandit, *The Scope of Happiness*, 237.

[30] The episode is discussed by Mohammad Riaz, *Dawn*, 1 Feb. 1985.

Attlee an important appreciation: 'It seems to us . . . that the need of South Asian territories is not so much primarily to build up military strength against the threat of armed Russian aggression, as to establish conditions of stability which will defeat the Stalinist technique'.[31]

In June Nye made a shrewd assessment of the position.[32] India's decision had been carried with almost no criticism within Congress, though the small Socialist, Communist, and Hindu Mahasabha parties had opposed it. The remarkable change of Indian opinion in a mere two years was attributable to the manner of Britain's departure from India, the belief that imperialism was virtually dead, and the real Soviet threat to Asia. India was 'not likely to be a very good "club" member' in the sense of accepting obligations. But this seemed of secondary importance. He had never expected that India would contribute much to Commonwealth defence. What mattered was that the Commonwealth could now help India with her economic problems which, were they not solved, would leave India 'a prey to Communist agitators and quite incapable of becoming the much hoped for bastion against the spread of Communism in South-East Asia. . . . The task before India is anything but easy, but, without the decision to keep India in the Commonwealth, it might well have been an impossible one.' In one way or another the new Commonwealth did assume a viable alternative to Communism, and of its forty-nine eventual members only Grenada has experienced a Marxist regime.

Yet old hopes of integrating South Asia within a Commonwealth defence structure died hard. At the end of the year Noel-Baker ruminated that if India and Pakistan 'should . . . settle their differences they are likely to be the only two members of the Commonwealth who are in a position to put reasonably equipped and trained forces into the field at short notice'.[33] He still viewed the final settlement of the Kashmir dispute as 'really a major objective in Commonwealth defence policy', for the conflict consumed enormous funds that might support forces 'integrated into

---

[31] Bevin to PM, 21 Apr. 1949, encl. FO memo, 'South Asia', 14 Apr. 1949, FO 800/462.

[32] UK High Commissioner to Secretary of State for CR, 15 June 1949, CAB 21/1824.

[33] Noel-Baker's memo, 'Defence Burdens and the Commonwealth', 30 Dec. 1949, cited in P.S. Gupta, 'Imperialism and the Labour Government of 1945–51', loc. cit., n. 41.

Commonwealth defence generally'.[34] Dr Anita Inder Singh expresses justifiable surprise at the belated abandonment of such dreams, which, as she shows, came to an end in mid-1950, when India remained neutral towards Korea.[35] With the increasing involvement of the USA in Asia and the Middle East, Britain came to accept the case for defence collaboration with Pakistan alone. In Cold War terms, Britain's new Commonwealth diplomacy for South Asia indicates an appraisal consistent with recent judgements on her Mediterranean and Middle Eastern policies. A study of the Greek case concludes: 'At best, it can be argued that Britain's achievement in Greece was to prevent the communists from attaining power until the Americans decided to take up the load'.[36] Bullock sums up for the Middle East:

. . . there is a case for arguing that the minimum Bevin succeeded in maintaining for the ten years after the War was worth the effort by providing Western control of the Middle East and access to its oil during the most dangerous years of the Cold War when the division between Eastern and Western spheres of influence was not yet stabilized. By the time Britain's power in the Middle East was ended, the Americans were willing to take their place.[37]

Large claims have been made for Nehru as the key figure in the making of the new Commonwealth. At the time of the Declaration Cripps wrote to him:

I have somewhat looked upon this meeting as the climax of our mutual efforts over the last 9 years—more! I am very happy and I do believe that you have done something really big in world history. It is not only—or perhaps so much—what we have written down or arranged but it is that 8 nations have settled a most difficult and troublesome question with great friendliness and simplicity. We have again shown what can be done by sincere and honest individuals determined to accommodate one another and to have regard for the good of humanity.[38]

It was recently said in the *Times of India* that 'Jawaharlal Nehru was the Father of the New Commonwealth. It was Nehru's

---

[34] Noel-Baker's memo, cited in A.I. Singh, 'Post-Imperial British Attitudes to India, 1947–51', loc. cit., 368.

[35] Ibid.

[36] Alexander, *The Prelude to the Truman Doctrine: British Policy in Greece, 1944–1947* (1982), 251.

[37] Bullock, op. cit., 842.

[38] Cripps to Nehru, 28 Apr. 1949, CAB 127/143.

revolutionary formula of a Republic remaining within the Commonwealth that saved that institution and made it relevant to the needs of the times.'[39] Professor Bimal Prasad elaborates:

Nehru's contribution to the emergence of the new, multiracial, multinational Commonwealth is now beyond dispute. But for India's decision to remain in the Commonwealth in 1949, for which he had been primarily responsible, the Commonwealth must of course have continued, but with a limited membership confined largely to the Anglo-Saxon group of nations. It was India's example which paved the way for all parts of the British Empire emerging into freedom automatically taking their place in the Commonwealth, thereby continuously enlarging its membership and adding to its significance.[40]

He cites Professor Mansergh with approval:

But for him, India almost certainly would not have become the first republican member-state of the Commonwealth, and but for Indian membership almost certainly nationalists elsewhere in Asia and, still more, in Africa would not in their turn have opted also for membership. In the consequent addition of anti-imperialist Asian and African states to a Commonwealth which had grown out of an Empire, by procedures that became so conventional as to cease to cause remark, an idea achieved its most spectacular triumph. Not Smuts, not Mackenzie King, but Nehru was the principal architect of that achievement.[41]

Nehru's decision, writes Prasad, helped transform 'a club of white, Anglo-Saxon nations and a bulwark of British imperialism in various parts of the world . . . into a multiracial and multinational grouping of nations working for the promotion of peace freedom and racial equality in the world'.[42] Hugh Tinker sees Nehru as 'the key figure' at the London Conference, 'flexible yet firm on essentials'.[43] Mansergh praises his magnanimity. Only four years earlier he had completed 3,262 days as a prisoner in the gaols of the Raj.

[39] K.N. Singh's review of *Don't Spare Me Shanker*, repr. in *Indian and Foreign Review*, 21 (31 Jan. 1984), 28–9.

[40] Prasad, 'Nehru and the New Commonwealth', *India Quarterly*, 39 (1983), 432–46, p. 432.

[41] Ibid. See Mansergh, *Commonwealth Experience*, ii, 235.

[42] Prasad, op. cit. Laithwaite had put the point differently in August 1948: 'There may be some advantage, given the great negro population of the Colonial Empire, in avoiding any suggestion that the Commonwealth is a White Man's Club' (cited in A.I. Singh, op. cit., 366).

[43] Tinker, *Separate and Unequal*, 387.

It was remarkable that an association rejected by the kith and kin of Ireland, and a royal title unpalatable to the old Dominions of Canada and South Africa, should have been accepted by free India. In November 1948 Cripps had said that 'it was quite impossible for any Indian to accept the Crown in any sort of way'.[44] Nehru disliked the term 'Head of the Commonwealth' and his acceptance of it was indeed magnanimous.[45] Of other Indians, Krishna Menon, Rau, and Bajpai contributed most to the London Declaration. Cripps marvelled at the conversion of Menon—'the revolutionary, the Anti-British India Leaguer, has become one of the chief architects of the new and invigorated Commonwealth of Nations'.[46] Still, Menon grossly exaggerated his own importance in this matter when he spoke of it in years to come.[47] Rau was indefatigable. He was a gentle man whom Mrs Pandit described as 'a bridge builder'.[48] From his early enunciation of the common citizenship formula that Nehru espoused he contributed consistently to his Prime Minister's receptiveness to the advantages of the Commonwealth to India. Bajpai's supreme moment came when he recognized the 'Head of Commonwealth' as the formula that would satisfy the old Dominions yet avoid problems with the Congress. After Merton College, Oxford, Bajpai had joined the ICS in 1914, visited Commonwealth countries in 1921–22, and attended Imperial Conferences in 1921, 1930, and 1937. He had served as the Viceroy's Agent to the US during the war. Josef Korbel described him as 'a small man with a shy smile, perfect manners, and ivory-cut hands, with the English of Shakespeare'.[49] He was a patrician Anglophile, who might hold up 'a sentence in perfectionist pedantry until he had found the right word', leaving 'the listener . . . all the more impressed because of the classically pure English'.[50] It was he who found the right words and impressed Nehru with them in March 1949. Menon conveyed to India an appreciation of Labour's ministers, Rau communicated a respect for British law and tradition, and Bajpai, from long experience as

[44] Gordon Walker's Diary fragment, 11 Nov. 1948, GNWR 1/7.
[45] Nehru to Patel, 23 Apr. 1949, Das, op. cit., viii, 12–13.
[46] Cripps to Nehru, 28 Apr. 1949, CAB 127/143.
[47] Brecher, op. cit., esp. 75–7.
[48] Mrs Pandit, op. cit., 213.
[49] Korbel, *Danger in Kashmir*, 123.
[50] Grafftey-Smith, *Hands to Play*, 87.

an imperial envoy, imparted an understanding of the Dominions' outlook.

Nehru himself had a genius for finding words to persuade and convince. When he returned from London he broadcast in terms of India's advantage: 'I have naturally looked to the interests of India, for that is my first duty'.[51] No 'commitments of any kind limiting our sovereignty or our internal or external policy have been made'. The Commonwealth was 'not a super State', the King had 'no function' as its 'Head', and any member could leave it at will. At the same time 'the London decision on the Commonwealth gave India certain temporary advantages of co-operation in industry and trade, and certain psychological advantages in regard to world peace'.[52] He dealt summarily with the opposition:

The world may change, and the problems of the world may change, but they only think of those problems in terms of a generation back. The biggest thing that has happened in the world is the emergence of Asia, and it is quite impossible for you to judge of this emergence in some hard and fast way, applying the same simple slogans which you might have used 10 or 15 years ago. I find that the Socialist Party for the moment is stuck in past grooves of thought and is unable to get out of it and adjust itself.

He reserved a visionary tone for the Constituent Assembly:

In this world which is today sick and which has not recovered from so many wounds during the last decade or more, it is necessary that we touch upon the world problems, not with passion and prejudice and with too much repetition of what has ceased to be, but in a friendly way and with a touch of healing, and I think the chief value of this declaration and of what preceded it was that it did bring a touch of healing in our relations with certain countries. We are in no way subordinate to them and they are in no way subordinate to us. We shall go our way and they shall go their way. But our ways, unless something happens, will be friendly ways; at any rate, attempts will be made to understand each other, to be friends with each other and to co-operate with each other. And the fact that we have begun this new type of association with a touch of healing will be good for us, good for them, and I think good for the world.[53]

The Assembly approved the London agreement on 16–17 May and the All-India Congress Committee on 21 May.

---

[51] Broadcast of 10 May 1949, *Hindustan Times*, 11 May 1949.
[52] Press Conference on 11 May 1949, *National Herald*, 12 May 1949.
[53] Constituent Assembly speech, 16 May 1949.

'In a sense the Commonwealth was invented at Adelaide', wrote a recent visitor to Australia.[54] He was making rather a lot of Rosebery's statement at the Adelaide Town Hall on 18 January 1884 that 'There is no need for any nation, however great, leaving the Empire, because the Empire is a commonwealth of Nations'.[55] In the summer of India's Independence another visitor gave a somewhat surprising answer to a question:

Where is the core of the British Empire? London, perhaps, imagines that it is the heart? Calcutta, Vancouver, Cape Town, Edinburgh, may all have their claims, but in the Adelaide Club you will find the answer! Here, far removed from any suspicion of an idea that Queen Victoria is not still on the throne, you will find something that I thought had ceased to exist—the England we were taught about at school, the England of Kipling or even of Dickens![56]

With its verandah cooled by *khush khush tatties*, sporting trophies on the walls, a Roll of Honour surmounted by the words 'For King and Empire', and sited opposite a Governor's House screened by palm trees, the Adelaide Club had a proud colonial air. To a Mountbatten 'clubland' seemed as inimical as *koi-hais* to the spirit of the new Commonwealth.[57] Yet it was not so, as the persistence of the club from Ootacamund to Peshawar, from Calcutta to Karachi, at Colombo, Penang, Hong Kong, and Nairobi, in Canada and every major Australasian city, testifies. So usual did it become to find a club at Commonwealth centres of government and administration that when General K.M. Cariappa arrived in Canberra as India's High Commissioner in 1953 he noted: 'I need not say how surprised I was to learn that there was no such club in a place like this'.[58] He mentioned the omission to many people, from the Prime Minister down, 'both official and non-official', and founded one. The founder members wanted to call it 'the Cariappa Club', but concerned at the possibility of the name one day embarrassing Indo-Australian relations he suggested the title 'Common-Wealth

[54] John Grigg, *Sunday Telegraph*, 26 May 1985.

[55] Cited in Mehrotra, *The Commonwealth and the Nation*, 4.

[56] Boyd Neel, *The Story of an Orchestra* (1950), 111.

[57] Ziegler, op. cit., 472.

[58] Cariappa's circular letter to 20 'important people' in Canberra, 19 Jan. 1954, and attached note on 'The Common-Wealth Club, Canberra', d. July 1954, in possession of the Commonwealth Club, to whose Secretary, Mr J.E.T. Stubbs, I am indebted for copies.

Club'. He became the patron of the 'Commonwealth Club' and the New Zealand High Commissioner its first president. Today the name is assumed to refer to the Commonwealth of Australia. In the early post-imperial 'golden years of hope', however, it perhaps blended the concepts of Club and Commonwealth, which were so often conjoined.[59] As a High Commissioner in Canberra Cariappa might have claimed for the Commonwealth Club what the recently installed Smuts Professor at Cambridge claims for the Commonwealth, that 'it provides the readiest means available to us for orienting ourselves sensibly to the most of our fellow humans'.[60]

[59] Mansergh's phrase, *Commonwealth Experience*, ii, 160.
[60] D.A. Low, '*The Contraction of England*',Inaugural Lecture, 22 Oct. 1984 (Cambridge, 1985), 28-9.

Bibliography

A. PRIVATE PAPERS

1. India Office Library, London

Christie Collection, MSS Eur.
D718

Cunningham Collection, MSS
Eur. D670

Jenkins Collection, MSS Eur.
D807

Mountbatten Collection, xerox

copies from the Broadlands
Archives

Mudie Collection, MSS Eur.
F164

Short Collection, MSS Eur. F189

Templewood Collection, MSS
Eur. E240

2. Public Record Office, London

Brook Papers, CAB 127/343-4

Cripps Collection, CAB 127/57-154

Bevin Papers, FO 800

3. Liddell Hart Centre for Military Archives, King's College, London

Ismay Papers

4. Bodleian Library, Oxford

Attlee Papers

5. Churchill College, Cambridge

A.V. Alexander Papers

Attlee's Draft Memoirs

Gordon Walker Papers

Noel-Baker Papers

6. Cambridge: University Library

Templewood Papers

7. National Archives of India, New Delhi

Rajendra Prasad Papers

8. Nehru Memorial Library, New Delhi

All-India Congress Committee
Papers

K.P.S. Menon Papers

B.N. Rau Papers

9. Flinders University of South Australia

Evatt Collection

B. OFFICIAL PAPERS

1. *Public Record Office, London*

Cabinet Conclusions (CAB 128)
Cabinet Memoranda (CAB 129)
Cabinet Registered Files (CAB 21)
Commonwealth Conference
  Papers (CAB 133/89)
Commonwealth Affairs
  Committee Minutes and

Memoranda (CAB 134/54–5)
Commonwealth Relations
  Committee Minutes and
  Memoranda (CAB 134/117–19)
Foreign Office Files (FO 371,
  FO 800 IND.)
Prime Minister's Files (PREM)

2. *India Office Library, London*

Political Department, Transfer of
  Power Papers (L/P & J/10)
Private Office Papers (L/PO)

Private Secretary to the Viceroy's
  Papers (R/3/1)

3. *National Archives of India, New Delhi*

Ministry of External Affairs Files
Ministry of External Affairs and

Commonwealth Relations Files

4. *Australian National Archives*

Cabinet Agenda Papers and
  Minutes

Department of External Affairs,
  A1838

C. NEWSPAPERS

Age
Cape Times
Daily Express
Daily Telegraph
Dawn
Economist

Hindu
Hindustan Times
Manchester Guardian
Observer
Sydney Morning Herald
The Times

D. PARLIAMENTARY DEBATES

United Kingdom: Commons and
  Lords
India: Constituent Assembly
Canada: House of Commons

Australia: Senate and House of
  Representatives
South Africa: House of Assembly

E. PRINTED BOOKS

Alexander, G.M., *The Prelude to the Truman Doctrine: British Policy in Greece, 1944–1947*, Oxford, 1984

Ali, Chaudhri Muhammad, *The Emergence of Pakistan*, New York, 1967

Aron, Raymond, *Peace and War: A Theory of International Relations*, 1966

Birdwood, Lord, *A Continent Decides*, 1953

——, *Two Nations and Kashmir*, 1956

Bowra, C.M., *Memories 1898-1939*, 1966

Bullock, Alan, *Ernest Bevin: Foreign Secretary, 1945-1951*, 1983

Burridge, Trevor, *Clement Attlee: A Political Biography, 1986*

Campbell-Johnson, Alan, *Mission with Mountbatten*, 1951

Caroe, Olaf, *The Pathans 500 BC-AD 1975*, 1976

Coen, T. Creagh, *The Indian Political Service: A Study in Indirect Rule*, 1971

Collins, L., and Lapierre, D., *Freedom at Midnight*, 1975

Collins, L., and Lapierre, D. (eds.), *Mountbatten and Independent India, 16 August 1947-18 June 1948*, New Delhi, 1984

Connell, John, *Auchinleck*, 1959

Dani, A.H. (ed.), *World Scholars on Quaid-i-Azam Mohammad Ali Jinnah*, Islamabad, 1979

——, (ed.), *Quaid-i-Azam and Pakistan*, Islamabad, 1981

Darling, M.L., *Wisdom and Waste in the Punjab Village*, 1934

Das, Durga (ed.), *Sardar Patel's Correspondence, 1945-50*, 10 vols., Ahmedabad, 1971-4

Dichter, D., *The North-West Frontier of Pakistan: A Study in Regional Geography*, Oxford, 1967

Eayrs, J., *In Defence of Canada: Peacemaking and Deterrence*, Toronto, 1972

Foreign Relations of the United States: Diplomatic Papers, 1948, Washington

Garner, J., *The Commonwealth Office, 1925-68*, 1978

Gopal, Sarvepalli (ed.), *Selected Works of Jawaharlal Nehru*, 15 vols. to date, New Delhi, 1972-

Gopal, Sarvepalli, *Jawaharlal Nehru: A Biography*, 3 vols. Delhi, 1979-84

Gordon Walker, Patrick, *The Commonwealth*, 1962

——, *The Cabinet*, 1970

Grafftey-Smith, Laurence, *Hands to Play*, 1975

Gupta, Partha Sarathi, *Imperialism and the British Labour Movement, 1914-1964*, 1975

Gupta, Sisir, *Kashmir: A Study in India-Pakistan Relations*, Bombay, 1966

Hall, H.D., *Commonwealth: A History of the British Commonwealth of Nations*, 1971

Harris, Kenneth, *Attlee*, 1982

Hasan, K. Sarwar, *Pakistan and the Commonwealth*, Karachi, 1950

Hodson, H.V., *The Great Divide: Britain-India-Pakistan*, 1969

Holland, R.F., *European Decolonization, 1918-1981: An Introductory Survey*, 1985

Hunt, Roland, and Harrison, John, *The District Officer in India, 1930–1947*, 1980

Irving, Robert Grant, *Indian Summer: Lutyens, Baker and Imperial Delhi*, New Haven, 1981

Jalal, Ayesha, *The Sole Spokesman: Jinnah, the Muslim League and the Demand for Pakistan*, Cambridge, 1985

Jansson, Erland, *India, Pakistan or Pakhtunistan: The Nationalist Movements in the North-West Frontier Province, 1937–47*, Uppsala, 1981

Keesing's Contemporary Archives, 1946–7

Korbel, Josef, *Danger in Kashmir* (1954), Princeton, rev. edn. 1966

Lamb, Alastair, *The Kashmir Problem: A Historical Survey*, New York, 1967

Lipton, Michael, *The Erosion of a Relationship: India and Britain since 1960*, 1975

Louis, W. Roger, *The British Empire in the Middle East, 1945–1951: Arab Nationalism, The United States, and Postwar Imperialism*, Oxford, 1984

Lyon, Peter, and Manor, James (eds.), *Transfer and Transformation: Political Institutions in the New Commonwealth*, Leicester, 1983

Mahajan, Mehr Chand, *Looking Back*, 1963

Mansergh, N., Lumby, E.W.R., and Moon, E.P. (eds.), *The Transfer of Power, 1942–7*, 12 vols., 1970–83

Mansergh, Nicholas, *The Commonwealth Experience*, 2 vols., 2nd edn., 1982

Mehrotra, S.R., *The Commonwealth and the Nation*, New Delhi, 1978

Michel, Aloys A., *The Indus Rivers: A Study of the Effects of Partition*, New Haven, 1967

Mitchell, Norval, *Sir George Cunningham: A Memoir*, 1968

Moon, Penderel, *Divide and Quit*, 1961

Moon, Penderel (ed.), *Wavell: The Viceroy's Journal*, 1973

Moore, R.J., *The Crisis of Indian Unity, 1917–40*, 1974

——, *Churchill, Cripps and India, 1939–45*, 1979

——, *Escape from Empire: The Attlee Government and the Indian Problem*, 1983

Morgan, Kenneth, *Labour in Power, 1945–1951*, 1984

Morris-Jones, W.H., and Fischer, Georges (eds.), *Decolonization and After: The British and French Experience*, 1980

Murti, B.S.N., *India and the Commonwealth*, New Delhi, 1953

Nagai, Yonosuke, and Iriye, Akira (eds.), *The Origins of the Cold War in Asia*, New York, 1977

National Documentation Centre, *The Partition of the Punjab, 1947, Official Documents*, 4 vols., Lahore, 1983

Neel, Boyd, *The Story of an Orchestra*, 1950

Ovendale, Ritchie (ed.), *The Foreign Policy of the British Labour Governments, 1945-1951*, Leicester, 1984

Pandey, B.N., *Nehru*, 1976

Pandit, Vijaya Lakshmi, *The Scope of Happiness: A Personal Memoir*, 1979

Pelling, Henry, *The Labour Governments, 1945-51*, 1984

Radcliffe, Lord, *Not in Feather Beds: Some Collected Papers*, 1968

Rau, B.N., *India's Constitution in the Making*, 1960

Raza, S. Hashim (ed.), *Mountbatten and Pakistan*, Karachi, 1982

Rothwell, Victor, *Britain and the Cold War, 1941-1947*, 1982

Sain, Kanwar, *Reminiscences of an Engineer*, New Delhi, 1978

Singh, Khushwant, *A History of the Sikhs*, 2 vols., Princeton, 1966

Stephens, Ian, *Horned Moon*, 1953

——, *Pakistan*, 1963

Stevens, Bertram, *New Horizons: A Study of Australian-Indian Relations*, Sydney, 1946

Strang, Lord, *Home and Abroad*, 1956

Symonds, Richard, *The Making of Pakistan*, 1950

Tinker, H.R., *Separate and Unequal: India and the Indians in the British Commonwealth, 1920-1950*, 1976

Tinker, H.R. (ed.), *Burma: The Struggle for Independence, 1944-1948*, 2 vols., 1983-4

Tuker, Francis, *While Memory Serves*, 1950

Watt, D.C., *Succeeding John Bull: America in Britain's Place, 1900-1975*, Cambridge, 1984

Wheeler-Bennett, J.W., *King George VI: His Life and Reign*, New York, 1958

Wilson, A. Jeyaratnam, and Dalton, Dennis (eds.), *The States of South Asia: Problems of National Integration* (Essays in Honour of W.H. Morris-Jones), 1982

Wolpert, Stanley, *Jinnah of Pakistan*, New York, 1984

Ziegler, Philip, *Mountbatten: The Official Biography*, 1985

Zinkin, Maurice and Taya, *Britain and India: Requiem for Empire*, 1964

F. ARTICLES AND PAPERS

Adamthwaite, Anthony, 'Britain and the World, 1945-9: The View from the Foreign Office', *International Affairs*, 61.2 (1985), 223-35.

Brecher, Michael, 'India's Decision to Remain in the Commonwealth', *Journal of Commonwealth and Comparative Politics*, 12 (1975), 62-90.

Copland, Ian, 'Islam and Political Mobilization in Kashmir, 1931–34', *Pacific Affairs* 54.2 (1981), 228–59.

Critchley, T.K., 'Prospects of Trade between India and Australia', *India Quarterly*, 1:1 (1945), 45–56.

Darwin, John, 'British Decolonization since 1945: A Pattern or a Puzzle?', *Journal of Imperial and Commonwealth History*, 12.2 (1984), 187–209.

De Silva, K.M., 'Sri Lanka: D.S. Senanayake and the Passage to Dominion Status', *Sri Lanka Journal of Social Sciences*, 3.2, n.d., 1–14.

—— ' "The Model Colony": Reflections on the Transfer of Power in Sri Lanka', in A.J. Wilson and D.G. Dalton (eds.), *The States of South Asia*, 1982.

Gopal, Sarvepalli, 'Nehru and the Commonwealth', in D. Dilks (ed.), *Retreat from Power*, II, 1981, 138–151.

Gupta, Partha Sarathi, 'Imperialism and the Labour Government of 1945–51', in Jay Winter (ed.), *The Working Class in Modern British History: Essays in Honour of Henry Pelling*, Cambridge, 1983.

Hill, Peter, 'Towards an Indian Dominion: Lord Zetland and the Indian Constitutional Problem, 1939–40', *Journal of Indian History*, Diamond Jubilee Volume (1982), 199–226.

Holland, R.F., 'The Imperial Factor in British Strategies from Attlee to Macmillan, 1945–63', *Journal of Imperial and Commonwealth History*, 12.2 (1984), 165–86.

Jalal, Ayesha, 'Inheriting the Raj: Jinnah and the Governor-Generalship Issue', *Modern Asian Studies*, 19.1 (1985), 29–53.

Jeffrey, Robin, 'The Punjab Boundary Force and the Problem of Order, August 1947', *Modern Asian Studies*, 8.4 (1974), 491–520.

Keenleyside, T.A., 'Nationalist India and the Issue of Commonwealth Membership', *Journal of Indian History*, Diamond Jubilee Volume (1982), 227–50.

Krishna, Y., 'Mountbatten and the Partition of India', *History*, 68 (1983), 22–37.

Low, D.A., '*The Contraction of England*' (An Inaugural Lecture), Cambridge, 1984.

Millar, T.B., 'Kashmir, the Commonwealth and the United Nations', *Australian Outlook*, 17.1 (1963), 54–73.

Morris-Jones, W.H., 'The Transfer of Power, 1947: A View from the Sidelines', *Modern Asian Studies*, 16.1 (1982), 1–32.

Newton, C.C.S., 'The Sterling Crisis of 1947 and the British Response to the Marshall Plan', *Economic History Review*, 37.3 (1984), 391–408.

O'Brien, John B., 'Australia and the Repeal of the [Irish] External Relations Act', unpublished paper delivered at the Australian Irish Bicentennial Conference, Kilkenny, 20 October 1983.

Prasad, Bimal, 'Nehru and the New Commonwealth', *India Quarterly*, 39.4 (1983), 432–46.

Singh, Anita Inder, 'Imperial Defence and the Transfer of Power in India, 1946–1947', *International History Review*, 4.4 (1982), 568–88.

——, 'Decolonization in India: The Statement of 20 February 1947', *International History Review*, 6.2 (1984), 191–209.

——, 'Economic Consequences of India's Position in the Commonwealth: The British Official Thinking in 1949', *Indo-British Review*, 9.1 (1984), 106–111.

——, 'Keeping India in the Commonwealth: British Political and Military Aims, 1947–49', *Journal of Contemporary History*, 20 (1985), 469–81.

——, 'Post-Imperial British Attitudes to India: The Military Aspect, 1947–51', *Round Table* (1985), 360–75.

Smith, Raymond, and Zametica, John, 'The Cold Warrior: Clement Attlee Reconsidered, 1945–7', *International Affairs*, 61.2 (1985), 237–52.

Spens, Lord, 'The Arbitral Tribunal in India, 1947–48', paper read before the Grotius Society, 1 February 1950.

Talbot, I.A., 'Mountbatten and the Partition of India: A Rejoinder', *History*, 69 (1984), 29–35.

Tinker, Hugh, 'Pressure, Persuasion, Decision: Factors in the Partition of the Punjab, August 1947', *Journal of Asian Studies*, 36.4 (1977), 695–704.

Tomlinson, B.R., 'Foreign Private Investment in India, 1920–1950', *Modern Asian Studies*, 12.4 (1978), 655–77.

——, 'Indo-British Relations in the Post-Colonial Era: The Sterling Balances Negotiations, 1947–49', *Journal of Imperial and Commonwealth History*, 13 (1985), 142–62.

Index